STEVEN BELL
FROM TRIUMPH TO TRAGEDY
THE CHAPECOENSE STORY
THE GAFFER TAPES PRESENT
THE A-Z OF FANTASY FOOTBALL
A HILARIOUS GUIDE FILLED WITH ANECDOTES AND EXPERT ADVICE
TOM HOLMES, CRAIG HAZELL AND ASH KERNSWORTH
FOOT SOLDIERS
EXCESS
BENJAMIN ROBERTS
DAVID BAIL
MAGIC MAGYA
THE RISE AND FALL
WORLD'S ONCE GREATEST F
The Beautiful Badge
THE STORIES BEHIND THE FOOTBALL CLUB BADGE
MARTYN ROUTLEDGE & ELSPETH WILLS
SPORTS BOOK AWARDS 2019
WINNER
FILIPE D'AVILLEZ
One Thousand Miles to
JAMOR
A JOURNEY INTO PORTUGUESE FOOTBALL
GRAND
RICHARD CROOKS
T0307327
MICHAEL
EVEN HESKEY SCORED
EMILE HESKEY
MY STORY
WITH DEAN ELDREDGE
SECOND YELLOW
THE FURTHER ADVENTURES OF OUR FOOTBALL HEROES
JOHN SMITH AND DAN TREFLER
WAYNE BARTON
Barton has an encyclopaedic knowledge and passion for United - telling stories in fascinating detail.
James Robson, Evening Standard
BECKHAM
THE MAKING OF A MEGASTAR
Stahl aus Brandenburg
STAHL BRANDENBURG 0:0 LOKOMOTIVE LEIPZIG
British Football's Greatest Grounds
ONE HUNDRED MUST-SEE FOOTBALL VENUES
Mike Bayly
THE PRIDE OF THE LIONESSES
The Changing Face of Women's Football in England
Carrie Dunn
FOOTBALL'S
STEVEN SCRAGG
SPORTS BOOK AWARDS 2020
WHY ARE WE ALWAYS ON LAST?

In 1888, when he retired from football, a newspaper reported that Andrew Watson, 'has entered upon another phase of his straggling life by taking to the sea'. The curious phrase 'a straggling life' implied there was more to know about the world's first black footballer.

A Straggling Life

A Straggling Life

ANDREW WATSON

The Story of the World's First Black International Footballer

LLEW WALKER

pitch

First published by Pitch Publishing, 2021

Pitch Publishing
A2 Yeoman Gate
Yeoman Way
Worthing
Sussex
BN13 3QZ
www.pitchpublishing.co.uk
info@pitchpublishing.co.uk

© 2021, Llew Walker

Every effort has been made to trace the copyright.
Any oversight will be rectified in future editions at the
earliest opportunity by the publisher.

All rights reserved. No part of this book may be reproduced,
sold or utilised in any form or transmitted in any form or by
any means, electronic or mechanical, including photocopying,
recording or by any information storage and retrieval system,
without prior permission in writing from the Publisher.

A CIP catalogue record is available for this book
from the British Library.

ISBN 978 1 78531 820 7

Typesetting and origination by Pitch Publishing

Printed and bound in India by Replika Press Pvt. Ltd.

Contents

Acknowledgements

Chris Watney for support, guidance and motivational assurance. Norman Epps, the archivist and custodian of the history of Corinthian and Casuals Football Clubs. Richard McBrearty at the Scottish Football Museum for permitting me to use the Andrew Watson pictures, and Ged O'Brien, Tommy Malcolm and Brian McColl, the history men of Scottish football. Gary Ralston for support and guidance. Alex Jackson at the National Football Museum. Many, many thanks to Andy Mitchell for generously sharing his time, exceptional knowledge and sound advice.

Natasha Muluswela for her vision and lending her talent to the project.

Katrina DiMuro and Joan Burgess at King's College London Archives. Libby Holmes at the University of Glasgow and Nerys Tunnicliffe at Glasgow Life. Rod Van Cooten and Tikwis Begbie at the BG Colonists Index. Lucy Gibbon and Sarah Maclean at the Orkney Library & Archive.

David Alston at Slaves & Highlanders for a unique website and sharing his exceptional knowledge.

Matthew Lowing at Bloomsbury for guidance, and Malik Al Nasir for sharing his thoughts.

Jonathan Lees at Crossley Heath School in Halifax for information and permission to use the images.

For permission to use images or sharing information: Louise Elizabeth Boyd for help with Agnes Ann Millett

Dods; Bridget Farmer for her help and permission to use the image of her great-great-great aunt, Elizabeth Pinder née Buchanan; David Baird for help and permission to use the images of his great-great-grandfather, George Baird; Neil Scarrow for permission to use the image of Demerara; and Fawaz Khan in Guiana for use of the Sandbach Parker image, and Jon Martin for use of Willie Clarke image.

Dedication and Author's Note

To Sally, for everything.

At the time of publication, all the facts in this book had been verified as accurate and true. Some interpretations have been made on available facts. However, as the research of the founding fathers of football continues, new information will surface and change again what we know about Andrew Watson. My hope is that this book will inspire further research and discussion, not only about Andrew Watson, but many of his contemporaries who have also disappeared from the historical record. I also hope this book will open more avenues, promote further research and perhaps one day we will know all there is to know about the world's first black international footballer. LW

Preface

In November and December of 1898, the British press serialised a 'brilliant' series of articles entitled 'Association Football'. Charles Wreford Brown's columns were syndicated to dozens of newspapers nationwide and included topics such as 'How to Play Association Football' and 'Pressing Questions Affecting the Future of the Game'. Brown was held in very high esteem and considered one of the all-time footballing dignitaries.[1]

In the first of two articles entitled 'Some Famous Footballers', Brown praised Andrew Watson:

> '… a West Indian, but of Scottish origin, was another very fine back.' But in further editions, this brief acknowledgement included the view that 'unfortunately, he never kept himself in proper condition, and was therefore unable to utilise to the full, the abilities he possessed'.[2]

Wreford Brown's inclusion of Watson, albeit brief, was very high praise indeed, even if he felt that Watson had

1 Ex-Charterhouse, former captain of both the Oxford University AFC and the English national team, who would later become the vice-president of the English Football Association.

2 The second sentence was deleted from some syndicated versions, but it is unclear whether this was for typesetting purposes or not. The articles were reprinted in 1900.

squandered his talents. Still, the undeniable pathos echoed a tone occasionally found in other articles about Watson. Earlier, in 1888, when Watson announced his retirement from football, one journalist wrote:

> '... Andrew Watson ... has entered upon another phase of his straggling life by taking to the sea as a profession'.[3]

The reference to 'a straggling life' and Wreford Brown's suggestion that Watson wasted his talent are surprising and unexpected opinions. They shed new light on Watson's story. When Tony Talburt's biography was published in 2017, it appeared Watson's life and his many achievements had finally been recognised and celebrated.[4] But these obscure references to the human side of Andrew Watson suggested there was more to discover.

It is perhaps astonishing that any information about Watson has survived, considering how little remains of many of his contemporaries or team-mates. In truth, Watson's historical record, as well as that of the football players from more than a dozen decades ago, began to erode as soon as they had hung up their boots. It was not until nearly 100 years later that the history of football became legitimate territory for scholarly research. By that time, much of the historical record had been lost or erased. Ostensibly, the players in Watson's era are a forgotten sporting generation, only recently being rediscovered and recognised for their contributions to the birth of the game.

---

3 *Glasgow Evening Post*, Friday, 31 August 1888.

4 Talburt (2017).

The disappearance of Watson's generation from the record books was a gradual process. The rise of professionalism monopolised and eclipsed the formative years of association football, and this dominance affected subtle changes, reinforcing the superiority of the professional game over the amateur code. The wholesale assimilation of professionalism in football is revealed in the subtle change to the definition of the word 'amateur'. Once used to refer to an honourable sporting ethos, the term is now used to refer to something or someone inexperienced or incompetent. Similarly, the word 'professional', once used to describe 'an activity for gain or as a means of livelihood', now tends to mean competence, efficiency and experience.

Watson's generation were all amateurs. Along with their code, their memory gradually faded, and a century later, in 1975, when the Football Association (FA) removed the word 'amateur' from the rule book, their disappearance was complete.

Some mistakenly believe Watson's achievements were deliberately wiped from the records due to his ethnicity, but as the Wreford Brown quote confirms, he was mentioned in books and articles for years after his playing days were over. The fact that more information about Watson has survived is a testament to his fame, talent and the high regard he was held in by his peers, rather than his colour.

After almost a century, the Scottish Football Museum's research produced a list of Watson's accomplishments, and he is now acknowledged as the first black player to:

- represent a British football team internationally
- captain an international football team
- play for the Scottish national team
- captain the Scottish national team

- win a major cup competition
- play in the English FA Cup
- hold the role of a football club administrator

Some suggest he was also the first black professional too, although this accolade probably belongs to Arthur Wharton.

Watson was schooled in the code of amateurism. Through the influence of his public school education and his membership of both the Corinthian and Queen's Park football clubs, he would have been a strict amateur. Like his team-mates, he would have frowned on professionalism.

However, the passionate revelations that accompanied the 'discovery' of Andrew Watson and the eagerness of writers to broadcast the news have resulted in a blurred and inaccurate biography. Since his restoration to the pages of football history, his story has been reduced to a few bullet points:

- black man
- slavery
- fortune
- public school
- wealthy
- first black footballer
- no racism
- erased because of his colour

Such a simplistic and misleading 'e-biog' is almost as sad as forgetting him again, but fresh research has corrected several misconceptions and has fashioned a more complete and detailed picture of Andrew Watson's life and times. For example, he was not an independently wealthy gentleman as his current biography asserts. In truth, he received only a small amount of his father's estate. After his football career had ended, far from being a rich man, he led a quiet, modest life. There is no evidence to prove that Watson or his heirs possessed any significant wealth, even though his extended family contained several of the wealthiest individuals in the country.

What we do know is that Watson was well-liked, affable, had a good sense of humour and made friends easily. He was a gentleman, perhaps not an accomplished scholar, but had a kind heart, was courteous and polite.

As a footballer, he was a leader, captaining the teams he played for and earning the respect of spectators, players and journalists. The appointments to committees at clubs and associations suggest he was a hard worker, capable, organised, diligent and possessed all the qualities needed for positions of responsibility.

Having been raised in the homes of two senior church officials, it is likely Watson was a man of faith, perhaps devout. He would have been acutely aware of the Church's expectations of each member of the congregation. Growing up in a religious environment and with a public school background, Watson would have been well-versed in Christian principles and morals, yet, like his own father, he was an absent parent. He relinquished the responsibility for the upbringing of the children from his first marriage, then later, after his football career was over, he worked as an engineer on steamships, traversing the Atlantic several times a year. This effectively meant leaving his second wife and their two children alone in Liverpool for months at a time.

He twice uprooted his family to pursue employment opportunities in other parts of the country, revealing that financial security was more important, or perhaps more necessary to him, than football.

But being accused of professionalism at the end of his career would have wounded him deeply and may have been a factor in his choice to lead a very private life, one that left an almost indecipherable trace of his last 20 years.

Playing an active role in the formative years of the development of the beautiful game, Watson appeared to transcend obstacles faced by many black athletes in the years since. His parentage and ethnicity were both details that could have easily prevented his progress. Instead, the sporting public and the media on both sides of the border fell in love with him.

In a society that ignored or excluded everything outside a contrived image of itself, the opportunities for an illegitimate, mixed-race son of a plantation owner would have been rare or non-existent. The fact that Watson became so admired and was held in such high esteem makes him exceptional.

Andrew Watson is a sporting and cultural icon: a black footballer who succeeded despite the conventions and morals of Victorian society. He was a footballing pioneer when the love affair with the beautiful game was taking its first few steps. Yet, at the end of his career, when he fell from the public gaze, he disappeared and eventually became lost to history.

A Man of Colour

No heads turned when a dark-skinned, well-dressed young man with an impeccable English accent and the suspicion of wealth, enrolled in the University of Glasgow in 1875. Universities were expected to attract members of Britain's global dominion, colonists with a thirst for universal knowledge. When this man fell in love and married a girl from the local tenements, he was welcomed into the family. When he opened a shop, invested money in a small but ambitious football club, and showed an ability to play, people would remark on his talents. When he joined the city's most prominent and most loved football team and walked out at Hampden, first for Glasgow, then for Queen's Park, and eventually for the national team, heads would turn to admire one of Scotland's most exceptional sportsmen.

A father of two, in business and an international football player, his neighbours would call out greetings in the street and wishes of good fortune in the upcoming match. When he left Glasgow and moved to London, people were sorry to see him go, but they followed his fortunes and misfortunes from afar, proud that a Scot was playing with some of the best football teams in the land. He would be welcomed on his frequent returns to Scotland and once brought with him the best team in English football for the entertainment of his fellow Glaswegians. When he remarried to a shop girl from a local business, people were pleased and wished him lasting happiness. When he finally moved south for good, he was missed but always remembered as being an excellent footballer, a Scot with an English accent.

The colour of Andrew Watson's skin would not have passed unnoticed in the latter part of 19th-century Glasgow. When people came to watch him play, his mixed heritage would undoubtedly have been mentioned. Even though, during his lifetime, no records exist in the print media of any verbal discrimination, after his death it was no surprise to discover that, beyond the printed word, he had been commonly known as 'Black Watson'.

There is a belief that the absence of racism in connection with Watson was a Scottish cultural manifestation, a characteristic of the difference between England and Scotland. The often-repeated adage of 'no problem here'[5] has been rolled out on numerous occasions but has long since been discredited.[6] Some suggest that 'racism' evolved after Watson's time and, before this, all were treated equally. This belief is also nonsense, and even though instances of specific acts of racism do not appear in the Scottish historical record for Andrew Watson, there are plenty of examples to confirm that racism was a disease not belonging solely to the English. Similarly, there are no reports of discrimination connected with Watson in the English historical record either. Still, no one would be naïve enough to advocate that the British were multiculturally sensitive and it is wrong to believe that just because racist terminology had not been used in the Scottish or English media, that Watson did not experience this throughout his life.

---

5 The often-quoted belief that Scotland was free from racism.

6 Dimeo & Finn (2001).

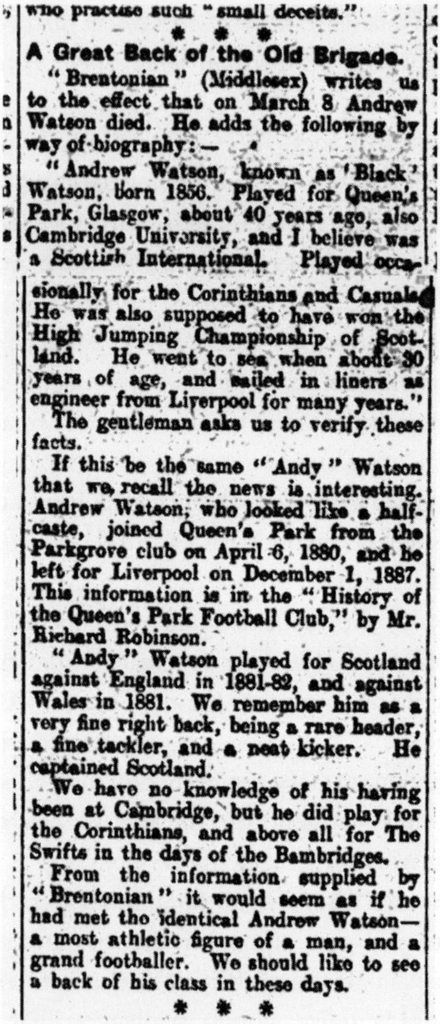
who practise such "small deceits."

* * *

A Great Back of the Old Brigade.

"Brentonian" (Middlesex) writes us to the effect that on March 8 Andrew Watson died. He adds the following by way of biography:—

"Andrew Watson, known as 'Black' Watson, born 1856. Played for Queen's Park, Glasgow, about 40 years ago, also Cambridge University, and I believe was a Scottish International. Played occasionally for the Corinthians and Casuals. He was also supposed to have won the High Jumping Championship of Scotland. He went to sea when about 30 years of age, and sailed in liners as engineer from Liverpool for many years."

The gentleman asks us to verify these facts.

If this be the same "Andy" Watson that we recall the news is interesting. Andrew Watson, who looked like a half-caste, joined Queen's Park from the Parkgrove club on April 6, 1880, and he left for Liverpool on December 1, 1887. This information is in the "History of the Queen's Park Football Club," by Mr. Richard Robinson.

"Andy" Watson played for Scotland against England in 1881-82, and against Wales in 1881. We remember him as a very fine right back, being a rare header, a fine tackler, and a neat kicker. He captained Scotland.

We have no knowledge of his having been at Cambridge, but he did play for the Corinthians, and above all for The Swifts in the days of the Bambridges.

From the information supplied by "Brentonian" it would seem as if he had met the identical Andrew Watson—a most athletic figure of a man, and a grand footballer. We should like to see a back of his class in these days.

* * *

Athletic News – *Monday, 4 April 1921*

Ironically, it is a Scottish anatomist, zoologist and physician, Robert Knox, whose best-selling book, *The Races of Men*, published in 1850, pioneered a theory in which he proposed the 'science' of identifying racial characteristics and a hierarchy of races. His 'scientific' work sparked much discussion, and its theme would eventually lead to the premise for 'scientific racism'.[7] From this, the emergence of eugenics would pollute European society for the next hundred years.

As Victorian society changed, most people had more leisure time, and a large section of the working classes discovered football, while many in the middle classes pursued science and scientific research. 'Science', the study of the material and physical world, became a disciplined search for facts, knowledge and, ultimately, truth. This new discipline would be applied to everything from race and ethnicity to football. The assumption that 'scientific football' was not only intellectually but practically superior hung around the game for many years. Even though the term 'scientific football' was a misnomer, it confirms the Victorian obsession with science.

In general, the British Victorians believed they were superior to all other races, and they turned to science to prove this. They founded a proliferation of scientific institutes and associations that embodied the Victorian thirst for knowledge. But as the British Empire grew, the strange and exotic cultures visited by a series of famous Victorian explorers and adventurers would begin to sow seeds of doubt. The vast 'Dark Continent', for example, was considered mysterious and terrifying, and people hoped that science would provide reassurances against the unknown. Knowledge would help in not only understanding what criminal or evil thoughts were in the minds of these foreign people, but it would ultimately reveal how to rule and control them.

Scientific discussions and publications about race were no longer confined to the halls of learning but had found a new audience in the growing numbers of the educated middle

---

7 The belief that empirical evidence exists to support or justify racism (racial discrimination), racial inferiority or racial superiority.

class. The downward dissemination of these ideas meant the increasingly literate masses could now also participate in the debate. Instead of providing clear and accessible answers, knowledge only brought more questions and doubts. It was left to the individual to choose the simplest theories that best suited their hopes and fears and, in general, Victorian society settled for what supported their view of themselves, even if this supported racial stereotypes and institutionalised racism.

When the average Victorian read the following description of the white Anglo-Saxon and compared it to the list of traits of numerous other ethnic groups, they would be comforted and reassured of their place in the universe:

> 'The Saxon also still remains the Saxon, stolid, and solid, outwardly abrupt but warm-hearted and true, haughty and even over-bearing through an innate sense of superiority, yet at heart sympathetic and always just, hence the ruler of men; seemingly dull or slow, yet preeminent in the realms of philosophy and imagination.'[8]

Ultimately, this 'Age of Empire' searched for confirmation that they were the peak of the evolutionary scale, and some scientific studies supported the theory that the Anglo-Saxon was the superior race. If science could confirm this and it was considered respectable and decent to discuss race and ethnicity in a public forum, then it was acceptable for the masses too. Of course, there were dissenters, but the concepts of power, superiority and race filtered into the Victorian consciousness.

It is noticeable that the media contained fewer ethnic terms in the 1870s and 1880s, and the following quotation

8 Lorimer (1988).

is an example of the struggle journalists had with referencing the colour or ethnicity of a player in print. Although the full meaning has been lost, the article appeared in *Athletic News* in May 1880, a month after Watson joined Queen's Park, and appears to reveal how reluctant the reporter is to identify Watson by his ethnicity, without causing offence:

> 'A certain Queen's Park full-back, who is a strong believer in the Darwinian theory, and who therefore looks upon man as nothing short of a chrystallised [*sic*] ape, has done more by his faultless kicking these three weeks to prove his unfitness to sit in the Dundas-street sanctuary than all the eloquence of a Tennyson or a Somers, between whom some people think there is only a "leetle"[9] difference, but with all his analytical genius he could not say whether the chips of wood were bones on Wednesday evening.'[10]

This article refers to a Charity Cup replay between Queen's Park and Rangers, which was criticised for the rough play and the injuries sustained by several players. The 'Dundas-street sanctuary' refers to the premises of the Scottish FA before it moved to Carlton Place. 'Somers' is William Scott Somers, the Queen's Park full-back, who, due to the abundance of quality they had in the backs, caused Queen's Park to experiment with a new formation. This meant

---

9 Perhaps used in reference to the popularity of poets from America adopting 'negro dialect', such as Irvin Russell (1853–1879). 'Leetle' means 'little', as in the poem, 'Christmas-Night in the Quarters'.
We labors in de'ya'd, wukin hard an' wukin' true;
Now, shorely yo' won't notus, ef we eats a grape or two,
An' takes a leetle holiday – a leetle restin' spell
Bekase, nex' week, we'll start in fresh, an' labor twicet as well.

10 *Athletic News*, Wednesday, 19 May 1880.

pushing Watson into the midfield, criticised as 'not being conducive to good play'.[11] Although the article appears to refer to Watson, it is clear that the journalist struggles with referring to the colour of his skin or his heritage.

However, even though racist terminology may not have been in frequent use in the media, tolerance of racial stereotypes was evident. Shortly after Watson signed for Queen's Park in 1880, the Sheffield Zulus arranged a fixture at Hampden for Wednesday, 21 April. Even though the game had been widely advertised, poor weather and lack of interest meant a paltry crowd of only about a hundred witnessed it, the home side ending up resounding winners by 7-0. The Zulus had initially been created to raise money for the relief of widows and orphans of the Anglo-Zulu War of the previous year. However, realising there was money to be made from the team, they dropped the charitable cause and became a touring side, sharing the gate receipts among themselves.

GRAND FOOTBALL MATCH.

QUEEN'S PARK *versus* SHEFFIELD ZULUS,
HAMPDEN PARK, MOUNT FLORIDA,
ON WEDNESDAY, 21ST APRIL.
Kick-Off at 5-45 P.M. prompt.
Admission 6d.; Ladies free. To Grand Stand, 6d. each person.

Glasgow Evening Citizen – *Friday, 16 April 1880*

The Zulus had played a series of games in the Midlands and the north of England, attracting large crowds, and, like minstrels, they would black up, carry shields and spears and perform war dances to entertain the crowds. However, this team were not entertainers but were players of a high calibre, and until they played in Scotland, had only been beaten by the FA Cup winners, Blackburn Olympic. One member

11 *Glasgow Evening Post*, Saturday, 15 May 1880.

of the Zulu squad would go on to play for the English national team.[12]

The effect of the Anglo-Zulu War had raised tensions in all parts of the country. Reports appeared in the newspapers of men and women of colour being abused in the streets, and in Scotland a letter appeared in the *Glasgow Herald* from 'A Man of Colour':

> 'I have the misfortune to be, or rather it has pleased God to create me, a man of colour, and my well-educated wife and daughter are of the same caste as myself. Though I am in a respectable business here my wife and daughter have been subjected to gross insults by crowds of howling men and women, who call them Zulus, & c., even by the very men who ought to protect them – viz., the police – as a young lady in my shop can testify … my wife and daughter cannot go out either by tramway car or on foot without being subject to outrage and insult.'

Watson may have been subjected to abuse also, as stories in the press from across the country report incidents directed at people with darker-coloured skin and at non-Africans. Some reports suggest Watson played against the Sheffield team and that he was 'amused' by the event.[13] However, it is unlikely, as he had played for the Scottish Canadian team two days before and was due to play for the Glasgow Pilgrims the day after, not to mention the Glasgow Charity Cup two days after that.

---

12 John Hunter, 1852–1903. Sheffield Wednesday player and FA Cup winner with Blackburn Olympic in 1883.

13 http://inbedwithmaradona.com/sheffield-2/2015/11/2/sheffield-zulus-victorian-showmen

Tolerance of this 'minstrel' football reflects the times. Heightened by the loss of British lives at the hands of the tribesmen the previous year, the racial parody and its charitable connotations seemed to sanction open hostility towards anyone with darker skin than themselves.

But as the Sheffield Zulus became more popular and no longer a charitable entity, they were charged with professionalism, and the Sheffield FA banned them. The team disbanded in 1882, but clearly racial persecution and jingoism were secondary to the Sheffield FA's laws on professionalism in football. But 'Minstrelism' would remain an acceptable form of entertainment right through to prime-time television in the 1960s.

One of the few references to abuse Watson received appeared in the *Scottish Athletic Journal* 1885:

> 'Both on and off the field he is courtesy, and unostentation personified and although of a most powerful build he invariably plays a sterling honest game ... Although on more than one occasion subjected to vulgar insults by splenetic,[14] ill-tempered players, he uniformly preserved that gentlemanly demeanour ... he is the embodiment of rare geniality and kind-heartedness.'

This brief reference to 'vulgar insults' presumably would include references to his ethnicity and may not have been the sole preserve of opposition players. However, the article is otherwise wholly complimentary towards Watson, with no reference to ethnicity or colour.

In recent years, the history of black footballers in Scotland has been fertile ground for scholarly research, and with the

14 Used to describe a person who easily becomes angry or annoyed, or their behaviour – Cambridge Dictionary.

rediscovery of players like Robert Walker and Willie Clarke, it becomes obvious that Watson was not the only man of colour to disappear from the record books.

Like Watson, Walker and Clarke owe their existence to Scottish fathers and their business interests in the colonies of the Empire. Robert Gustave Walker (1857–1936) was born in Sierra Leone to a Scottish father and a local woman, but was brought up in Preston Mill, Kirkcudbrightshire, Scotland. He played for Third Lanark between 1875 and 1877 and was the first man of colour to play in a senior cup competition in 1875. He was also the first man of colour to play in a major cup final when Lanark met Queen's Park in the 1877 Scottish Cup. He may also have been the first man of colour to trial for the national team, when in February 1876 he played for Wallace's team against Dickson's team, at the Scottish trials, losing 2-1. He would be invited to trial for the national team twice more. He played for Parkgrove during the 1877/78 season, alongside Watson, but after Parkgrove he does not appear to have played football regularly again. Like Watson, he left Scotland for Liverpool to become a marine engineer, and like Watson, later in life moved with his family to London, to Hammersmith, where he died in 1936.

D.D. Bone mentioned Robert Walker in 1890:

> 'The half-back line was thoroughly consistent with the rest of the team – smart and quick on the ball. In the attacking row were, with successive changes, a curly-haired son of Africa, named Walker – a misnomer, however, so far as his pace on the extreme right was concerned ...'[15]

15 Bone (1890).

The Parkgrove Football Club not only included two men of colour, they included Tommy Marten, a player with Asian ancestry.[16] This makes Parkgrove a unique club as they are almost certainly the first team to play at a high level with such ethnic diversity.

> Third Lanark are the only team to have a half caste playing for them; this was Darkey Walker, a familiar and conspicuous figure from 1874 to 1878. Andrew Watson, the famous Queen's Park back, and he were almost of a colour, Andrew being born in Jamaica.

Scottish Referee – *Monday, 8 February 1904*

Before Watson was rediscovered, John Walker (no relation to Robert) was believed to have been the first black football player in Scotland. Labelled with the same racial epithet, John Walker was born in 1876 to a West Indian father and a Scottish mother and played for Leith Primrose in junior league football. He then played as a professional for Leith Athletic, before being transferred for the princely sum of £50 to Hearts in 1898. This made John Walker the first black player to command a transfer fee in the Scottish League. In 1900, he crossed the border as many Scotsmen had done in previous decades and became the first man of colour to play for Lincoln City. Sadly, he died of consumption in 1900 at the age of 22.

Willie Clarke would join the list of black Victorian men of colour to play a high standard of football in Scotland. Like Watson, Clarke's father was from Guyana and mother from Kilmarnock. Clarke was born in Mauchline, Ayr, but moved to Glasgow where he would play at Kelburn, Crown Athletic, Third Lanark, Arthurlie and East Stirlingshire

---

16 Thomas William Henry Marten (1857–1911) – born in Surakarta, Java.

(but not in the Scottish League). He was a Scotland junior internationalist in 1897 and was the second man of colour to wear the Scotland shirt at any level. Moving south, he became the first man of colour to play for Bristol Rovers (1900), Aston Villa (1901) and Bradford City (1905). He was the first man of colour to score a goal in the Football League, when Aston Villa beat Everton 3-2 in the FA Cup on Christmas Day 1901.[17]

But the list of black Scottish Victorian footballers is short. It may grow as the period is researched further, but it is highly unlikely there will be another discovery of the calibre of player such as Andrew Watson. In a period before Britain celebrated its diversity, these players are all pioneers.

All these black or Asian sportsmen appear to have been judged on their skill rather than their race and were able to compete without any obvious discrimination or adverse comment in the press. This is in stark contrast to, say, attitudes towards the first women footballers, or the sectarianism and racism that became so pervasive in the 20th century.[18]

After Watson, it would be over 100 years before the next man of colour played for Scotland, when Nigel Quashie appeared against Estonia in 2004 but, throughout Europe, Watson would be the only man of colour to represent a national team in the Victorian era.

In England, the list of black Victorian footballers is equally as short. Walter Tull was the first black outfield player to play in the English League, and goalkeeper Arthur Wharton was the first black English professional footballer. Tull would later fall in the First World War.

---

17 Gleave (2020).

18 Andy Mitchell – https://www.scottishsporthistory.com/sports-history-news-and-blog/scotlands-first-black-footballer-robert-walker-the-curly-haired-son-of-africa

It would be well into the next century before another man of colour would be associated with a national squad. John Leslie would have been the first to play for England in 1925 but, having been selected to play, he was mysteriously dropped when the International Selection Committee, who picked the squad before a manager was appointed, realised Leslie was a man of colour. Picked to play against Ireland, Leslie remains the first black player to be 'selected' to play for England, even though he does not appear in the records.

It was not until the modern era that Viv Anderson became the first black footballer to play for the senior England national side when he turned out in 1978 against Czechoslovakia, almost 100 years since Watson first pulled on the Scotland shirt and almost 50 years since Eddie Parris pulled on the national shirt for Wales. It was not until 1997 that Jeff Whitley played for the Northern Ireland team against Belgium, then Chris Hughton for the Republic of Ireland against the USA in 1979.

Arguably, Andrew Watson could have played for England, having spent most of his early life there, but the opportunity never arose. Playing for Corinthian and for Surrey County was the closest he would get.

The rediscovery of Andrew Watson is as remarkable as it is unfathomable. How can the captain of a national team be forgotten, especially as the team he captained thumped the English 6-1 at The Oval, one of Scotland's most historic sporting achievements? It is unconvincing to argue that he was deleted from the record books due to his ethnicity when many of the names of Watson's team-mates in that Scottish side and linked to the Scottish contribution to the evolution of the world's beautiful game have also been forgotten.

The Game

When Watson first moved to Scotland and began a career in football, various elements within the game were reluctantly coalescing. A decade later, as Watson's career was coming to an end, many of the loose threads had been pulled together, and the intervening years of negotiation and compromise had provided the coherence required to allow the game to evolve exponentially.

In the 1870s, the social and political changes affected all corners of the country. Increasing industrialisation drove an agrarian population into the cities, creating new communities. The middle classes expanded, cities grew, and everyone felt the changes. The working classes found they had slightly more money in their pockets and more free time to spend it, so were turning to football, both as spectators and as participants. As the momentum grew, this intense period of adjustment propelled 'the beautiful game' forward.

It was at this time that Andrew Watson first began playing football, and he would play through the years when remarkable changes were taking place around him. From his first games in Glasgow in 1875 to his last games in Liverpool in the late 1880s, he was perhaps unaware that he was living through the birth of the modern game. To understand the historical context is to appreciate how the game emerged from turmoil and discord into something that is today more familiar.

In the 1870s, the rules of the game could vary depending on where you were in the country, what school you attended, what team you played for or what social class you belonged to. There were no professional footballers, no nationwide leagues, no UEFA, FIFA or World Cup. By the early 1880s, the only international fixtures were friendlies between England, Scotland, Wales and Ireland. The principal governing body, the English FA, was set up in 1863 to help fashion a universal set of rules. Although superficially representative, it did not have a full consensus of football clubs in England or Scotland. Many in the north considered it an institution only interested in southern business. The game was socially and politically regionalised, with fraying tensions simmering just below the surface.

Meanwhile, the game was evolving from a provincial pastime to an organised sport. The elements vying for power, without adequately understanding the consequences of their actions, dug the foundations for the game we know today. But for a while, the game was on a knife-edge, precariously balanced between class ideology and regional differences.

On page i of the picture section is an early depiction of an England versus Scotland international at The Oval in London, played on 6 March 1875. This meeting was the fourth official international between the 'auld enemies' and resulted in a 2-2 draw. The previous three contests produced one draw and one win apiece. However, of the following nine games Scotland would win eight, forcing the English FA into a period of introspection, consolidation and compromise, changing the game forever.

Watson's whereabouts at the time are unclear. He may have still been in London with his sister and, if so, may have even attended the game. However, evidence suggests he was already in Glasgow and may have become a member of Maxwell Football Club. If he arrived around Easter, there would only be two games left in the season, and his membership of Maxwell would be short-lived.

Having exchanged London for Glasgow, Watson would quickly become aware of the differences in the game north of the border. He may have also been aware of the various elements attempting to exert control over the governance, constitution and legislation of the sport at that time. Amateurs argued with professionals over the integrity of the game, the north resented southern governance, northern working classes found little in common with the southern amateur gentlemen, and the Scottish and English fought for dominance on the field.

In 1863, the English FA published 'The Rules of Association Football', which heralded years of disagreement between the supporters of the different rules and codes. Unable to align the squabbling parties over the handling or not of the ball, the establishment of the rugby code finally settled the argument and separated it from the football code in 1870.

The Oval image was published only five years after the split of the codes and may explain why it looks more like action from a game of rugby than something we might recognise today as 'soccer'. However, issues in rugby remained unhealed, and the inability of the north and south to find a middle ground would later lead to a division into the two forms of the discipline we know today – union and league. Miraculously, those driving football at the time managed to avoid a similar outcome, but for a while there was a real fear that the game might end up split on a regional basis.

Versions of the game where players would kick a sphere with their feet have been traced back to ancient times, but 'folk football' has been identified as the precursor to the game that would become association football. The Shrove

Tuesday festivals at Corfe Castle and Kingston upon Thames are well-known examples of English folk football. The 'Ball of Scone' or 'Fastern's Eve' festivals are similar pre-industrial rituals found in Scotland. These ball games, played in towns or communities across the kingdom, could involve hundreds of people, with the whole town providing the pitch. The object of the game was to move a 'foot-ball' to a designated point on either side of the town, using hands and feet, or sometimes only hands.

Games could be extremely physical and often considered rites of passage for young men or women. The teams were spilt via arbitrary designations, such as 'married' versus 'unmarried' or those living in the north of the town versus those from the south. Some of the festivals were perceived as ancient sports, and research has suggested they were of a deep cultural significance, offering social value and cohesion. However, although folk football in Scotland was remarkably like the English rituals, this similarity would not be reflected in the development of football on each side of the border.

In the mid-1800s, when the English public schools and universities embraced the facets of folk football, the game became more organised and structured, with rules and codes, and less like the mayhem of the provincial festivals.

The emergence of Muscular Christianity in public schools and the introduction and application of a set of rules and regulations transformed the pastime into a legitimate sport.[19] Applying a code of conduct to the game also meant it had a moral component. Football became a rational recreation, embodying a moral superiority, public duty

---

19 Muscular Christianity was a philosophical movement, originating in England in the mid-19th century. It believed in 'a healthy mind and a healthy body'. It also included concepts of patriotic duty, the moral and physical beauty of athleticism, discipline, self-sacrifice and manliness.

and responsibility.[20] This became manifest in 'amateurism'. The game should be played for enjoyment and personal improvement, reflected in the adage 'it's not whether you win or lose, it's how you play the game'. One key factor kept their code clean and pure: amateurism. The amateur and the professional dichotomies would create deep-seated divisions in the game but would also compound and drive its evolution.

What emerged from these schools were physically healthy gentlemen, imbued with moral fibre and of sound character. Destined to be the next generation of politicians, business leaders, military and clergy, they were expected to use what they had learned on the playing fields of their schools to lead the Empire into the next century. When they left their schools and universities, the 'gentlemen' migrated to towns and villages all over the country, taking their game with them and sharing the rules and enthusiasm with local communities.

Perceived by the middle classes as an effective method of social control and a means of building character, participation was encouraged. Every conceivable institution, organisation and community across the country adopted football. What was once the province of the privileged few was spiralling into a national obsession and was well on its way to becoming the people's game.

Meanwhile, the evolution of the game in Scotland had taken an alternative route. As business opportunities began transforming Glasgow into an important business centre, an influx of middle-class Highlanders migrating to the large cities fed football. This distanced the game in Scotland from the English public school version. Redirecting interest

---

20 A rational recreation was a productive and socially responsible recreation, which transformed a traditional rural leisure activity, like football, by imbuing ideological principles of obedience to given rules, discipline, hygienic living, teamwork, masculinity and a projection of a national identity.

from their traditional Highland games, the Highlanders embraced the new sport. They experimented with techniques and introduced their own rules that allowed their version of the game to evolve, gradually producing a style of play unique to Scotland.

In England, different football philosophies began to create regional divisions. Based in London and administered primarily by public school and university graduates, the English FA governed the game throughout the country. It was also a resolutely amateur organisation. But in the industrial north of England, the capitalist ethic was strong, and this code would influence the business of football. Clubs realised they could make profits from football, and new clubs were formed or grew to accommodate the demand from their local communities. Local rivalries developed and pressure to win became a driving force. These clubs felt that the FA was unsympathetic and aloof, and they wanted to be free to pursue their own business interests without interference from the south. It did not help that the opposing force in the south appeared to consist of a group of financially secure 'old-boys' who could afford to be amateurs!

By the beginning of the 1880s, there were four distinct footballing regions, each with their own version of the rules: Scotland remained staunchly amateur well into the 1890s; the north of England wanted to be professional; the Midlands was amateur, but the potential to embrace professionalism was growing; and in the south, the amateur gentlemen dominated.

The 'southern gentlemen' faced the problem of controlling 'their' sport and preserving its moral integrity.[21]

---

21 Charles Clegg, chair of the Sheffield Association and later chair of the English FA, said, 'They should play football as a friendly game and not as a matter of business.'

They saw the emergence of professionalism in the north as particularly disturbing. The gentlemen believed professionalism would corrupt or replace their amateur code with an all-encompassing desire to win by fair means or foul. The introduction of professional money had polluted boxing and horse racing and they feared it would do the same for football. If left unchecked, professionalism would inevitably lead to cheating, dishonesty and gambling.

There followed an uneasy peace where the northern club owners, all businessmen, paid lip service to the English FA's amateur ethos, while at the same time looking around for ways to attract bigger crowds, more receipts and cementing stronger local allegiances.

By the 1880s, the style of football played by the Scottish and English was significantly different. The English favoured the 'kick and rush' style, seen in the England versus Scotland image from The Oval in 1875. In the picture, the ball has been kicked forward and the English are rushing to intercept it. As a variant to this, they would employ the dribbling game, where one of the eight forwards, usually the biggest and toughest, would run with the ball at his feet, knocking opponents out of the way. It was an individualistic approach to the game, lacking teamwork and interplay.

The English team in the image are advancing, barging the Scottish players and preparing to bundle the ball into the goal. The Scots look in disarray, but with 14 players in the penalty box, the pushing and kicking that followed would not only resemble a rugby maul but would probably not achieve the desired English goal.

The Scottish employed the 'passing' game, known as 'combination' football. The players took up positions and would work together, passing between themselves to get the ball up the field and into their opponent's half. This was a far less individualistic style, more appropriate to the smaller physical attributes of many Scottish players, as opposed to the well-fed, robust English public school physique.

The Oval picture shows that solid crossbars, nets, goalkeeper shirts and goal lines were not in use. Also, the fact that the Scottish and English had not yet agreed a universal set of rules meant that one of these teams was playing by rules they may have been unfamiliar with.

Scotland's dominance in winning eight of the next nine matches would not go unnoticed by clubs in the north of England. In 1878, Darwen, a mill town in Lancashire, were dazzled by the superior Scottish style of Glaswegians Jimmy Love and Fergus Suter. Blackburn Rovers were so impressed that they poached Suter with a surreptitious offer of pub ownership.

Other northern clubs followed suit, and soon a stream of Scottish players had been tempted south with clandestine offers of wages and positions of employment. Consequently, many of the top clubs in the north included a considerable number of Scottish footballers. In 1883, Burnley played with ten Scots in the team and, a year later, the Preston North End squad included nine Scots. As Richard Robinson said in 1920:

> '... [Blackburn Rovers] were among the first to induce Scots to cross the border. F. Suter and Hugh M'Intyre led the way, and others followed until it became quite the fashion in Lancashire to leaven the teams with imported Scottish players. What the inducements were that enticed these players, and a hundred others, to go south can only be surmised. In some cases, an upholsterer was transformed into a thriving publican, and an iron moulder, and even

> labourers, into flourishing tobacconists. Other Scots went about with their hands in their pockets, gentlemen at large, yet nothing could be proved against any of the clubs.'[22]

These players would eventually be referred to as the 'Scottish professors', bringing their skills and advanced theories with them.[23] But, at the time, the practice of rewarding players for their services became known as 'shamateurism'.

Now the northern clubs set their sights on the jewel of the English football crown, the FA Cup, and yearned to be the best team in England.

The southern amateurs were also keen to understand the Scottish game and, thanks to the spread of the railways, arranged numerous fixtures with teams north of the border. However, the journeys were perhaps driven less by the prospect of competition but were more for reconnaissance purposes. The resulting influence of the Scottish style on the English game cannot be overstated.

But the professionalism question remained unaddressed and, fearing a split along professional and amateur lines and the disastrous loss of governing power, the FA chose to turn a blind eye to the practice.

However, not all northern clubs were supportive of legalising professionalism. In contrast, some of the increasingly politically motivated working classes saw the introduction of money into the game as removing it from the people and into the hands of privately owned businessmen.

But the die was cast, and it was becoming increasingly evident that the amateur principles defended so vehemently

---

22 Robinson (1920).

23 A modern term used to describe the influence of migrating Scottish footballers who took the game to all corners of the globe.

in the south were losing ground when Blackburn Olympic (northern professionals) beat Old Etonians (southern amateurs) in the FA Cup Final of 1883, the first northern team to win the trophy. Previously dominated by southern amateur clubs and 'old boys' teams, never again would this footballing genre win the FA Cup. The dominance of the northern teams in the last decades of the 18th century was almost comprehensive. In fact, the cup would not return south until 1901 when, after a replay, Tottenham Hotspur beat Sheffield United. But by that time, most teams were thoroughly professional.

The legitimisation of professionalism finally came in 1885 when the FA was forced to address the issue. After losing an FA Cup match against Preston North End, Upton Park protested to the FA that the Preston team was 'packed full' of professionals. The uncomfortable candour of the Preston North End chairman, William Sudell, preferring not to lie to the FA commission, told the truth:

> 'Preston are all professionals, but if you refuse to legalise them, they will be amateurs. We shall all be amateurs, and you cannot prove otherwise.'[24]

Sudell's honesty and the support he received from northern clubs eventually forced the FA's hand and professionalism became legitimised, but it would be stringently controlled. Ironically, Sudell, who had vigorously championed the rights of professionals, was later convicted of embezzling money from the mill where he worked as a manager to help pay for player wages and expenses. He received a three-year prison sentence and, even though by now it was far too late to

---

24 Catton, J.A.H., *The Story of Association Football* (1926).

reverse the decision, perhaps the worst fears of the amateurs had been realised.

The legitimisation of professionalism was ultimately a capitulation to the north. Having threatened to set up their own football association, they had challenged the power of the FA and forced them into a compromise to save their governing monopoly.

BRITISH FOOTBALL ASSOCIATION.

A meeting of the British Football Association was held at the Bay Horse Hotel, Blackburn, last night to consider what action should be taken respecting the result of the general meeting of the English Association. A letter was read from one of the leading Midland clubs suggesting the holding of a conference, and expressing a hope that professionalism might be legalised. It was decided to appoint a sub-committee to go over the rules of the English Association, with a view of suggesting several amendments to be made at the next annual meeting in March. The question of assistance by members of clubs belonging to the British Association was also considered, but the result was not allowed to transpire.

HEELEY v. MEXBOROUGH.

Sheffield Daily Telegraph – *Tuesday, 3 February 1885*

However, Scotland would hold on to its amateur status for another seven years. Their policy of disowning players tempted south by offers of 'filthy lucre' meant that the Scottish national football team were never able to field a team of their best players. However, Scotland continued to match and regularly defeat the English.

When a young Andrew Watson arrived in Scotland around 1875, he would have been an amateur. Having just left an English public school, bound for university, the differences of the Scottish game would have fascinated him. He was in the right place at the right time and willing to learn, not from the university professors but from their footballing counterparts. He would become a professor himself but a variation of northern practice. He would become one of only a handful of Scottish players who journeyed south to bring the Scottish game to the English amateurs.

By the end of Watson's career in 1888, football had transformed from the disparate elements of the 1870s to a properly organised, governed and administered sport. William McGregor's Football League was underway, and numerous cup competitions favoured professionalism, reducing the attraction of amateur contests. Professional footballers were commonplace, the game had a universally accepted set of rules and a far more recognisable form of the modern game was beginning to emerge.

During the seven years between professionalism being legitimised in England and Scotland, armies of Scots went south and accepted professional terms. It was a skill migration that shaped the English game forever.

Watson made the journey south twice in his career, demonstrating his celebrated talent to English audiences. In doing so, he would never again be selected to play for his homeland. After his three appearances, including one captaincy, his international career was over. It could be said that Watson sacrificed his international career to demonstrate the finer points of the Scottish game to the English. His short career straddled the years when the dominance of power in the game shifted from the gentleman amateur to professional business, from regional divisions to a nationwide obsession, and from the preserve of a few to entertainment for the masses.

Origins

Countless children of mixed heritage were conceived throughout the British Empire due to the enormous fortunes to be made from the production, processing and sale of sugar. By the time Andrew Watson was born, even though it had been years since the abolition of slavery, the communities created by the trade in sugar had changed little.

Demerara came late to the sugar trade. After the 1807 abolition of the slave trade and the vast fortunes made in the West Indies in the production of sugar, British entrepreneurs saw the fertile flood plains of the Demerara river as a new opportunity and perfect location for growing sugar cane of high quality. The predominantly Dutch plantations had been producing a variety of crops for centuries, and as the necessary slave labour was already in place, British traders began purchasing estates and repurposing them to grow the superior product called 'Demerara Sugar'.

It would take another 26 years before the slave trade was finally abolished. The abolitionists eventually agreed to allow compensation payments, not to the slaves but to the slave owners. The equivalent of over £20 billion was distributed to claimants, the beneficiaries ranging from politicians, business owners and aristocrats to members of the middle or lower-middle classes, widowed annuitants and members of the clergy. Over 50 per cent of the claimants lived in Britain and had never seen a plantation.[25]

It was around the time that the Slave Trade Act of 1807 was passed that the four Watson brothers sailed to Demerara to make their fortunes. Two brothers would never return to Scotland, and of the two that did return, one would be mentally or psychologically damaged. Only Peter Miller Watson would produce offspring, a daughter named Annette (or Annetta) and a son called Andrew.

The Watson Family

There are records of an 'Andrew Watson' in Crantit, near Kirkwall in the Orkney Islands as far back as the 16th century.

Through advantageous marriages, the Watson family tree was full of wealthy and influential relations, many having made fortunes in Demerara and the West Indies.[26]

At the turn of the 18th century, the 'Factor' in Kirkwall was James Watson. Essentially a property manager acting on behalf of the landowner, Lord Dundas, the Factor had the power to evict tenants. This role often made them unpopular in the local community, especially during the Highland and Island Clearances.[27] James Watson married Christian Robertson, whose family can be traced back to the Plantagenets, Bruces, Stewarts and as far back as Edward I.[28] She was considered a rare beauty and was known as 'the second of the Three Fair Maids of Kiltearn'.

---

25 *Britain's Forgotten Slave Owners,* a two-part BBC programme presented by David Olusoga in 2015.

26 The familial relationships are expertly examined by Ian Campbell Whittle at: https://www.scotsfootballworldwide.scot/andrewwatson

27 https://en.wikipedia.org/wiki/Highland_Clearances

28 Ross (1895).

By the time she was 29 years old, Christian had produced five sons. Each would be expected to work hard and pursue their own destinies. While four brothers sailed off to Demerara to make their fortunes, the youngest, also named James, went to London and became a barrister.

The middle child, Peter Miller Watson, became a lawyer in Demerara, his name appearing on many legal documents and acting as an executor for the wills of deceased local plantation owners. This role placed him in the advantageous position of being kept informed of bankrupt estates or if a widow wanted to settle her affairs and leave the colony. He helped with the transactions of the sale and purchasing of estates. He later entered into a partnership and invested his own money in two plantations.

The two eldest sons, Harry and Andrew, both died in Demerara at the age of 34. Peter Miller and William Robertson Watson remained, eventually leaving Demerara in the 1850s as wealthy men. Of the remaining Watsons, only Peter Miller Watson had children, his brothers dying leaving no known issue. It is likely that if there were illegitimate children of any of the brothers, decency would have dictated they provide for their offspring as Miller Watson had for Andrew and Annetta.

When James died in 1808, a year after the Slave Trade Act, Christian married Thomas Stewart Traill, professor of medical jurisprudence at Edinburgh University.[29] Also born in Kirkwall, Traill and Christian would produce six more children.[30],[31]

---

29 Thomas Stewart Traill, 1781–1862. Professor of medical jurisprudence at Edinburgh University. National Galleries of Scotland Collection.

30 One stillborn in 1824.

31 One daughter, Ann Traill, left Andrew and Annetta £1,000 each in her will.

Christian's father and grandfather were both ordained in the Presbyterian ministry. Her father had married the daughter of the Attorney General of Barbados. The family had business interests in Demerara, and two uncles and three of Christian's brothers either died there or en route to or from British Guiana. These familial connections would no doubt have helped find her sons opportunities in Demerara, with the added bonus of removing them from her new family home.

Miller Watson eventually became joint owner of two sugar plantations in Demerara: 'La Bonne Intention'[32] ('The Good Intention'), and 'Zeeburg'[33] (Sea Town), a former Dutch estate. His partner in those ventures was Alexander McLaren, another Scot, to whom Miller Watson would sell his holdings before returning to Europe.

After the abolition of slavery in 1833, the compensation payments made to Demerara claimants were the highest of all awarded to plantation owners throughout the Empire. In 1832, Miller Watson filed four claims for 18 slaves, receiving over £800 in compensation.[34] His brother, Andrew, made one claim for six slaves, worth close to £300.[35] Another brother, Henry Robertson Watson, made two claims for seven slaves and received over £350 in compensation.[36] Overall, the Watson brothers owned 31 souls.

Rather than giving them their freedom, the Slavery Abolition Act of 1833 bound the slaves to 'an apprenticeship' for four years after 1834. Then in the 1840s, labour

---

32 Sugar plantation producing rum. In 1829, La Bonne Intention had 300 slaves.

33 Sugar, cotton and coffee, but also produced rum. In 1829, Zeeburg had 200 slaves.

34 Equivalent to over £80,000 in 2018.

35 Equivalent to over £33,000 in 2018.

36 Equivalent to over £38,000 in 2018.

problems, taxation and the falling price of sugar made plantation owning less profitable for many. This meant that, from emancipation to 1850, the number of working estates in Demerara halved, the production of sugar and coffee fell dramatically, and the production of cotton ceased completely.[37] Perhaps due to the challenging economy in Demerara, Miller Watson and his surviving brother Henry returned home.

Andrew Watson's current biography says Miller Watson left Demerara between 1857 and 1858 when the mother of his children, Hannah (or Anna Rose), died. Instead of returning to Scotland, where most expats brought their offspring, Miller Watson chose to live in England. Logic suggests that his children, Andrew and Annetta, accompanied him at that time.

In 1857, records show that Miller Watson had an account at the Union Bank of London. Two years later, the electoral roll places him at Shagden Farm or Weylea near Worplesdon, in Surrey, which suggests he took up residence in 1858.[38]

When the children arrived in Britain, Andrew would have been only two or three years old and Annetta seven or eight. There are no records of their mother travelling with them to England. As the children grew, their memories of Demerara and their mother would have become vague and indistinct. The children had been transported to an unfamiliar country of manners, respectability and wealth they must have found

---

37 Brumell (1853).

38 Name listed in electoral register. Maps of the period list Weylea, but not Shagden Farm, the assumption being they are one and the same, as the London Road reference is consistent through all directories and electoral registers. Weylea was demolished in the 1980s and replaced by new housing, but the name survives in Weylea Avenue. Also, the public house opposite, the Anchor and Horseshoes, which Peter Watson must surely have frequented, remains to this day.

hard to comprehend. Their father would have met all their needs, but the children's shared anxieties would surely make them inseparable. This bond might explain why the 1861 census shows Andrew, a four-year-old boy, living with his sister in a school for young women.

The children would also be aware of the attention they attracted but would be unable to grasp the more profound, complex issues they would have to deal with as they grew older.

The British climate would require them to wear new, bulky, perhaps uncomfortable clothes, causing them both to feel awkward, self-aware and physically restricted. They would be exposed to the Victorian adage that children should be seen and not heard, constraining them further and driving them closer together.

Research suggests the children did not live with their father, and the record of the 1861 census seems to confirm this. Appearing at such a young age in the Elizabeth Buchanan household in Staffordshire, in a school for young ladies, might be seen as a father distancing himself from his offspring. Victorian respectability may have inclined Miller Watson to remove the children, but decency dictated he should provide for them financially, and leave them to others to raise. In his last will and testament, Miller Watson consistently refers to his daughter as 'Annette or Annetta'. This indecision by a father towards his daughter is telling – perhaps indicating his unfamiliarity with or his detachment from his daughter – and it follows that Andrew was treated similarly.

Later in his life, to confirm his eligibility to play for Surrey County, Watson would associate himself with Dorking, Worplesdon and Godalming. All these towns were within easy reach of his father's estate and close to his father's final resting place. Connecting himself with these towns suggests that Watson may have been more familiar with Surrey than is currently understood.

Death of Peter Miller Watson

After a protracted illness, Peter Miller Watson died on 22 April 1869 at 2 Chandos Street, London, in the house of his friend, Francis Courtnay. He was 65 years old. Andrew was 12 years old and Annetta 18 or 19. It is unknown whether they were with their father at the end or whether they attended his funeral.

Miller Watson was buried seven days later in St Luke's, Burpham, Surrey, in a grave marked by an expensive and rugged monument that remains at the forefront of the churchyard 150 years later. Francis Courtnay's groom and housekeeper witnessed his last will and testament, suggesting he had written it in haste, that he fully understood he was on his deathbed and was getting his affairs in order.

Even though he rushed his will, it was complicated and full of legalese. There were precise instructions for the allocation of funds and legacies, and he also named three executors. One surprise beneficiary was 'Hannah' Rose, the children's mother, obviously still alive and living in Demerara. Previously believed dead, this meant that Miller Watson had taken Andrew and Annetta from her when he decided to return to Europe. She was bequeathed £250.[39]

Watson's Mother

Little is known of Andrew's mother, Anna or Hannah Rose, but she is believed to have been a freed slave and of mixed race. As far as research can tell, Anna and Miller

39 Equivalent to approximately £30,000 in 2018.

Watson were not married, at least not in Britain. On both his wedding certificates, Andrew stated that his parents were married, but this may have been only to hide his illegitimacy.

Confirming the lack of a marital bond, in his last will and testament, Miller Watson named both Andrew and Annette or Annetta as his 'natural' offspring. Similarly, in her will, Miller Watson's stepsister, Ann Traill, confirmed this, and her bequest to Peter's children states:

> 'To my brother Peter's natural children, Andrew Watson, £1,000 and, Annette Watson, £1,000.'[40]

Liaisons between Europeans and locals with an African heritage, either free slaves or those emancipated by the Slavery Abolition Act, continued to produce children. Although a few of these liaisons may have been bound in legal matrimony, most were not. The lives of mixed heritage children were uncertain, and many endured miserable lives, usually separated from one or both of their parents.

Demerara, Essequibo and Berbice, on the Caribbean coast of South America, had been exploited for sugar, coffee and cotton for 200 years before Andrew Watson was born. The 1819 Slave Register records almost 80,000 slaves living in or around Demerara. Fewer than 3,000 of the population were of European origin, of whom the majority were either Dutch or Scottish. Ownership of slaves by the minority white population was widespread, from doctors to clergy, to military and local government.

Although most slaves worked on the plantations, housemaids, house boys, gardeners, nurses and various household slaves were also owned. Although they may

40 The term 'natural child' was used to name offspring that belong to the family even though their parents were not legally bound.

not have had to experience the often brutal conditions of the plantations, they could not expect benevolence from all the households where they were employed. Exposure to various forms of exploitation was usually, but not exclusively, towards young females. Demerara-born historian Henry Dalton (1818–74) wrote of the 1850s:

> '... a large proportion of the white Europeans had come from Scotland and were for the most part of humble extraction, uneducated, and glad to accept any opening that presented itself.'

David Alston commented:

> 'Dalton believed that most Scots in Guyana had lost what he considered their characteristic "reserve, temperance, and zeal for religion" and "separated from the austere influence of domestic examples at home . . . [had] plunged as readily as others into the vortex of dissipation".'[41]

David Alston's examination of relationships between Europeans and enslaved or 'free coloured' women in Guyana is an ugly account of this often ignored and uncomfortable history.[42]

It was common for plantation owners and their European employees to take slaves, freed or not, as mistresses. Peter's business partner, Alexander McLaren, fathered several children with a woman called Fatima Pau (or Pan or Parr), who was a 'free black woman in Guyana'.[43]

41 Alston (2015).

42 Alston (2015).

43 https://www.geni.com/people/Alexander-McLaren/6000000052160238865

After that relationship ended, McLaren fathered more children by another woman of colour.[44] Although little is known of the relationship between McLaren and Miller Watson, they were clearly close friends. McLaren named one of his children Peter Miller Watson McLaren, and Watson was likely to have been a godparent. Alexander died in 1872 and was still living on the Zeeburg plantation.

Anna's surname 'Rose' may be attributed to the owner of the plantation where her mother lived and worked. There were numerous claimants in the records of compensation paid to slave owners with the surname Rose, and it was a common occurrence for slaves to adopt their owner's name or for plantation owners to label slaves with their surname as a mark of possession. The Slave Registers only supplied the first name for all slaves; therefore, the addition of a surname assumes not only that of a father but, potentially, a freed slave. Andrew Rose was a plantation owner in Demerara and research shows that he may have had a link to Anna or Hannah Rose.

In letters from Andrew Rose's sister in Demerara to their mother in Scotland, it becomes clear he was engaged in a relationship with a local woman. On Andrew Rose's advice, his sister, also named Anna, had travelled to Demerara to find a husband, and the suggestion had been successful. She met, married and produced a son for her husband. In 1807, in a letter home, she alluded to Andrew's relationship:

> **I told you in my last letter that Andrew (her brother) had lost his little Mary. Upon the whole it is a fortunate circumstance as 'tis next to impossible to bring up any girl of that colour virtuously."**

The Domestic Papers of the Rose Family – Chapter XI. Anna 1785–1827

44 https://www.wikitree.com/wiki/McLaren-473

Anna Rose is expressing an opinion that would have been generally accepted in Victorian Britain. However, in Demerara and other slave colonies, there would have been a tolerance of unions between locals and Europeans, as David Alston quotes on his Spanglefish website:

> 'When a European arrives, he finds it necessary to provide himself with a housekeeper or mistress – the children are sent back to England for education.' Henry Bolinbroke, 1807[45]

Four years after Anna Rose's letter home, an official notice appeared in the *Essequebo & Demerary Royal Gazette* of 12 October 1811, stating that Andrew Rose had petitioned:

> '... the Court of Policy of the Colonies of Demerary and Essequebo, for Letters of Manumission for the negro woman named Minkie, and her mulatto child Anna'.

Andrew Rose was applying to the court to free the mother and her daughter, Anna Rose. In the Slave Registers for 1819, 'Minky', 'Minkie' or 'Minchy Rose' described herself as 'an agent to Susan Waddell' and owned one slave. Ten years later, this would increase to five slaves. 'Minchy Rose' also filed for compensation for the ownership of two slaves, receiving £76.

The petition meant that Minkie's daughter, Anna Rose, would not only be 'free' but would have been a contemporary of Miller Watson.[46] Due to the low percentage (3 per cent) of

45 http://www.spanglefish.com/slavesandhighlanders/index.asp?pageid=222459

46 P.M. Miller was born 1805 and Anna Rose before 1811.

Europeans in the Demerara population at that time, Anna Rose may have been Miller Watson's partner, the union producing Andrew and Annetta. If correct, Andrew Watson had one parent of mixed race and one of European descent, so was of one-quarter African ancestry. This union would have produced offspring with a pale complexion, perhaps contributing to Andrew Watson's successful engagement with Victorian society. The famous image of Watson with the Corinthians in 1883 (page iii of picture section), shows a pale young man, not too dissimilar to his team-mates.

The implications of Watson's complexion might also have contributed to his apparent disappearance from the historical register. As can be seen in the image, the offspring of a union between a European and a person of mixed heritage can produce children of a fair complexion. Watson's fair skin may be the reason he remained so unobtrusive for so long. There are only a few pictures of Watson, and it is not immediately evident he is a person of colour. Not until the 1980s, while examining a photograph of the Scottish team, did Tommy Malcolm begin to suspect he was looking at a person of colour.[47] Much later, while researching another topic, he came across an article where Watson was referred to as a 'coloured gentleman'. With this discovery, Tommy Malcolm and Ged O'Brien began work in earnest to discover the story of the man in the images.

Watson was 12 years old when he lost his father and may not have been aware that his mother was still alive. The only connections Watson had with Demerara were the heirlooms from his father, his elder sister and the colour of his skin. Research has yet to discover any evidence of

47 Tommy Malcolm, Ged O'Brien and Richard McBrearty, from the Scottish Museum, are credited with establishing Watson's place in football history.

Watson's curiosity of either his African or Guyanese heritage, but there are indications he saw himself as Scottish. The choice of a Celtic cross for the grave of his first wife, Jessie, could suggest a personal affiliation with his ancestral home. However, he would eventually choose to live in England for the last 40 years of his life.

Many children of mixed race were brought home to be educated. Those with Scottish fathers were usually sent to school in Scotland. Why Andrew and Annetta were brought to England to be educated is a mystery.

Footnote

The *Richmond and Twickenham Times* published an obituary on 21 March 1921, two weeks after Andrew Watson's death, saying:

> 'Watson – On March 8th at 88 Forest Road, Kew. Andrew Watson, aged 64, son of the late Peter Miller Watson, of Guildford, cousin of the late Right Honourable, William Ewart Gladstone and C.S. Parker.'[48]

Not only is the link to the British Prime Minister surprising, but it also conceals solid links to slavery, Demerara, and Sandbach, Tinne & Company in Liverpool. Andrew Watson was related to many traders who made vast profits from the production of sugar and the slave trade. Both Watson children were provided with the means to occupy a position in the Victorian middle classes, derived from their family's

48 The Gladstone family and Charles Stuart Parker each received over £110,000 in compensation payments after the abolition of slavery, the equivalent of over £11 million each in modern currency. C.S. Parker was Andrew Watson's step-uncle.

links to the production of sugar and, by association, the slave trade. But it would be wrong to classify the Watson children as mere beneficiaries, as their very existence was a consequence of the same business that enslaved their maternal forebears. This disconcerting truth must have troubled both Andrew and Annetta throughout their lives.

Education

Unlike most illegitimate, mixed-race children in the Victorian era, Andrew Watson had an excellent education. It would provide him with the bearing and self-assurance he would need to cement himself firmly as an upstanding member of the middle class.

Before Andrew entered the public school system, Elizabeth Buchanan had tutored both him and his sister. Perhaps as an acknowledgement of her role in the education of both his children, Buchanan was a beneficiary in Miller Watson's will. She had run the Fisherhill School for Ladies in Preston, Lancashire and had passed the school over to her daughter, also Elizabeth, before opening a school for young ladies in Colton, Staffordshire.

This school catered to young women between the ages of 11 and 19. The 1861 census includes, along with both Watson children, a 'visitor' named as 19-year-old Emma E. McLagen, a pupil who had attended Buchanan's previous school in Preston.

Like Andrew and Annetta, Emma Eugene McLagen was born in Demerara. She was the daughter of John McLagen M.D. and an unknown local woman.[49] She married Elizabeth Buchanan's son Robert and moved to Skipton, Yorkshire, where Elizabeth joined them, dying there in 1869. Accepting the marriage of her son to a woman of

49 John McLagen's brother Peter became the long-serving Member of Parliament for Linlithgowshire from 1865 until 1893.

mixed heritage suggests that the Buchanan family's social consciousness set them apart from the norms of the day and that the family may have extended this open-mindedness to both Watson children.

Elizabeth's father, George Pinder, a minister, and his wife, Frances Baynes, were acquaintances of William Wilberforce and Benjamin Franklin, both leading abolitionists of the day, and Elizabeth likely held similar views.[50]

In 1861, the presence of a young boy, barely four years old, in a school for young women, perhaps confirms Miller Watson's preference to keep the children together rather than separate them and keep Andrew with him in his large house in Surrey until he was of school age.

Nevertheless, Andrew received a primary education of a sufficient standard to pass the examinations for entry into Queen Elizabeth's Free Grammar School in Heath near Halifax, Yorkshire (Heath School). He was registered with the School in August 1866.[51] Of note, this was just three years after the foundation of the English FA and the publication of 'The Rule Book of Association Football'.

Heath School

The decision to attend Heath was perhaps predetermined, as the headmaster of the school, the Reverend Thomas Cox, was the husband of Elizabeth Buchanan's daughter.[52] Cox had previously run the grammar school in Preston, perhaps where the connection with the Buchanans was first established.

Andrew Watson was ten years old when he entered Heath School on 1 August 1866 and, along with seven other boys,

---

50 From correspondence with great-great-great niece, Bridget Farmer, 2019.

51 Archives, The Crossley Heath School, Savile Park, Halifax.

52 Author of *Popular History of the Grammar School of Queen Elizabeth, at Heath, near Halifax (1880).*

Thomas Cox officially registered Watson. In 1867, the school comprised 40 boys – five boarders of whom Watson was one, and 35 day scholars from the local area.

The origins of the Heath School date back to the reign of Queen Elizabeth I, but pupil numbers had been dropping steadily since the boom of the industrial revolution in the 1850s and 60s. Cox was doing his best to recruit new fee-paying boarders, but the preference of local Halifax families was to send their boys to Bradford Grammar and other city schools. Consequently, he failed to make Heath a 'public school' (funded by fees), so the school had to exist as a publicly funded 'Endowed School', accepting all pupils, a situation Cox found frustrating. In the year before Watson joined the school, Cox wrote:

> 'The proportion of idle, ignorant, incompetent and low class boys here has exceeded all my former notions on the subject.'

Cox worked hard to keep the school alive and relevant to the local community. A few years after Watson left the school, Cox managed to oversee the construction of an enormous Gothic edifice, able to house 250 pupils. Watson would have been familiar with the old, Elizabethan, stone-floored classroom pictured on page iv of picture section. It was levelled to make way for the new school, the only remnant saved being the 'apple and pear' window incorporated into the north end of the new school, overlooking the bicycle sheds.[53]

---

53 Historic England says the first school on this particular site was established in 1597 and the original 'apple and pear' rose-window from the building is preserved in the north gable wall of the 1878–79 drill shed, and is likely to be the oldest known example of a Halifax rose-window. https://historicengland.org.uk/listing/the-list/list-entry/1410047

However, Cox was unable to change the fortunes of the school, so retired in 1883, and the school closed. At the time of closure, the population of the school comprised one master (Cox) and 13 pupils. He died before the school reopened under new management in 1887.

The school accepted junior boys from eight years old and seniors between the ages of 14 and 19. The school fees were £8 a year for juniors and £12 for seniors, including an extra payment for French. William Wightman's accountancy firm in Liverpool paid Watson's fees. Mentioned as an executor in Miller Watson's will, Wightman managed the particulars of Watson's education and appears on the registry for King's College. Charles Wightman, a year younger than Watson, was William Wightman's son and a fellow pupil and boarder at Heath School.

Boys applying to enter the 'Junior Department' of Heath School had to pass an examination that included reading easy narrative, writing small text-hand and simple sums in the first four rules of arithmetic with the multiplication table.[54]

Obviously, Elizabeth Buchanan's tutoring had been of a sufficient standard to get Watson over this academic hurdle and gain acceptance into the school. For the next four years he could expect to take classes in English grammar, composition and literature; arithmetic, elements of algebra and geometry; history; geography; Latin and some modern language other than English; natural science; drawing; and vocal music.[55]

Watson's school day started at 6am and ended at 5pm, with only one break, between 10am and 11am, except on

---

54 Halifax, Heath Grammar School: Endowed Schools Scheme: 1873 – National Archives.

55 Halifax, Heath Grammar School: Endowed Schools Scheme: 1873 – National Archives.

Thursdays when school ended at 11am, and Saturdays at 1pm. Cox was responsible for the introduction of 'games', which included rugby and cricket. There were three terms to a year, and Watson could look forward to four weeks' holiday at Christmas, four days at Easter, two weeks at Whitsuntide, and six weeks in the summer. He presumably spent his holidays with the Cox family, as there is no indication of him ever spending time with his father in Surrey.

mono.

FOOTBALL PLAYERS.

To the Editor of The Yorkshire Post.

SIR,—Having lately had my attention attracted to a letter in your paper from an old Huddersfield College boy, claiming that his school had had the honour of producing several noted football players, whose names he gives, I, as an old Heath Grammar School (Halifax) scholar, wish to claim for my school similar honours. Heath has produced many excellent football players, such as George Thomson (International, &c.), A. Walsh (late captain of Halifax Football Club), J. E. Wood (Halifax and Yorkshire County), J. Robinson (late half back of Halifax), W. Crabtree (late of Halifax 1st), T. Chambers (of Halifax 1st, and who has only lately left Heath), and many others of local fame. Apologising for trespassing in your valuable paper.—I am, &c.,

AN OLD HEATH SCHOLAR.

Yorkshire Post and Leeds Intelligencer – *Saturday, 24 January 1880*

Thursday afternoons were 'play-days', and this is likely where Watson first discovered his athletic abilities. No records have been found of him taking part in any sport while at the school, although there were competitions between local schools.

In a letter to the *Yorkshire Post* in 1880, the correspondent suggests that football (rugby) was of a high standard at Heath.

There are reports of the school cricket team, which would occasionally supplement the lack of players with teachers, and local newspapers published several scorecards. The

Reverend Cox's sons appear in many of the games, and even though both are younger than Watson, no mention of him appears in any games for the school or the orphanage, who were regular opponents.

Some research has suggested that Watson was placed in the Crossley orphanage, but further research suggests this was not the case.[56] The Crossley Heath Orphanage opened its doors a year before Watson arrived at Heath and the intake was eight boys. During the ensuing years the numbers increased, but admission was by application, and each petition was carefully investigated. The orphanage's prospectus stipulated preference be given to orphans born in the county of York who have lost both father and mother and whose families have been reduced in their 'temporal circumstances'. Watson would not have met any of these requirements, having not been born in Yorkshire, and his father being alive and financially secure.

The 1871 census records Watson as a 'boarder', along with eight other scholars, in the home of the Reverend Thomas Cox. Providing board and lodging to students by educators was common practice and would give the Reverend extra income to supplement his salary. He later complained that in writing his history of the school he lost about £10 in publishing the book, which suggests he was not an affluent man. Of the boarders staying with Cox, Watson was the only one not born in England and one of only three not born or living in Yorkshire or Lancashire. It would have been at Heath where Watson faced the inevitable challenges regarding his parentage and skin colour.

---

56 The orphanage did not become the Crossley and Porter Orphanage until 1885, merging with Heath School in 1985. The resulting Crossley Heath School inhabits the old Crossley and Porter orphanage building.

Andrew's last year at Heath was in 1871 and, according to the school curriculum, he would have left Heath being able to read Latin, and perhaps speak it also, as well as being grounded in literature, mathematics and the scriptures. He would also be able to call himself a 'Heathen', as alumni chose to do.

> 'To say that a boy had been educated at Heath stamped him at once with a hallmark. Many old scholars had attained eminence in many parts of the world, and it was true to say that if a record could be made of all the boys who had left the school and the positions of eminence they had attained, they would find a roll of honour which would be difficult to beat.'[57] Mayor of Halifax, Alderman John Radcliffe

King's College School

King's College was an institution with an exceptional reputation and a progressive curriculum, obviously considered by Wightman as superior to the senior department at Heath.

> 'King's College's junior department was tucked away in its "subterranean" or "infernal regions" (Hearnshaw 103, 153), i.e., its basement. To begin with, it was the most successful part of the new college, growing from 85 pupils in 1829 to 500 in 1843 (Weinreb and Hibbert 447). Not that many of these boys rose to "the airier amplitudes of the professorial lecture-rooms" upstairs (Hearnshaw 153): most either took wing for Oxford or Cambridge or, especially after the introduction of a "modern" as

57 *Halifax Courier*, Saturday, 10 June 1939.

> well as classical section in January 1851, disappeared into what we might now call the business sector.'[58]

On Watson's assessment form completed before admission to King's College School, he was assessed as a 'B' student, having indicated he had studied Latin, including Caesar, Ovid, Virgil, Horace and Juvenal. In arithmetic, he was familiar with proportion, compound rules and reduction, and vulgar fractions, plus had studied Euclidean geometry and algebra.

King's College, London – the School – occupied the basement of the senior college on Strand in the centre of London. King's moved to Wimbledon in 1897. Fees were £24 2s 6d a year, paid in advance, plus £5 5s per term for meals, 'without beer'! The day started at 9.30am with Divine Service in the College Chapel. No pupil could absent themselves 'without the special permission of the Headmaster'. Matriculated students had to wear a cap and gown, which the student paid for.

Watson's registration form at King's was signed by 'Mrs Wightman, at 6 Bentley Road, Liverpool'. It is not clear why it was necessary for William Wightman's wife to sign the forms and not William himself. Perhaps Wightman's role as executor conflicted with his other business, so he recruited his wife's services, assuming, now that Miller Watson was dead, the role of an executor was provided pro bono.

The matriculation records state Watson boarded with the Reverend Blomfield Jackson and his wife, Elizabeth Anne, at their home, Smith House in Stoke Newington. Having lived under the guiding light of the Reverend Cox in Yorkshire, lodging with the Reverend Blomfield

58 Banerjee, J., 'The University of London and Its Boys' Schools', www.victorianweb.org

Jackson would continue Watson's moral and religious training.

Boarding with educators was a common occurrence, and teachers would advertise their homes to students. In the King's College Calendars from 1875–76, Blomfield regularly placed advertisements:

> 'Rev. Blomfield Jackson, M.A. of Exeter College, Oxfford [sic]; South House, Stoke Newington. Mr Jackson's residence offers the advantages of a very healthy neighbourhood and a large garden. It is within walking distance of the School and can be reached in a short time either by train from Temple Station or by omnibuses which travel between it and King's College in forty minutes.'[59]

Jackson was the curate of St Mary's, Stoke Newington, a classical master at King's College, an Oxford graduate and tutor to the daughters of King Edward VII – Princess Louise, Princess Victoria and Maud, who later became Queen of Norway. When Andrew arrived at the school, Jackson was teaching sacred history, catechism, English history, geography, parsing, poetry, dictation, easy composition and Latin.

Boarding fees with the Reverend Jackson were 20 guineas per term, one guinea per term for washing, plus one guinea overall for the use of linen and plate, etc. The total cost of a year's board and tuition at King's would have been around £156, or £18,000 a year in today's currency, a significant sum.

Watson would be familiar with the potentially austere religious and moralistic environment, regular church

59 King's College London College Archives.

attendance, observation of holy days and festivals. He would have a good knowledge of the Bible, and most of his social life would have revolved around the church. Although the respectability, high moral standards and social approval of the church would have shaped his life, he would also have been exposed to the works of Darwin and Marx. Their ideas had been shaking the establishment at the time.

Compared to Halifax, London must have been a revelation to Watson. Being in easy reach of the centre of London, the scale and activity of the city would have overwhelmed him. Close by was Hackney Downs, where rugby, cricket and athletic events regularly attracted large crowds. It was home to numerous football clubs, including Pilgrims and Clapton, and it is likely Watson witnessed games and may have been familiar with the top teams of the time.

Academically, Watson appears to have been a moderate pupil and appeared only once in the school magazine, in the Lent Term 1874 for the Upper School Class prize, Division B! He was never mentioned on the school's speech day, where awards were given to the worthiest pupils in subjects such as mathematics, Latin prose, drawing and the best collection of mounted insects. The school was very proud of their alumni and would follow the honours gained by ex-pupils at Oxford, Cambridge and King's College. Watson's name never appeared in the list of candidates who passed the examination for matriculation at any university.

King's sports days were social occasions, with brass bands and local civic leaders, and were patronised by the stylish and elegant classes filling the Grand Stand Polo Pavilion. The sports days had been held on the Lillie Bridge ground in

Charles Wreford Brown (1867–1952)

Reproduced from: The Illustrated Sporting and Dramatic News – *13 March 1875*

Illustrated Weekly News – *Saturday, 18 March 1865*

William Gibb Clarke (1878–1949) Permission: Jon Martin. Footballs Black Pioneers - https://footballs-black-pioneers.com

Darwen team that won the first Lancashire Challenge Cup in the 1879/80 season, with Fergus Suter lying at the front.
Image provided by Blackburn with Darwen Borough Council for use in the Cotton Town digitisation project: www.cottontown.org

Blackburn Olympic 1882

Georgetown Harbour, circa 1850
http://www.cumberlandscarrow.com/demerara.htm

Crantit House, Kirkwall, Orkney https://www.visitscotland.com

Peter Miller Watson's grave (with chains) at St Luke's, Burpham, Surrey

Alexander McLaren *Avie McLaren* *McLaren's children*

Permission granted Kevin Huscroft, a descendant of Alexander McLaren – 2019

Andrew is sitting at the bottom left, holding his knee. The gentleman in the middle left with the handlebar moustache is E.C. Bambridge, England international and Corinthian, who would play a key role in Andrew's footballing career. The unlabelled player is Frank Etheridge Saunders (1864–1905), England international, who made 50 appearances for Corinthian. He also played six of the seven games in the 1884 tour.

Elizabeth Pinder, nee Buchanan (1805–1869). Image reproduced by permission of Bridget Farmer, great- great-great niece.

Thomas Cox (1822–1887)

'Old Heath School', prior to the rebuild in 1879.
From: A Popular History of the Grammar School of Queen Elizabeth at Heath, Near Halifax. *By Thomas Cox, M.A. 1879*

'Often however did he feel annoyed by the stone floor on which he had to stand, […], and at the distance which lay between him and the fire, a distance so severely felt on a cold day.' From: A Popular History of the Grammar School of Queen Elizabeth at Heath, Near Halifax. *By Thomas Cox, M.A. 1879*

From: A Popular History of the Grammar School of Queen Elizabeth at Heath, Near Halifax. *By Thomas Cox, M.A. 1879*

Reverend Blomfield Jackson, The Graphic – *Saturday, 17 June 1905*

Kings College, Strand

George Osborne Baird (1848–1940). Image courtesy of D. Baird

Andrew Watson's grave in Richmond Cemetery, Surrey

Edward Charles Bambridge (1858–1935)

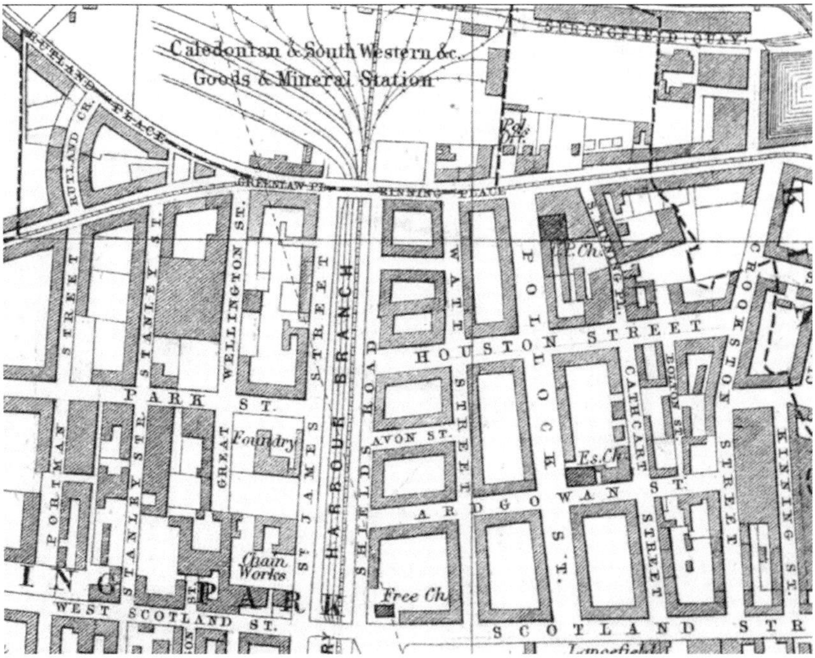

Shields Road, where Watson lived, runs north and south next to the train lines. Watt Street, where the Armour family lived, runs parallel. Houston Street, where J.J. Gow, George and James Miller and George Urquhart lived, intercepts both. National Library of Scotland.

John James Gow, 1859–1932

Thomas Johnson Britten 1858–1910

Crown Hotel, Camsie Glen.

This remarkable picture is the Scottish Canadian team that played Darwen at the Barley Bank Ground in Darwen, on 7 February 1880. The Canadians won 7-3. Watson had chosen to stay behind for the Glasgow trials. He joined the team two days later, and beat Manchester Warriors 8-1. A day after that, the Canadians played Notts Forest and won 2-1. Back Row LtoR: David Davidson (QP), Alexander Vallance (Rangers), John Smith MA (Edinburgh Uni), R. Fraser (Glasgow Uni), James Duncan (Alexandra Athletic). Front Row LtoR: William Wightman Beveridge (Edinburgh Uni), William Scott Somers (QP), William Giffen Struthers (Rangers), Tom Vallance (Rangers), John Leck Kay (QP), Harry McNeil (QP) – © Scottish Football Museum

West Brompton since 1865 and results of the various events could be found in the daily newspapers.[60]

Athletically, Watson does not appear to have been anything out of the ordinary. In his second year at King's he was captain of the third-string rugby team. Apparently missing from the 1872 sports day, he was entered into several events the following year.

Of note, two months earlier, the FA Cup had been played on the Lillie grounds. Wanderers, the first winners, could choose where they would defend the cup, and they decided on Lillie Bridge, the only time the FA Cup Final was held there. Being a ground familiar to the boys from King's College, Watson and his school friends may have attended, especially as the Boat Race was due to take place not far away later that afternoon. If they had been witnesses, they would have seen 'a game of giants'.[61] Cuthbert John Ottaway, all-round sportsman, the first captain of an official England national team and of Oxford University, faced a Wanderers team containing Arthur Fitzgerald Kinnaird, who had two weeks earlier played for Scotland at The Oval.

> 'Bell's Life went into ecstasies over the way in which Kinnaird dribbled right through the Oxford team to score his side's second goal, and anyone with a spark of imagination can surely picture that red beard flowing in the breeze and the white trousers threading a way between the forest of Oxford legs.'[62]

If Watson was there, the effect of watching the two best teams in the country battle it out for the FA Cup may have left an

---

60 Now Lillie Square, close to Chelsea FC's home of Stamford Bridge.

61 Green (1949).

62 Green (1949).

indelible impression, one that he wanted to pursue. However, the truth behind the win for the English lies in the fact that Queen's Park could only afford to send seven players and an umpire to London but had to use four London-based players with an affiliation to Scotland.[63] Even though two of the players had experience of playing in Scotland, the importation of these players, nevertheless, weakened the Scottish team.

At the sports day of 1873, Watson won the drop-kicking competition, came second in the place kicking, third in the 100 yards hurdles and was awarded his 'cap' as captain of the 3rd XV. It is odd that although he went on to achieve greatness in association football, and even though he was selected as captain, he only played third string in rugby.

A year later, in June 1874, perhaps surprisingly, Watson came fourth in the football kicking contest, last in the place kicking competition and did not finish in the 100 yards hurdles, but was first in the high jump with a leap of five feet one inch. He would later excel in this event when he lived north of the border. His ability to kick a ball would also be commented on throughout his footballing years.

A newspaper cutting of a rugby game on 16 November 1872, between King's College and University College School, lists Watson as captain of the 3rd XV, and the report mentions that '... the game was chiefly remarkable for the number of disputes, which could not be settled owing to the absence of umpires.'[64] Watson scored three goals as King's won the game by five goals, two touchdowns and four touches, to nothing!

There are no comments or references to Watson being involved in the association game. If he played football at

63 The Scottish Football Association did not exist at this time.

64 Similar to the role of a linesman.

King's, as other commentaries have suggested, reports of his participation may have been lost. However, within two years of leaving King's, Watson was playing a good standard of football, and four years later was close to joining the Scottish national team. It is, therefore, difficult to believe he did not have experience of the association game before he arrived in Glasgow.

As graduates from King's were expected to go up to the senior college, Oxford or Cambridge, Watson choosing to move to Scotland instead would have been considered an opportunity squandered. Assuming he went against the advice of his tutors or legal guardians, he would have been reminded he was an illegitimate, mixed heritage orphan, in a society ready to reject him for his parentage and colour. An offer from either Oxford or Cambridge might have cemented his social standing, and he would have been conscious of this.

Not returning to King's in September 1874, it would be another year before Watson entered Glasgow University but, in the meantime, it appears he stayed by his sister's side. Her marriage had been a series of disasters: a shotgun wedding, adultery, venereal disease, the loss of a baby and eventually divorce. Annetta had been living in Putney in the summer of 1874 and, presumably, Andrew stayed by her side.

Glasgow University

Andrew enrolled in the University of Glasgow for the 1875–76 session to study 'Arts', which included three classes: natural philosophy, mathematics (senior class) and civil engineering and mechanics.

Brian McColl, from the Scottish Football History Archive,[65] accessed Watson's records at the university and believes Watson might have intended to obtain a Certificate

---

65 Brian McColl – © Scottish Football *Historical Archive: www.oocities.org/br1anmccoll/andrewwatson.htm (unresponsive July 2020)*

of Proficiency in Engineering. However, this qualification was replaced in 1872 by a Bachelor of Science degree for science subjects, including engineering.

On 8 November 1875, Watson paid £4 4s to take a course called 'Natural Philosophy' under Professor Sir William Thomson, who would later become Lord Kelvin. The classes covered mechanics, hydrostatics, pneumatics, optics, astronomy and natural history. Later, Thomson introduced thermodynamics, magnetism, electricity and telegraphy. Under Thomson's influence, the department gained international recognition, and his work on telegraphy, specifically the transatlantic telegraph system, earned him a knighthood from Queen Victoria.

However, Watson missed 18 of the 20 weekly examinations, did not borrow any books from the library and achieved a total of eight marks, compared to a classmate who had accrued a total of 1,548. This less than glowing report indicates that Watson withdrew from the course less than a month after enrolling.

He had also enrolled to take a senior class in mathematics at the cost of £3 3s, under Professor Hugh Blackburn. Professor of Mathematics at Glasgow University for over 30 years, Blackburn was a friend of and worked closely with Thomson. Of note, Blackburn's father, Hugh, owed his wealth to the possession of sugar plantations in Jamaica and, after the repeal of slavery in 1833, filed for compensation for 550 slaves.

The third of the three classes Watson signed up to study was 'Civil Engineering & Mechanics' under Professor James Thomson. The future Lord Kelvin's younger brother, James Thomson was elected Regus Professor of Civil Engineering and Mechanics in 1873 and, even though he was very highly regarded as a mathematician and an engineer, was overshadowed by his famous elder brother. No records exist on the cost of the course or concerning Watson's performance or attendance in either senior mathematics or civil engineering, but it is likely he dropped out of these courses too.

McColl states that there are no records of a bursary but, as with Watson's other educational costs, Wightman would have handled these. Although no records exist of a reaction to Watson's decision to drop out of university and the squandering of fees, it can be assumed that Wightman would have offered Watson the benefit of his opinion.

The courses that Watson chose show his interest in subjects considered to be cutting edge at the time. It is difficult to understand why he decided to withdraw from the classes, as William Thomson's department and the professor himself were very highly regarded and at the cutting edge of invention and research at that time. Being under the influence and the celebrity of Professor Thomson could have steered Watson's life in a completely different direction. However, with a young man's impetuosity and the total and complete belief in his own destiny, Watson chose a different path to follow. But perhaps this lost opportunity may have haunted him in years to come?

Watson was only 19 years old, had played football with Maxwell before their amalgamation with Parkgrove and had already been elected as vice-president of the club. Plus, the season had been underway for around three months. For Watson, the lure of football was too much for him to ignore.

Although no evidence has yet been found to confirm why he dropped out of Glasgow University, it does seem reasonable to believe that football had an influence on Watson's change of direction. He may also have been courting Jessie Armour at the time, whom he would marry a year later. He stated on their marriage certificate that he was an 'apprentice mechanical engineer', but this may only refer to his abandoned studies.

It was around this time that Watson would have been considering ways in which to invest the inheritance he would collect within a year, and ideas for the warehouse business with William Miller, his Parkgrove team-mate, and George Baird may have been forming. There are no indications that he was receiving an income from any other source than his father's annuity, so, for the time being, Andrew Watson would appear to be an independently wealthy gentleman.

Although Annetta's education does not appear to have been as expensive as her brother's, her career as a music teacher shows a high standard of schooling and training. Therefore, it is clear that their father considered education a priority. But by the time Andrew left King's College, their father was dead and presumably their mother too, so the only close blood relatives they had were each other.

By 1876, Watson's education was at an end. He was about to start another phase in his life in business, as a footballer, a father and husband.

Estate

Even though it was his father's wealth that provided Watson with many advantages, there can be no doubt it was Watson's unique ability as a footballer that cemented his place in that society. An examination of Watson's estate is valuable in understanding one of the many myths that have perpetuated about him, and the following looks to debunk the belief that he was an independently wealthy gentleman.

His family was related to some of the wealthiest people in the country, who not only owned plantations, but made huge profits from the production of cotton, coffee, molasses, rum and sugar. They also made money from the transportation of slaves from Africa to America and the West Indies.

The Watson family were bound by blood or marriage to names such as Sandbach, Parker, Robertson, Omond, McLagen, Traill and Tinne – names that held strong associations with Demerara. Relations included some prominent individuals, such as Charles Stuart Parker, Liberal MP for Perthshire, and British Prime Minister, William Ewart Gladstone. The families were so close that family names were interwoven, producing individuals such as Peter Miller Watson McLagen, Samuel Sandbach Parker, Alfred Traill Parker, Martha Tinne Sandbach and Robert Traill Omond.

Andrew's father, Peter Miller Watson, left £35,000 in his last will and testament, outlining gifts and bequests to a collection of individuals. However, most of the document focuses on providing for his natural children, and their 'maintenance and education'. He left detailed instructions, explicitly stating that if Annetta were to be married, her husband would not be able to access her annuity. However, this appears to have eventually been neglected when the time came.

The complicated four-page document contains specific guidelines for the executors. They were charged with investing £6,000 for each child at their discretion in:

> '... any government stocks funds or securities (with power to vary such stocks funds or securities into or for others of the same or life nature)'.

Miller Watson instructed the executors to compound the interest until such time as each child reached the age of 21. Andrew would have to wait ten years before collecting his inheritance, whereas Annetta could expect to receive hers in around two to three years' time. With an annual growth of about 3 per cent, the interest would be close to £200 a year, more than enough to cover Andrew's school expenses. At maturity, Andrew and Annetta had the option to collect the whole sum, plus the compounded interest and investments, or receive the money as an annuity each year. Annetta chose the annuity, whereas Andrew had the amount and investments transferred to him.

Miller Watson also bequeathed a few of his personal effects to Andrew, including a hunting watch, a gold patina chain, a trunk of silver plate and all his books. The will did not specify any heirlooms for Annetta but, tellingly, neither child inherited any property, including their father's house, Weylea, in Guildford, Surrey. The property was described in the sale notice from a few years after Miller Watson's death:

> 'This valuable estate comprises a very pretty modern family residence with a newly erected lodge entrance, carriage drive, pleasure grounds, lawn gardens and orchard, tastefully laid out and planted with ornamental trees, evergreens, and flowering plants. Very superior newly erected carriage house, stables, excellent harness room, comfortable enclosed farmyard, barn, granary, cow-house, sheds, piggeries, and other farm buildings; and about 50 acres, (more or less), of exceedingly Rich Pastures and Arable Land, in a high state of cultivation, a portion of which is beautifully studded with fine growing oaks, presenting a park-like appearance.'[66]

Later, other advertisements appeared, adding more detail to the property:

> 'The Weylea Villa ... comprises 3 superior in calf Alderney Milch cows in full milk, splendid 6-year-old, 16 hands, carriage and riding mare, a handsome promising 4-year-old thoroughbred bay filly by Touchstone, brown mare and foal by Peon, and in foal again same horse. Powerful 7-year-old cart horse, 17 hands, large frame. Sussex breeding sow will 11 pigs. Quantity of white Dorking fowls. Farming and garden implements – ploughs, turnip cutters, scarifiers, oilcake crushers, chaff cutter, sheep and pig troughs, lawn mowing machine

66 *Surrey Advertiser*, Saturday, 2 October 1869.

> and a great variety of other farming and garden tools … Carriages and harness. Capital double-seated brougham complete in first-rate condition. Phaeton with pole and bar, complete, set of brass mounted carriage harness, 2 sets of black do., riding saddles and bridles, and a variety of capital stable implements. Quantity of straw and growing crops, viz., mangold wurzel, Swedes, turnips, carrots, etc.'[67]

Weylea became the property of Miller Watson's stepsisters, Ann Traill and Mary Eliza Omond, and was put up for rent, then later sold. In leaving the family home to his stepsisters, rather than his only male heir, it is clear Miller Watson saw Traill and Omond as right and proper beneficiaries of the property. Although generous to his natural children, he did not consider them as his legal heirs.

Miller Watson nominated three trustees to administer his will, each receiving a legacy. After the distribution of his assets and money, around £8,000 remained but, after fees and taxes, this would dwindle away. The three executors were Frances Whitaker, Robert Omond and William Wightman, who were charged with overseeing Andrew and Annetta's financial matters.

Frances Whitaker of London (1834–1900) was the solicitor for the Duchy of Lancaster, the private lands owned by the British Sovereign.[68] He married Catherine Bean Lucie-Smith, born in Demerara, and whose father received compensatory payments after the abolition of slavery. Her brother John Lucie-Smith was the Solicitor-General of British

67 *Surrey Advertiser*, Saturday, 13 November 1869.

68 Valued at around £20 million a year as private income to the Queen.

Guiana and became Chief Justice of Jamaica. Whitaker also managed the sale of Weylea after Miller Watson died.

Dr Robert Omond of Edinburgh (1801–81) was a relative through marriage and was born in Kirkwall, Watson's grandmother's home town. He had been the president of the Royal College of Surgeons of Edinburgh but was not a legal man. He had married Mary Eliza Traill, the daughter of Christian Robertson, Andrew Watson's grandmother, and is buried in the same plot as William Robertson Watson, Peter's brother, who shared a cottage in Innerleithen with Andrew Watson's sister, Annetta.

The most influential executor was William Wightman of Liverpool (1826–88), an accountant by profession and, judging by the available records, he was instrumental in the management of most of the Watson children's financial affairs. His father and grandfather also owned slaves in Tobago. The Wightman family filed claims for compensation for over 300 slaves in Tobago to the value of over £6,000.[69]

Omond and Wightman both died in the 1880s, leaving Whitaker to act as the sole executor, but it is doubtful he would have been able to spare much time away from his Duchy of Lancaster responsibilities. Therefore, both Watson children would have been left to manage their own affairs.

Andrew and Annetta both received a sum of £6,000 outlined in the will plus interest, and after that had been exhausted there would be nothing more.[70] The fact that both would have to find employment throughout their lives suggests that the money did not last long. Annetta became a music teacher at Bellahouston Academy and later a private

---

69 Equivalent to over £750,000 in 2018.

70 Equivalent to over £600,000 in 2018.

music teacher. When she died in 1889 at the age of 42, her overall wealth was valued at £213 7s 7d.

As Andrew's inheritance had been growing for ten years before he could access it, the sum he inherited would have been considerably more than Annetta's and, for a while at least, the annuity may have initially allowed Watson to live the life of an independently wealthy gentleman. Yet, if the assets were not appropriately managed, this would not last forever. Watson's 'ready purse' and his investment into the Parkgrove football club and the Watson, Miller and Baird warehouse business would account for most of his assets, as later in life there is no indication of substantial wealth.[71]

Watson, Miller and Baird

In 1877, Watson turned 21 years old and received his inheritance. He became a partner in Watson, Miller and Baird, a wholesale warehouse business that sold 'dry goods', textiles and materials from a shop at 54 Union Street, Glasgow, with offices at nearby 35 Mitchell Street. There is nothing to suggest that Watson knew anything about the warehouse business, so it is reasonable to assume that he was offered a partnership in exchange for investment. This might also be confirmed by the arrangement of the names in the title of the business. It is doubtful that he worked in the shop and he had little or no work experience. In the 1881 Scottish census, he described his occupation as 'Warehouseman (Dry goods)', suggesting that he had wholeheartedly adopted this new career.

Over the next few years, the post office directories for Glasgow included listings for Watson, Miller and Baird, and entries for his partners: George Osborne Baird (1848–

71 Bone (1890).

1940), a commercial traveller, and William Govan Miller (1852–98). Miller was the captain and match secretary for Parkgrove Football Club, a team where Watson invested some of his inheritance.

Watson was a partner in the business for five years, but in November 1883, while he was living in London, a fire broke out in a building adjacent to the Watson, Miller and Baird Union Street premises. It resulted in a wall collapsing and damaging the warehouse plus many other businesses.

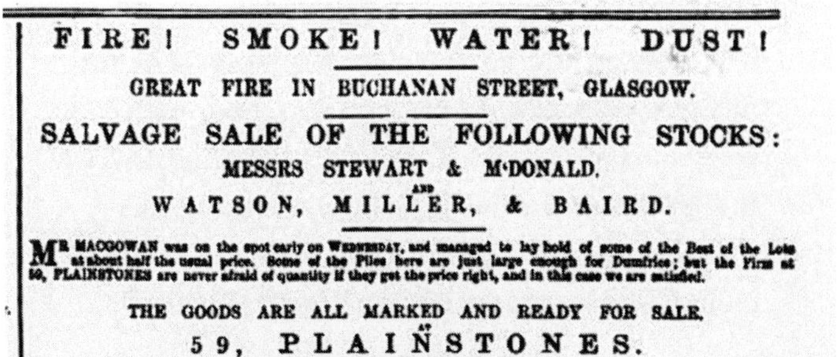
FIRE! SMOKE! WATER! DUST!

GREAT FIRE IN BUCHANAN STREET, GLASGOW.

SALVAGE SALE OF THE FOLLOWING STOCKS:

MESSRS STEWART & M'DONALD,

AND

WATSON, MILLER, & BAIRD.

MR MACGOWAN was on the spot early on WEDNESDAY, and managed to lay hold of some of the Best of the Lots at about half the usual price. Some of the Piles here are just large enough for Dumfries; but the Firm at 59, PLAINSTONES are never afraid of quantity if they get the price right, and in this case we are satisfied.

THE GOODS ARE ALL MARKED AND READY FOR SALE,

AT

59, PLAINSTONES.

THE STOCKS CONSIST OF:

75 LADIES' FUR CAPES.
60 CHILDREN'S FOUR-IN-HAND ULSTERS.
50 LADIES' FOUR-IN-HAND ULSTERS.
30 DOZ. LADIES' FANCY WOOL SQUARES.
120 GROSS DRESS BUTTONS—ALL NEWEST STYLES.
50 GROSS No. 81 BLACK MOHAIR BRAID.
19 FUR SETTS (Very Wide.)
50 PIECES UNBLEACHED COTTONS.
25 PIECES COTTON SHEETINGS.
200 PAIRS COTTON SHEETS.
50 PIECES WINCEY SHIRTINGS.
20 PIECES COTTON SHIRTINGS.
25 PIECES DRESS GOODS.
10 PIECES LINEN BED TICKS.
60 BED MATS.

MACGOWAN & CO.,

WHOLESALE AND RETAIL WAREHOUSEMEN,

59 PLAINSTONES,

DUMFRIES.

Dumfries and Galloway Standard – *Wednesday, 28 November 1883*

A year later, on 1 October 1884, Watson resigned as a partner in the company.[72] Perhaps due to the fire or to

72 *Edinburgh Gazette,* 17 October 1884.

Watson's settling in England, his partnership and income would have ended. In the years after, the post office directory held a listing for Miller and Baird, still working out of the Union Street and Mitchell Street premises, and the company continued trading until the death of William Govan Miller in 1899.

Parkgrove Investment

In 1890, D.D. Bone wrote:

> 'Mr Watson did a great deal for football in the Glasgow district a dozen years ago, both with his ready purse and personal ability in the game. It was in a great measure owing to his interest and energy, that the young Parkgrove Club obtained a proper ground and was fairly put on its way rejoicing.'[73]

This famous quote confirms that, after the receipt of his inheritance, Watson was able to contribute his 'interest and energy' and sums of money to Parkgrove Football Club. He was now involved financially with Miller in two ventures.

Finding sound investments would have been the advice of his father's executors, as this could provide him, if successful, with a comfortable income on top of his inheritance, allowing him to pursue his sporting activities and live comfortably for years to come. However, it is not exactly clear how the investment was made. This was years before clubs issued shares to finance their business and, if it were a loan, then there appears to be no security. It seems that Watson simply paid for everything from his own purse, and any guarantees were merely verbal.

---

73 Bone (1890).

At that time football was a new entertainment, with unknown business potential. An investment such as Watson's may have been considered foolhardy, but football clubs in Glasgow were beginning to realise that the public not only wanted to attend athletic events and football matches but were willing to pay for the privilege. This proved to be so financially attractive that clubs began looking around for larger venues where they could offer enclosures and cater for increased attendances. Investing his own money into a club would have been a gamble, but perhaps Watson felt he had identified a serious business opportunity. Alternatively, Watson may have simply been altruistic, intending to support his local football club, and the assurances that he would receive a return on his investment with dividends were less important than having a vehicle to pursue his footballing career.

Watson's investment in Parkgrove not only provided the club with a home ground in Trinidad Park, but the club's colours also changed from scarlet and blue to black and white. Obviously, Watson's finances were used for a variety of other purposes.

The year 1877 was an exciting one for Andrew, as not only did he take possession of his inheritance, but he married Jessie Nimmo Armour. By 1880 he was a father of two children, Rupert and Agnes.[74],[75] His reputation in football and athletics was growing, he was appearing regularly for Parkgrove and had been selected to play for Glasgow in the annual fixture with Sheffield. In athletics, he took part in many events in the Glasgow area and was rarely beaten in the high jump. He had also trialled for the Scottish national

---

74 Rupert Andrew Watson (1878–1948).

75 Agnes Maude (or Maud) Watson (1880–?).

football team and was beginning to receive accolades from journalists, the first of many he was to collect throughout his playing career.

As the business of football attracted more attention, clubs looked to improve their product. One idea that clubs were willing to explore was the potential for night-time games and the added revenue these could generate. Although the first-ever attempt at using floodlights at a football game was on 14 October 1878, at Bramall Lane, Sheffield, in front of 30,000 spectators, just two weeks later, Watson and Parkgrove participated in the second game of a series of three floodlit games, the first in Scottish football. The opening match of the three Scottish fixtures took place at Cathkin Park between Third Lanark and Vale of Leven, on 25 October 1878:

> 'It consisted of a stage, fifty feet in height, from the top of which the light was controlled by Mr Joshua Horton, Glasgow. The light itself was generated by a dynamo-electric machine of Gramme's, the motor power being supplied by a steam-engine of eight horsepower ... The experience gained was, that one machine is not sufficient to supply the requisite amount of light. When the reflector was adjusted so as to throw the light on to the centre of the field, both goals were quite in darkness, so that as the ball moved up and down the field, the light, by means of the adjustment of the reflector, had to follow the play as best it could. The consequence was that often kicking and dribbling were more a matter of chance than of judgement or good play, and the result of such a game cannot be taken as indicating the relative strength of the two teams. From a financial point of view, however, the game was a great success,

> the number of people inside the enclosure being at least between 8000 and 9000.'[76]

Six days later, after a 24-hour delay due to the weather, on 31 October, Parkgrove played the Shaftesbury Club at Trinidad Park. The owner of the apparatus, Joshua Horton, provided the equipment free of charge, and all profits went to local charities. But, if successful, the possibility of regular midweek games was exciting.

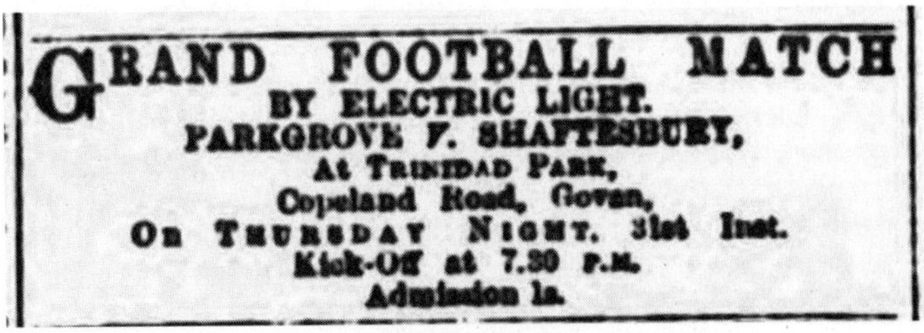

GRAND FOOTBALL MATCH
BY ELECTRIC LIGHT.
PARKGROVE V. SHAFTESBURY,
At Trinidad Park,
Copeland Road, Govan,
On Thursday Night, 31st Inst.
Kick-Off at 7.30 P.M.
Admission 1s.

North British Daily Mail – *Wednesday, 30 October 1878*

Unfortunately, fewer than a thousand spectators attended the game, and the press described the event as a 'greater failure' than at Cathkin Park a week earlier. *The Scotsman* reported:

> 'The beam of light reflected on the field was certainly wider and longer, but everything outside the reach of the rays from the reflector was in comparative darkness …'[77]

The venture at Trinidad Park raised £50 for charity, but there are no records of any further experiments with floodlights at Parkgrove.

76 *The Scotsman*, Saturday, 26 October 1878.
77 *The Scotsman*, Friday, 1 November, 1878.

At the end of the 1879/80 season, several unexpected events occurred. The Parkgrove club collapsed and lost its ground, Trinidad Park. Many of the best players left and formed a new club called Pilgrims, and Watson became a member of Queen's Park. Even though Parkgrove continued as a junior club, the hopes and dreams for the club were no more and, presumably, neither was Andrew's investment!

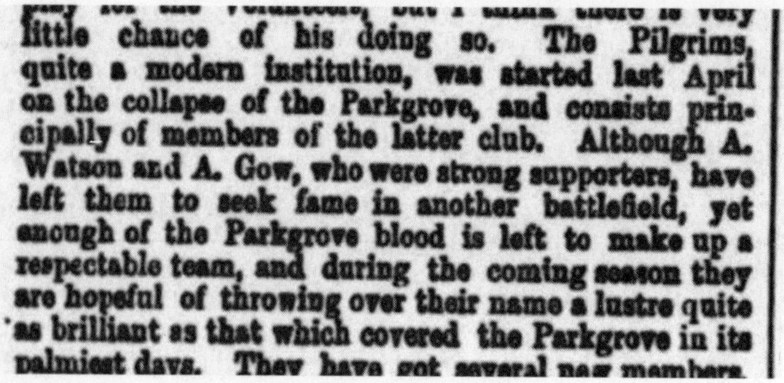

little chance of his doing so. The Pilgrims, quite a modern institution, was started last April on the collapse of the Parkgrove, and consists principally of members of the latter club. Although A. Watson and A. Gow, who were strong supporters, have left them to seek fame in another battlefield, yet enough of the Parkgrove blood is left to make up a respectable team, and during the coming season they are hopeful of throwing over their name a lustre quite as brilliant as that which covered the Parkgrove in its palmiest days. They have got several new members.

Athletic News – *Wednesday, 15 September 1880*

But Watson's triumphs were unrivalled. By 1882, he had represented the Scottish national team three times, once as captain, beating England (twice) and Wales. With Queen's Park he had won the Scottish Charity Cup, and the Scottish Challenge Cup twice. He contributed to notable victories over teams from south of the border and was a shining star of Scottish football, receiving regular plaudits in the media:

> 'Andrew Watson (Queen's Park, late of Parkgrove), right back. One of the very best backs we have; since joining the Queen's Park has made rapid strides to the front as a player; has great speed, and tackles splendidly; powerful and sure kick; well worth of a place in any representative team.'[78]

---

78 *Glasgow Evening Post*, Monday, 7 March 1881.

Andrew Watson was at the height of his career, with a long and glorious football future ahead of him, but he then made the unfathomable decision to leave Glasgow and move to London. The disruption this would cause his football career and his family would be considerable. Plus, he would not be able to play for the Scottish national team again. The move appeared to be inexplicable and can perhaps only be explained by the simple need to earn a living.

A Civil Servant

On 31 May 1882, Watson stood down from Queen's Park and the very next day he moved to London. This 'appointment' to 'Government offices' was as abrupt as it was unexpected, and contradicted reports in the press that Watson had confirmed he would be club secretary at Queen's Park for the coming season.

The suddenness of Watson's departure appears to suggest an urgency to take up the appointment. He was still a partner in Watson, Miller and Baird, and presumably continued to draw a salary, but it is feasible to suggest that the collapse of Parkgrove Football Club and the loss of his investment may have significantly eroded his inheritance, so he needed to find another source of income. The position in the civil service could offer not only a government salary and financial security but also a social status. Although football brought him a lot of pleasure, he was an amateur and could never make a living from it.

Arguably, the opportunity appeared to be exceptionally fortuitous and too good to refuse. Watson would have been aware that he was not qualified for any career at that time. Besides not having impressive results from school, he had failed to complete his university qualification and had a mediocre résumé (excluding football). The list of occupations he provided on official documents between 1875 and 1881 were varied: on his university matriculation form, he stated he was a 'Merchant'; on his wedding certificate, 'a mechanical engineer (apprentice)'; on Rupert and Maude's birth certificates, a 'Railway Shareholder'; and he described himself in the 1881 census as a 'Warehouseman (Dry Goods)'.

This was not a résumé of a person the civil service would be looking to headhunt. Applying for a position would have required interviews and correspondence, something that would have taken time and preparation. The abruptness of his departure does not suggest any planning, but a reaction to an unexpected opportunity. Either way, he would most likely need someone to intermediate for him, someone in London willing and able to liaise on his behalf. If this person had influence and was ready to act for Watson, then perhaps this person had an ulterior motive.

In March, Scotland had humiliated England at football again. Present at both matches was famous amateur and English top goalscorer E.C. Bambridge. It seems that Bambridge acted on Watson's behalf and used his influence to bring him to London.

E.C. Bambridge, affectionately known as 'Charlie Bam', was born in Windsor, Berkshire in 1858 to an ex-missionary, Eton tutor, and the royal photographer to Queen Victoria. 'Bam' was the most famous of five brothers, three of whom played for England and all were members of Swifts Football Club.[79]

Although founded in 1867, Swifts will forever be associated with the Bambridge family. Under their control, the club became one of the greatest amateur teams in England

79 Edward Charles (E.C.), Arthur Leopold (A.L.), William Samuel (W.S.), George Frederick (G.F.) and Ernest Henry (E.H.).

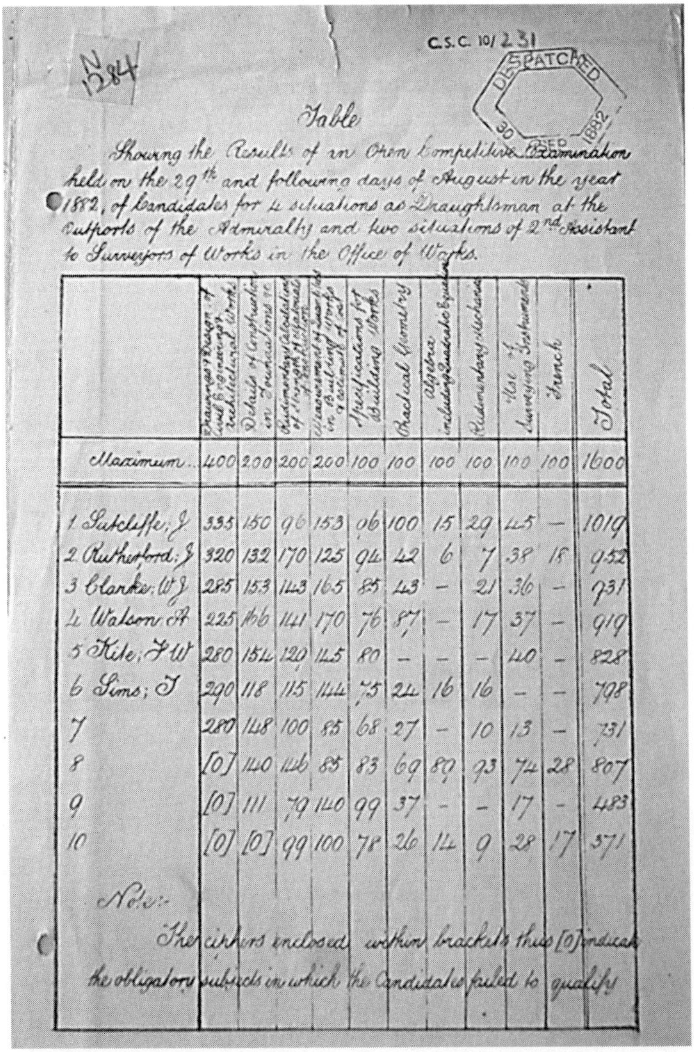

C.S.C. 10/231

N 1284

DESPATCHED 30 SEP 1882

Table

Showing the Results of an Open Competitive Examination held on the 29th and following days of August in the year 1882, of Candidates for 4 situations as Draughtsman at the Outports of the Admiralty and two situations of 2nd Assistant to Surveyors of Works in the Office of Works.

	Drawings & Design of Civil Engineering & Architectural Works	Details of Construction in Foundations &c	Rudimentary Calculation of Strength of Materials [illegible]	Measurement of Quantities in Building Works & Estimates of [illegible]	Specifications for Building Works	Practical Geometry	Algebra including Quadratic Equations	Rudimentary Mechanics	Use of Surveying Instruments	French	Total
Maximum..	400	200	200	200	100	100	100	100	100	100	1600
1 Sutcliffe; J.	335	150	96	153	96	100	15	29	45	–	1019
2 Rutherford; J.	320	132	170	125	94	42	6	7	38	18	952
3 Clarke; W. J.	285	153	143	165	85	43	–	21	36	–	931
4 Watson; A.	225	166	141	170	76	87	–	17	37	–	919
5 Kite; F. W.	280	154	120	145	80	–	–	–	40	–	828
6 Sims; T.	290	118	115	144	75	24	16	16	–	–	798
7	280	148	100	85	68	27	–	10	13	–	731
8	[0]	140	146	85	83	69	89	93	74	28	807
9	[0]	111	79	140	99	37	–	–	17	–	483
10	[0]	[0]	99	100	78	26	14	9	28	17	371

Note:- The ciphers enclosed within brackets thus [0] indicate the obligatory subjects in which the Candidates failed to qualify

The record sheet of the 'Results of an Open Competitive Examination held on the 29th and following days of August in the year 1882, of Candidates for four situations as Draughtsman at the Admiralty' – National Archives

at that time. Under Bambridge's influence, Swifts could draw on some of the most talented footballers of the day.

Bambridge was ambitious and would have acknowledged the superiority of the Scottish game, having played against the national team and best clubs in Scotland. Conscious that northern clubs were improving with the importation of Scottish players, he would have been aware of how this practice was changing the game.

However, as an amateur, Bambridge could not condone the payment of players in any team in the south. But if Scottish players could be attracted to amateur teams, not only would his Swifts learn a thing or two, but the English national team might also benefit.

Having played against Watson for England and Swifts, Bambridge would have known he was one of the best amateur players at Queen's Park. But he was also a perfect gentleman, educated in England and, maybe crucially, of the same social class. It was said of Bambridge that he '... had hosts of friends and no one could be his enemy', and through his natural geniality probably found an ally and friend in Watson.[80]

By profession, Bambridge was an insurance underwriter for Lloyd's and had played for and organised the Lloyd's football team.[81] Finding Watson a position would have been easy for the genial and popular Bambridge. Using his connections, doors could be opened to individuals looking for career opportunities. This type of assistance was a widespread practice among Freemasons, of which Bambridge was a member. Watson would later also become a member.

Whether Watson asked Bambridge to help or Bambridge initiated it is unknown, but once the plans had been made, Watson moved quickly. By June 1882, Watson had moved south and Bambridge may have used his connections to find Watson a suitable home, but not too close to Slough,

---

80 www.corinthian-casuals.com

81 At that time, Lloyd's focused mainly on marine coverage and would have had strong links with the Admiralty.

where Swifts were based. Watson set up home at Langham Road in West Green, Tottenham.[82] His new address, and its proximity to Stoke Newington, suggests that he had returned to the area he was familiar with, having lived in the vicinity while at King's College.

Having entered the civil service, Watson sat an open competitive examination and applied for one of four situations in the draughtsman and surveyor offices of the Admiralty. The results record dated 29 August 1882 shows that Watson achieved the fourth-highest score for the exams, enough to secure one of the situations as the Second Assistant to Surveyors.

However, disaster struck in October 1882, four months after moving to London, when his wife Jessie became ill with 'gastro bilious fever'. She died five weeks later. The death certificate stated her husband's occupation as 'A Civil Servant'.

Two weeks before Jessie's death, Andrew had played his first football match in England, for a select XI in a game that Bambridge organised. Drawing with an excellent Clapham Rovers team, he would then play for Bambridge's Swifts three days before Jessie died, beating Bradfield College 4-0. As Jessie became increasingly sick, Andrew should have dismissed any commitment to play football, but he did play, and perhaps the activity came as a welcome release from the angst of nursing an ailing wife. We may never know why he played these games, but it may reveal the sway that Bambridge could exert on Watson and the importance of gratitude and honouring commitments.

When Jessie died, Rupert was aged four and Agnes two, and for a single parent with a new job and unavoidable

82 House no longer standing.

commitments, the loss of a wife could not have come at a worse time. The most straightforward solution at the time was to send the children back to Glasgow, to their maternal grandparents. Presumably, if it had been practical, Watson would have employed a governess or nanny, but no records have been found to suggest this occurred. It is also possible that Andrew and Jessie left the children in Glasgow while they set up home but, in the three months since leaving, it is likely they had already sent for them. By the next census in 1891, Rupert and Agnes were living in Glasgow with Jessie's parents. They would both remain with their grandmother for the next 30 years.

THAT is a very sad bereavement which has befallen A. Watson. His wife, who was a most excellent woman, breathed her last on Tuesday of last week, and besides leaving a sorrowing husband behind her, she leaves three of a family, all of whom are very young, as it is only about six years since they were married.

Athletic News – *Wednesday, 8 November 1882*

In 1884, Agnes Gilmour, Watson's stepmother-in-law filed a decree for payment against the father of Agnes and Rupert. Watson had obviously neglected to send money for the maintenance of his children, and this is a disturbing turn of events. Perhaps Watson had simply forgotten, and Agnes Gilmour, facing the same issues that we know E.C. Bambridge occasionally had in contacting Watson, filed a case. This reflects on Watson's personal finances and confirms a financial obligation that he failed to honour. Oddly, Watson had won the Glasgow Charity Cup with Queen's Park three days before the summons had been filed and was obviously in Glasgow. Perhaps by returning to Glasgow, the issue was resolved as no further legal action is recorded.

Two weeks after his wife's death, Watson played for Pilgrims (including Bambridge), beating United Hospitals in Wandsworth 2-1. A week after that he won again with Swifts, against the Royal Military Academy. Watson continued to play game after game, and although this appears to have been inappropriate for a grieving widower, it may have been therapeutic and a release from the terrible circumstances he was being forced to manage.

Over the following year, Watson played for Corinthian, Swifts and Pilgrims, even playing once with the Bambridge brothers for West Surrey county.

Although Watson spent the next three seasons south of the border, he never thoroughly settled. He is regularly listed in games for Queen's Park over each season, plus a short series of games for Edinburgh University in April 1883. Visits to his children in Glasgow became longer and longer until, in April 1885, he remained in Scotland. Apart from two guest appearances, one for Scotch Crusaders and the other for I Zingari, he would not return to England again until moving to Liverpool two years later.

The return to Glasgow confirms that his civil service employment was over and may have been for some time. There is no mention of any occupation over the next couple of years, but he may have survived on any remaining investments.

Watson played two seasons in Scotland, primarily for Queen's Park, but towards the end of the 1885/86 season,

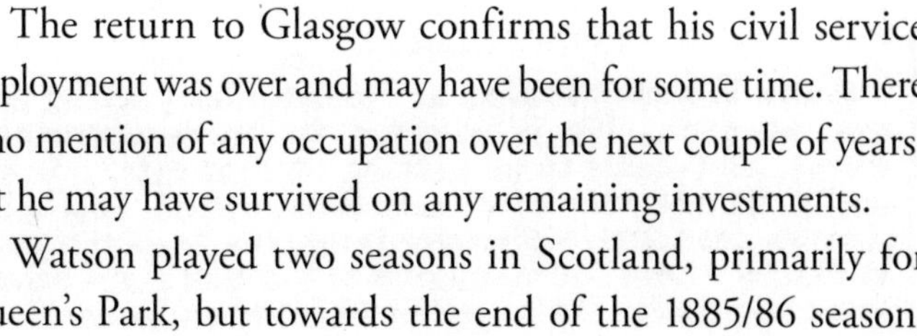
FOOTBALL.

It is said that Andrew Watson, the left back of the Queen's Park, intends leaving for California in little over a week. In that case Saturday's cup tie with the 3d L.R.V. will probably be his last match, at least for some time.

Dundee Evening Telegraph – *Wednesday, 13 January 1886*

stories began appearing in the press that he was retiring from football and leaving Glasgow to start a new life in California. Another suggested Bolivia, and other rumours stated that he was signing for other clubs in different parts of the country. Facing the end of his football career, Watson was obviously contemplating his future and exploring ideas for the next business opportunity. However, he remained with Queen's Park for the rest of the 1886/87 season, although his appearances reduced.

In April 1887, he married again, to Eliza Kate Tyler, an English shop girl living in Glasgow.[83] In the following month, an unexpected report appeared of Watson playing football for a team in Liverpool called Garston. Later that year, Andrew and his new wife left Glasgow and moved to Liverpool, where he joined Bootle Football Club.

Bootle was a well-funded club, and even though they claimed to be strictly amateur and would fiercely deny paying players, there were the usual tell-tale signs of Scottish players in the ranks. The details of the scandal Watson experienced in joining Bootle are covered later but, as part of

ANDY WATSON is also at Bootle, and playing as well as ever. He is engaged in an engineering works, and seems to be getting on first-rate. It is really wonderful how all these good football players manage to discover lucrative employment at places where the managers of football clubs have some influence. This applies to other clubs besides Bootle. Of course it is a coincidence—nothing more.

Athletic News – *Tuesday, 6 September 1887*

83 Eliza Kate Tyler (1863–1949). An English woman, Eliza was born on 16 June 1863 in Fareham, Hampshire. The Tyler family moved to Glasgow at some point in the 1870s.

the arrangement, he not only got to extend his career, but he was also able to follow a new calling as a sea-going engineer.

When he retired from football, for no discernible reason, Watson chose to take to the sea. He passed his Second-Class Engineering Certificates, then two years later qualified as a First-Class Engineer. For the next ten years the West India and Pacific Steamship Company Limited employed him, mostly as a second-class mate.[84] This work would have required him to remain at sea for months at a time, away from his family, and although it was a manual occupation, it would provide a regular income of around £11 a month.

Why an ex-public schoolboy and an English gentleman chose to spend the last dozen years of his working life in the engine rooms of transatlantic steamers and merchant ships can only be assigned to one reason: the need to earn a living. To choose to become an engineer may seem to have been below his station, the manual work beneath him, but it is clear his father's fortune was gone.

He could have turned to his extended family for support, but the only records of Watson's extended family offering any assistance are his step-aunt Ann Traill's bequest in her will. With so many affluent relatives in positions of power, it would have taken minimum effort to find Andrew a lucrative job somewhere in their many businesses. Perhaps he chose not to enter the company that had subjugated his ancestors and made fortunes from their misery.

Watson retired in the early years of the new century and spent the following 20 years living quietly and modestly. He moved to Surrey at the beginning of the First World War, and died there in 1921, at the age of 64.

---

84 The West India and Pacific Steamship Company Limited was later purchased by the Red Star Line.

Second wife Eliza survived him by almost 30 years and their daughter Phyllis by nearly 40 years. Watson may have retained some of the railway shares and other investments and may have had a pension from the Red Star Line, but no other form of income can be found. For three people to survive for so many years indicates a reasonably sized nest egg, but this would gradually erode over time.

Andrew Watson died intestate, leaving no will, and if he had inherited his father's wealth, very little found its way to his wife and daughter. Dying intestate seems unusual for someone who grew up being guided by three executors. Any officer with legal oversight of his assets, if he had any left, would have advised him of the need to produce a will. Therefore, it seems Watson had no advisors acting for him in the years before his death.

Nowhere in the probate documents of the members of the Watson family are there any indications of sizeable sums of money. Like his father, Henry died intestate, and Annetta Watson only left a little over £200. Eliza left close to £500, and their daughter Phyllis Kate under £700. In truth, the fortune talked about in the biographies was never really in Andrew Watson's hands. His father provided for an excellent education and a sum of money so his son could make his own way in life. Like his father and uncles when they left Kirkwall, Andrew was expected to find his own way and make a life for himself.

The most significant indication that Watson's father's fortune no longer existed can be found in Richmond Cemetery, Surrey. Andrew Watson's gravestone is not grand or ostentatious but a simple stone with inset letters, some now lost, but in need of care. It is not in a family plot but awkwardly positioned away from the path, somewhat isolated, behind other rows, and positioned contrary to the sequence of nearby graves. Kate and Phyllis are buried about 100 yards away. They share a plot in a different section, but unlike Andrew's grave, are in line with the others and next to the path.

Peter Miller Watson's wealth has long since dissolved. His estate in Surrey is now lost under a housing development. A name of a street is all that remains, with little else to recall what was there before. Miller Watson's heirlooms have been lost to house clearances and antique shops, and all that is left of the Watsons is what can be revealed from historical research and a few grainy photographs.

Perhaps the investments in a warehouse business and a football club drained Andrew Watson's 'ready purse', as there is no evidence of any wealth. In fact, after football, he became an average member of society, unremarkable and inconspicuous, his sparkling footballing career unknown to neighbours and locals. It can perhaps be understood why his last resting place would become lost to the passing years, and his achievements consigned to the pages of history, but it cannot be forgiven.

Footballer

The earliest account of Watson playing football was far from promising. In his book, *25 Years of Football*, Archie Steel wrote:

> 'Being but recently from a boarding-school in England, where rugby rules, of course, held sway, Andrew occasionally forgot the restrictions of the Association Game, and more than once stooped to pick up the ball. It was during one of these moments that, recollecting the attempted infringement, he drew himself up and attempted to clear his goal by one of his huge kicks. His foot, unluckily, struct the ground, the outcome of which was a slight dislocation of the hip joint.'[85]

The fact that the anecdote was worthy of inclusion in Steel's book recognises not only Watson's prominence in Scottish football history, but it also recognises his meteoric development as a player and his rise to celebrity. What is remarkable about Andrew Watson's football career is that from arriving in Scotland to being on the periphery of the national team was only a matter of a few years.

---

85 Steel (1896).

Andrew Watson's top-flight career was comparatively short, lasting just 13 seasons. Excluding the season with Maxwell Football Club, his first-class football career began around the time of his first appearances for Parkgrove in 1875. He was 19 years old at the time and continued playing until he retired from football at the age of 31.

Of the 13 playing seasons in his career, eight were in Scotland, with two excursions across the border, to London (three seasons) and Liverpool (one season). Even though personal tragedy, injury and migration interrupted his career, he was remembered for his achievements as one of the finest footballers of his age.

In his book published in 1926, J.A.H. Catton, an early sports journalist, included Watson in his all-time best Scottish team.[86] Catton was considered one of the greatest sportswriters of the day, and this selection emphasises Watson's remarkable development from the young man who arrived in Glasgow in 1875, with little or no football experience, to becoming the captain of the national team.[87]

The origins of Watson's first introduction to the association game are obscure, and there are no records of him playing before the 1875 season. Although documented as playing second- and third-string rugby at King's College School, his earliest involvements with the round ball game may have been recorded in the Archie Steel story mentioned above. This would have been around the time Watson first arrived in Glasgow and may have only been recalled as Watson was a man of colour and easily recognised and remembered.

---

86 *Catton* (1926).

87 Catton wrote for the *Athletic News* under the pseudonym 'Tityrus'.

Watson was still at King's College in late June 1874, where he had participated in the college sports day. He had taken part in the hurdles, won the high jump and been awarded a football 'cap' for his services to the 2nd XV. After three years at King's College, these would be his last activities with the school. His only living relative was his sister, Annetta, who had married the previous year but had disappeared to Brighton with her husband after a shotgun wedding. In the spring of 1874, Annetta had lost her baby, and Andrew probably stayed with her in Portland Place, London. Humiliated by a divorce from an adulterous husband, Annetta remained in London until the following summer.

There is no apparent reason why Watson chose to move to Glasgow, but the advanced science and engineering courses offered by Glasgow University may have proved attractive, so at some point later in 1874 or in 1875, Andrew Watson arrived in Glasgow.

Maxwell Football Club

The first football team Watson was associated with was the Maxwell Football Club. Based in the Govan area of Glasgow, it was probably named after local landowners, the Maxwell family. Watson found rooms on Shields Road in Govan, a short walk south to Pollokshields, where the Maxwell team played their matches. Perhaps Watson had been curious about the group of men kicking a ball around or passed a game in progress and decided to approach them. They would have been surprised to have a man of colour, with an impeccable English accent, asking them if they minded him joining in. However, the introductions were made, and he was not only accepted into their ranks, but there are indications he would take on an administrative role for the club too.

Research by Brian McColl at the Scottish Football Historical Archive has confirmed that a club called Maxwell FC existed in the Govan area of Glasgow for part of the 1874/75 season.[88] However, there are newspaper reports of a team called Maxwell from the 1873/74 season, so the club may have been in existence longer than previously believed.

The first directory of football clubs in Scotland was published in the *Scottish Football Association Annual* for the 1875/76 season.[89] The Maxwell club does not appear in the annual, indicating that they did not have a dedicated ground, a prerequisite for inclusion. They played their home games at Queen's Park, Kinning Park[90] and, for the final few games before their demise, Clifford Park. Fixtures have been found for games against Carrington, Kerland, Rosland, 2nd XI Junior Queen's Park, 2nd Woodbank, Bellahouston and Parkgrove, yet little else is known about the club.

However, Watson's time at Maxwell was short-lived as, during the summer of 1875, the club merged with another local team. Along with the rest of the Maxwell squad, he transferred his allegiance, unaware he was taking the first step on a trailblazing career that would see him recognised as one of the era's best exponents of the game.

Although published in 1890, the cartoon above is a comic representation of Queen's Park on any given Saturday. For many clubs in Glasgow, places like Queen's Park, Clifford Park and Kinning Park were their home grounds, and competition for space and the danger of flying objects caused concern in the early years of football in Glasgow.

---

88 http://www.scottish-football-historical-archive.co.nf/

89 A volume that lists all the season statistics for member clubs.

90 The Scottish Cup Final was played here in 1881.

Parkgrove Football Club

Named after a cluster of houses on the Paisley Road, before the urbanisation of Glasgow, Parkgrove was remembered by George Ernest Philip:

> 'To the west were waving fields of golden corn. Walmer Crescent was still unbuilt, and Bellahouston was innocent of villas, school or kirk. To the north lay the yet unbroken estate of Plantation, enclosed within high walls. To the south, and reaching as far as the Glasgow and South-Western railway, were yet more fields, partly under cultivation … but in part belonging to the Clydesdale Cricket Club, whose nightly practisings were a source of unfailing interest.'[91]

In the 1870s, the fields and houses were gradually covered by homes to accommodate the growth of the middle classes, and only the name remained.

The earliest reports of a club called 'Park Grove' or Parkgrove have been found at the end of the 1873/74 season, but it was not until the summer of 1875, and the amalgamation with Maxwell FC, that the new, enhanced Parkgrove Football Club came into being. A report in the press announced that Watson would be the club's vice-president, perhaps confirming that he had also been an official with Maxwell. Trusting the 19-year-old Watson with the role of vice-president seems unusual, as he had been in Glasgow for less than a year and may not have had a solid understanding of the association game played in Scotland. This could suggest that the club's committee was either

---

91 Philip (1922).

short-handed, or they had recognised Watson's abilities. He would later become captain and match secretary, perhaps confirming the latter.

FOOTBALL.

PARKGROVE CLUB.—At a meeting of the Parkgrove Football Club the following gentlemen were elected office-bearers for the incoming season:—President, Geo. Russell, Esq.; Vice-President, A. Watson, Esq.; Captain, William Docherty; Vice-Captain, Jas. Valentine; Treasurer, Geo. M. Miller; Secretary, Thomas C. Urquhart, 82 Houston Street.

North British Daily Mail – *Monday, 30 August 1875*

Throughout his football career, Watson would be elected on to numerous committees at clubs and associations. The significance of his election to the committees of Maxwell and Parkgrove confirms Watson as the first man of colour to become a football administrator. It would be the beginning of a series of 'firsts' bearing his name.

Of those on the Parkgrove committee, William Docherty, James Valentine and Thomas Urquhart were the team's star players, all living locally. Urquhart's address at 82 Houston Street was only a few doors away from Watson's soon-to-be in-laws, and just around the corner from his lodgings at Shields Road.

Of note, in the team sheet for Parkgrove's first game of the season against Govan, was a goalkeeper named as 'R. Armour', who was Robert S. Armour, Jessie Armour's uncle, so he may have been instrumental in introducing Watson to his first wife.[92]

The new, enhanced Parkgrove team arranged 21 fixtures for the upcoming season and would continue using Kinning

92 Janet (Jessie) Nimmo Armour (1860–82).

Park as their home field. Later, they moved to Clifford Park, both locations used by Maxwell. Parkgrove's first game, on 11 September 1875, was abandoned at 0-0, due to an injury to an Oxford player. A week later, they played away at Govan and lost 2-0. The team sheet included J.J. Gow, W. Docherty, D. Smith and W. Morris, who had been Maxwell players, which attests to the quality of football previously played at Maxwell before the amalgamation.

Fixtures against Hamilton Academical, Rosslyn, Stanley and Bellahouston failed to bring a win and, even though the games were closely fought affairs, the season was not turning out the way most had hoped. Parkgrove's first success came seven weeks into the season, away at Coatbridge, where they won 3-0.

Watson's performance in the Coatbridge game was worthy of acknowledgement in a match report, and this brief mention confirms that he was not only a first-team player but, considering the high standard of players at the club, is a remarkable testament to his development as a player. He had been in Glasgow for less than a year, and to be included in the 1st XI is an outstanding achievement for someone previously schooled in the laws of the rugby game. The following week, Watson enrolled at the University of Glasgow.

The merger of Maxwell and Parkgrove led to an excess of players, so fixtures for a '2nd Parkgrove' began appearing regularly in the press. A 2nd XI created competition for places, and it is likely that Watson played with the 2nd XI, improving his abilities and match fitness. Having two teams at the club would provide plenty of opportunities to work on his game.

The weather affected Parkgrove's first season, and several games in November and December were lost due to snow, but research shows that they won eight, drew four and lost three, with six results unreported. Several reports contain remarkably similar comments that during the game the Parkgrove goalkeeper either did not touch or barely touched the ball. This indicates that Watson's duties in the defensive unit were more than efficient.

In September 1876, Watson was an entrant in the high jump competition at the Queen's Park sports day. With a jump of 5ft 5in, he tied for first place with Dr John Smith from the Mauchline Football Club. At that time, high jumpers practised the 'standing leap', which had no run-up. They simply stood next to the bar, then projected themselves up and over. Watson's career-best was a leap of 5ft 9in.

This was the first of many high jump competitions featuring Dr John Smith and Watson. Both would end up playing for Queen's Park and would go on to share a similar footballing career. They would play for Corinthian, Swifts, Edinburgh University and the Scottish national team, and would become both rivals and great friends.[93] In years to come, at Smith's request, Watson would play alongside him in Edinburgh University games, even though Watson's allegiances were with the University of Glasgow. Their friendship contained a good deal of competitiveness.

> 'John Smith, it will be remembered, gave Andrew Watson a back seat at the Edinburgh Association Sports, and the latter, having had to bear a considerable amount of chaff over the head of that defeat, was determined to show his club mates that he could "do" for the popular "Varsity" athlete. And Watson did "do" for Smith, for when the pins were raised to 5ft. 6½ inches, the latter had to give in.'[94]

93 Robinson (1920).

94 *Athletic News, Wednesday, 7 September 1881.*

Like Watson, Smith's sporting achievements were many. He famously scored two of the six goals that defeated England at The Oval in March 1881, and became the third Queen's Park player and Scot, after Watson and J.W. Holm, to play for Corinthian. Smith had remarkable all-round sporting abilities and held the world long jump record for several years. He was also selected for the first British Lions rugby union tour of Australia in 1888.

The beginning of Parkgrove's second season began poorly, with both the 1st XI and the 2nd XI losing to Helensburgh. They beat Rosslyn 3-0 the following weekend, but a week later were then dumped out of the Scottish Cup in the first round, losing 2-1 to Lancefield. Although unsuccessful this time, Watson would go on to win the Scottish Cup and the Glasgow Charity Cup many times.

Meeting Queen's Park Juniors in the fourth game of the season, a reasonably even contest ended 1-0 to the Juniors. Watson and his fellow full-back, Armstrong, were singled out for praise, as were Valentine and Docherty. On 14 October 1876, Parkgrove secured their second win of the season, against Hamilton Academical, winning 2-1. They then went on a winning spree, beating Mount Vernon, 4th RRV, Wanderers and Abercorn.

The press began to notice Watson and acknowledgements increased. In a match against 4th RRV, the report said: 'A. Watson and R. Armstrong (backs) played in the usual brilliant and dashing style.'[95]

In the fixture against Wanderers, the report included:

> '... being ably tackled by Armstrong, Watson secured the ball, and by a splendid longshot, he sent it under

95 *North British Daily Mail*, Monday, 30 October 1876.

> the Wanderers tape, thus lowering their colours after twenty minutes play.'[96]

Although there are probably earlier instances, this was the first printed record of Watson scoring. The mention of putting the ball 'under the tape' underlines the elementary nature of the game at that time. The crossbar did not become mandatory until 1891, some 14 years later.

Parkgrove's second season consisted of 20 games – they won eight, lost four and drew four, with four games where the result has been lost in time. It was a transitory season where Parkgrove home fixtures were played at Clifford Park and generally against junior teams. But the ambitions of the club would become realised in their third season.

In May 1877, Watson turned 21 years old and received his inheritance from his father's will. He set about changing Parkgrove's fortunes.

Acquiring Trinidad Park established Parkgrove as a senior club in Glasgow and not only allowed them to arrange fixtures with the top teams in the city but also turned the club into a business, with an income and costs, requiring proper governance and administration. But it also set up mouth-watering clashes in which the Parkgrove players could measure themselves against the best players in Scotland and become visible to the Glasgow and Scottish selectors. The future of the club and its players looked very bright indeed.

In the same month, Parkgrove held its AGM and elected Watson as the captain for the 1st XI. This was the first time a man of colour had been selected as a captain for any club registered with their local Football Association.

---

96 *North British Daily Mail*, Monday, 20 November 1876.

The AGM introduced a new president, the Honorary Provost James Wilson of Govan.[97] Like Watson's Scottish father, Wilson had made considerable wealth in the colonies of the Empire. A shipping merchant in Trinidad, Wilson does not appear to have been a slave owner. His son, also James, would later marry a local woman of colour, Marion Archer. According to family sources, the Wilsons had a very close relationship with the Trinidadians and, in 1897, when he returned to Trinidad, it was said:

> '… the black people were so delighted to see their old friend that, without reserve, they went up to him, and threw their arms around his neck'.[98]

When Wilson first returned from Trinidad in 1859, he built a house on the Paisley Road called Trinidad Villa, near Bellahouston and Ibrox. The house and estate became associated with the local area and, when Watson turned 21 years old and received his inheritance, his 'ready purse' would procure Trinidad Park as Parkgrove's home ground.

Throughout the summer of 1877, Watson competed in many athletic events, usually winning the high jump but competing in various other competitions. He took part in the preliminary football heats for the Queen's Park sports day, where Parkgrove beat Oxford by two goals and one touchdown to nil, and Dumbarton by one goal and two touchdowns to one goal and one touchdown. These four-a-side contests used rules that were a hangover from before the rugby and association rules went their separate ways. However, in small-sided games, the ability to use

---

97 A provost is a civic position similar to that of a mayor.

98 http://meekwrite.blogspot.com/2016/04/north-bantaskin-forgotten-falkirk.html

a 'touchdown' (when the ball crosses the goal line, as in modern rugby, and the opponent manages to touch it first), was a sensible method of deciding games prone to concluding without a clear winner.

Acquiring their own ground immediately paid dividends for Parkgrove as the Scottish FA, in making the draw for the Scottish Cup in September 1877, refused admission to eight teams because '… they do not possess grounds of their own to play on'.[99] Parkgrove were drawn against Winton at home, a game lost to the passing of time, but the result either favoured Parkgrove or they received a bye, as they met Kelvinbank in the second round, losing 2-1.

In September 1877, the Scottish FA reported that there were 91 clubs registered with the association, with a membership of 4,470 players. This was an increase of 23 clubs (25 per cent) and 1,278 players (29 per cent) on the previous year. On Monday, 22 October 1877, the Glasgow press reported on over 80 games played on the past Saturday. In comparison, London's *Evening Standard* reported on five games and *The Sportsman* around 30 games. On the same day throughout the major cities in England, the local press covered on average around ten games and, of these, many were of the rugby variety.

The popularity of football in Scotland clearly eclipsed the English, and with so many players learning the game and regularly competing, the overall standard of football in Scotland remained unchallenged for years. But the speed at which the English fixtures changed over the following decade, and the interest the press began to take in football, would be astonishing, underlining the association football tsunami that swept across the country during these years.

99 *North British Daily Mail,* Wednesday, 12 September 1877.

The opening fixture of the 1877/78 season was a baptism of fire for the new ambitious club. They played a friendly game away at Rangers at Kinning Park, and although Parkgrove lost 5-1 or 7-0 (according to varying reports), Watson received praise in the newspapers. One said: 'Of the Parkgrove players, Watson (back) was undoubtedly the best man.'[100]

As if to underline their new status in the Glasgow football firmament, the first home game at their new Trinidad Park ground was against the best club in the world and current Scottish Cup holders, Queen's Park. Parkgrove were described in the match report as one of the 'coming young clubs'[101] in Glasgow, but their new pitch was criticised as being in 'rather a rough state'.[102] However, as the club had only taken over the field the previous Wednesday, they were forgiven for not having enough time to 'develop it'.

FOOTBALL.
PARKGROVE V. QUEEN'S PARK,
on SATURDAY, 22d September, TRINIDAD PARK, Copeland Road, Govan. Kick-off 3.45 P.M.
Admission Sixpence—Ladies Free.

North British Daily Mail – *Thursday, 20 September 1877*

On a glorious September day, around 1,000 spectators turned out to see how 'the youngsters' would fare against the best team in the land. Parkgrove held Queen's Park until the second half, when just before the close of play, Henry McNeil scored with a header.[103] Parkgrove were complimented on

100 *Glasgow Herald*, Monday, 17 September 1877.

101 *North British Daily Mail*, Monday, 17 September 1877.

102 *Glasgow Herald*, Monday, 24 September 1877.

103 Henry McNeil is credited with naming of the Rangers Football Club.

their confidence and their use of the passing game. Gow, Armstrong and Watson received praise.[104]

A testament to the standard of football played at Parkgrove would be the presence of J.J. Gow, who would later, like Watson, join Queen's Park and go on to captain the Scottish national side. They were obviously close friends as the following statement emphasises:

> '... and although John Gow was wooed hard by Rangers, Andrew Watson's influence prevailed, and he found his way to Hampden Park in 1880, there to play before his old Parkgrove clubmate, and to form with him a defence the like of which I venture to think in Queen's long career has not been surpassed.'[105]

The Gow family lived in the same neighbourhood and were not only neighbours and team-mates, but their football careers followed an identical path: Maxwell, Parkgrove, Pilgrims, Glasgow, Queen's Park and the national team. They would have played alongside each other at every level too, had it not been for the prowess of Vale of Leven's Andrew McIntyre, and Tom Vallance of Rangers, who were ever-present in the national team.

The last game of 1877 was a fifth-round cup game against Partick, who were looking to get their revenge for a match two months earlier, where they had led 3-0 but ended up losing 5-3. The game at Trinidad Park on 29 December ended in a draw, requiring a replay the following Saturday.

---

104 Richard Bentley Armstrong (1857–1891). A 'Stay Cutter Manager' and an Englishman, who ran away to Australia around 1884, leaving a wife and four children. His fate is unknown.

105 *Scottish Referee*, Friday, 8 December 1905.

However, before that, Partick had arranged two games in Lancashire, one against Darwen and the other against Blackburn Rovers. Losing both, they arrived back the day before the replay and, perhaps unsurprisingly, lost 2-1.

In the Partick team at the time was Fergus Suter and his brother Edward, plus Jimmy Love and his brother. Also in the squad was Darwen-born William Kirkham. These three represent not only the link between Partick and Darwen Football Club but the foundations of professional football. Love and Suter would make arrangements through Kirkham and, by the end of the year, both were Darwen players. Darwen would go on to become a powerhouse in Lancashire.

What is often overlooked in the history of football is that Suter and Love, even though they are considered pioneers in the professional game, were mercenaries at a time when professionalism was outlawed. They were not championing those who argued for broken time payments, compensation for the wages they lost by playing football, as it appears neither Suter nor Love actually worked but were paid only to play football. Suter, a stonemason in Scotland, became a 'licensed victualler' and owned several pubs in his life, a career change rumoured to have been financed by Blackburn Rovers, who tempted Suter from Darwen to Rovers.

Jimmy Love had a warrant for his arrest issued in Glasgow, which appears to have prompted his sudden move to Lancashire. After one season he joined the army to escape a paternity issue. In 1882 he died in Alexandria, Egypt of fever. His name appears on a brass war memorial in Rochester Cathedral to the memory of the fallen from the Royal Marine Light Infantry Chatham Division in the Egypt Campaign of 1882.

Parkgrove would become respected in Glasgow's football circles and, as they improved, they were not only able to hold their own but were able to beat some of the bigger teams in Glasgow. As a testament to the quality of the squad, in February 1878 Watson and four Parkgrove players were invited to trial for the prestigious annual inter-city fixture between Sheffield and Glasgow. Of note, there were only two Rangers and Queen's Park players present, along with four from Third Lanark and six from South Western.[106]

The Parkgrove team also contained several non-Scottish players, such as Thomas Marten, the goalkeeper described as a 'son of Japan', and another player with an African heritage in Robert Gustave Walker, the son of a Scottish merchant and a local Sierra Leonean woman.

Also in the team was the colourful character of T.J. Britten (*vii* of picture section) who, although an Englishman, played internationally for Wales and, surprisingly, trialled for the English team to face Scotland in 1879.[107] Born in Hertfordshire, Britten attended Brentwood School, Essex and later qualified as a mining engineer. In 1878, he was the first Parkgrove player to represent Glasgow, a year before William Docherty and two years before Watson. Britten played for Presteigne FC, Parkgrove, Grantham, Brentwood, Port Vale and Bootle. In 1887, he migrated to the Transvaal, South Africa as a mining engineer, where he was hugely successful, becoming an advisor to Rhodesia and marrying the cousin of South Africa's prime minister (General Louis Botha) in Johannesburg.

Towards the end of the summer, on Saturday, 3 August 1878, the Parkgrove team met at St Enoch's Square, Glasgow and were conveyed by horse-drawn carriages to Campsie Glen, a picturesque area of natural beauty around 15

---

106 South Western would later merge with the Glasgow Pilgrims, the club formed after the collapse of Parkgrove.

107 Image from http://www.s2a3.org.za/bio/Biograph_final.php?serial=365

miles north of Glasgow. Arriving around 3pm, they were entertained at the Crown Hotel and were able 'to do justice to the dinner prepared for them by Mrs Wilson'.[108] About 40 players, friends and family members ate lunch and listened to speeches before rambling over the hills and marvelling at the panoramic views. Later, accompanied by a group of musicians brought with them, they danced on the green as the light faded. Heading back to Glasgow, they arrived before midnight, 'thoroughly pleased with the day's outing'.

It is likely that the outing was arranged by Watson as, being club captain, he also chaired the lunch at the Crown Hotel. He was also an investor, having secured Trinidad Park and invested a sum from his inheritance in the club. It is also likely that he covered the cost of this extraordinary example of a Victorian team-building exercise.

Clearly, having moved to Trinidad Park, the club was keen to establish itself in the Glasgow football hierarchy. No doubt Watson too would want to see his investment lead to success and stability for the club. Nurturing the loyalty and team spirit of the players would be crucial, as unlike Queen's Park, the club was young, with little or no pedigree. The day out at Campsie Glen may have been an effort to retain their best players and attract more. It would also be essential to engage local fans and establish their allegiance to the club, not just during the football season, but also the summer months.

A few weeks later, on 24 August 1878, Parkgrove Football Club held its first annual athletics sports day and, even though the weather was dull, the event attracted a large turnout of spectators. Watson represented Parkgrove in a four-a-side football competition, losing to Rangers in

---

108 *North British Daily Mail*, Monday, 5 August 1878.

the final by two 'touch-downs'. As was becoming a regular occurrence at these events, Watson won the high jump, and Tom Vallance won the broad jump. Watson also won the ladies' 300 yards challenge cup, a race sponsored by the ladies of club.

PARKGROVE FOOTBALL CLUB
AMATEUR ATHLETIC SPORTS
Will be held on the CLUB'S GROUNDS, TRINIDAD PARK, COPELAND ROAD, GOVAN, on SATURDAY, 24TH AUGUST CURT.
PRELIMINARY TIES in FOOTBALL COMPETITION TO-DAY (SATURDAY), 17TH CURT., at 3.30 P.M.
Admission Sixpence. Ladies Free.

Glasgow Herald – *Saturday, 17 August 1878*

During the autumn of 1878, a few weeks after the first experiment with floodlights at Bramall Lane in Sheffield, Parkgrove became one of the first clubs in Scotland to attempt a game under floodlights. If successful, the receipts from midweek games at Trinidad Park could provide the club with a profitable revenue stream. Three matches were arranged in Scotland to showcase the invention, and even though the profits from the games were promised to charity, unfortunately, out of the three fixtures, the Parkgrove game raised the least revenue, and the experiment was dismissed as a failure.

In the following summer at the Parkgrove sports day, Watson continued his dominance in the high jump, came third in the 300 yards handicap, second in the broad jump (19ft 6in), third in the 120 yards hurdles, and he played for PFC in the football tournament. He also came first in a variation of his trademark event, the running high jump (5ft 1in). His commitment to the club could not be doubted, and his athletic abilities were evident.

During the summer months, many clubs and organisations held sports days in and around Glasgow.

Often, well-known local footballers participated, and even if this was an attempt to exploit their celebrity and attract paying customers, the number of events Watson, Vallance and others entered suggests it was not an obligation, but something they enjoyed.

In January 1878, Watson trialled for the Glasgow representative team to face the Sheffield Association in an annual inter-city fixture. It was a distinct honour to play for the Glasgow team, akin to being chosen to play for the national team, and even being asked to try out was equally prestigious. The trials took place at Hampden Park, Mount Florida, on a pitch covered in snow, and drew players from all the primary Glasgow clubs. 'Mr Dickson's team' played 'Mr Watson's team' and, even though one of the trial teams had been named after him, Watson failed selection. The following year he would be chosen as a reserve and would have to wait until 1880 before finally being included in the Glasgow team.

Of note, the game in 1878 was played before a universal set of rules had been agreed. Before the game, the teams decided to use the Scottish rules in the first half and Sheffield's for the second. Glasgow won 4-2.

Being selected to trial for the Glasgow team emphasises Watson's improvement over the few years he had been in Glasgow. As if to confirm his intentions to settle in the city, he had married and produced a son, Rupert, in 1878. He had also gone into business with William Miller and George Baird, in a textiles shop on Union Street. Andrew Watson was becoming a Glaswegian.

In June 1879, he was again elected as captain of the Parkgrove club, and match secretary. Donald Hamilton, the vice-president of the Scottish FA, was presented as the new president of the club and would later become president of the SFA. Hamilton's dual positions would appear to underline Parkgrove's growing prominence in Glasgow's football community, perhaps confirming high expectations of the club's future.

Between October 1876 and December 1879, Parkgrove played over 80 games, winning nearly 50 of them. Watson played in most but missed a handful. In an away fixture against Kilburnie, he missed the train and Parkgrove had to play a man short. Even with ten men, they still came away with a 3-1 win.

In 1879, Parkgrove entered the Scottish Cup again and were drawn to play Hibernian. The first game and the replay were both drawn. However, unlike today's use of penalty shoot-outs, both teams were returned to the draw and new fixtures arranged. Parkgrove met a strong South Western team, the game ending with one goal to South Western and a disputed goal to Parkgrove. At the time, Parkgrove could not convince the referee, who was nowhere near the play, that the ball had crossed the goal line. They appealed to the Scottish FA, and the game was replayed. Parkgrove lost 3-2 in the replay, and the fixture is only worthy of mention as Watson's name appeared on the scoresheet:

> 'On positions being changed the Parkgrove, with the wind in their favour, secured two goals – the first being obtained by Watson, whose play all through was very fine.'[109]

On New Year's Day 1880, Watson appeared in a scratch team organised by Rangers' Tom Vallance. Named the 'Scottish Canadians', it had been set up to raise money for a planned

109 *Glasgow Herald*, Monday, 29 December 1879.

tour of Canada. The team included many of Scotland's best players and, over the next year, Watson would be a regular participant. The exhibition games proved very popular, even though the tour of Canada failed to take place.[110]

The Scottish Canadians' first outing, against Rangers, drew a crowd of around 3,000 and, although Vallance loyally remained with his Rangers team, on display were a host of internationals, including Robert W. Gardner in his retirement year, a founder member of Queen's Park and the finest goalkeeper in the world in the 1870s. Watson was pushed into the half-back position to make way for Somers and Duncan. Dr John Smith and George Ker were part of a 2-2-6 formation, and the Scottish Canadians ran out 3-2 winners. The referee was Parkgrove president Donald Hamilton. A newspaper account of the game singled Watson out for praise:

> 'Watson, of Parkgrove renown, astonished all who saw him. It was pretty widely known that he was a careful player, but until Thursday few imagined he could kick or tackle with such ease.'[111]

The day after the Rangers game, on 2 January 1880, with Watson remaining in Glasgow, the Scottish Canadians went on a short tour, first to Newcastle, where they won 5-0, and then to Blackburn where they met Blackburn Rovers, arguably the best team in England at the time. Played in front of over 3,000 spectators, the Scots beat Rovers by a

110 The idea of the tour belonged to William Dick, secretary of the Scottish FA but, when he died, the tour was cancelled and the money raised was distributed between many worthy causes. The ten games raised over £400 and the Scottish Canadian team was never beaten.

111 *Athletic News*, Wednesday, 7 January 1880.

remarkable 8-1 scoreline. The game is significant because the only other time Rovers would be defeated by that scoreline was in 1884, by a Corinthian team that included Andrew Watson.

Watson missed the Darwen game as the Scottish Canadians arranged a fixture on the same day as the trials for the Glasgow Representative team to face Sheffield in the annual inter-city fixture. So concerned were the selectors that the Scottish Canadian team would draw on the best players and weaken the turnout at the trials, they threatened to bar any player invited who failed to attend.

These annual games against Sheffield were treated very seriously, and the committee that chose the players consisted mostly of the same people who made the national team selection. One of the best sporting occasions in the season for both cities, it produced football of a high standard and attracted large numbers of supporters. Since the fixture was first organised in 1874, Glasgow's home record was unblemished.

On Valentine's Day, Watson, having forsaken the Scottish Canadian team, took his chance and was selected to represent his home city. The Glasgow team beat Sheffield by one goal to nil.

Watson would represent Glasgow twice more, winning both games. His selection now brought him into contention for international honours, and two weeks after beating Sheffield, Watson trialled for the national team. He was not selected and would have to wait another year before receiving that honour.

The winter of 1879 had been one of the worst on record, and the freezing conditions affected the fixture schedule. There was also a marked lack of home fixtures for Parkgrove in the first few months of 1880, when only three games were

FOOTBALL IN SCOTLAND.

King Frost still holds undisputed sway in Scotland, and his reign for the last month has been uninterrupted. Snow fell very heavily in several places, and the wind shifted round to the south for a time, but by Wednesday evening the moon shone out as brilliantly as ever, and the frost was as hard, if not harder, than before. Supposing thaw were to set in to-day, it would take nearly a week of heavy rains to make the grounds playable.

Bell's Life in London and Sporting Chronicle – *Saturday, 11 January 1879*

played. Of those they played, Watson missed two, one to attend the Glasgow trials for the inter-city fixture against Sheffield and one to take part in the trials for the Scottish national team. He played against Kilmarnock Athletic in early January, and the next game was against Kilmarnock Portland in March. Even though the winter had frozen many grounds over many weeks, the lack of activity for Parkgrove was unusual.

That March, Watson failed again to make the national team but is likely to have attended the game at Hampden against England, a close affair, ending 5-4 to the Scots. He had joined up with the Scottish Canadians for two games, beating Hearts 5-1 and St Mirren and Abercorn 8-1.

It was around Easter 1880 that the Parkgrove Football Club ceased to be. The facts behind the closure of the club have been lost to time, but several theories exist. Douglas Lamming suggested Parkgrove folded due to Watson leaving, but this may not be entirely accurate.[112] Although Watson would eventually join Queen's Park, it did not happen immediately and not until weeks after Parkgrove's collapse. Besides, as an investor in the club, it is doubtful Watson would cause the failure of his investment.

112 Lamming, D., *A Scottish Soccer Internationalists' Who's Who, 1872–1986 (1987).*

FOOTBALL.

POSTPONED FOOTBALL MATCH.

The match (Dunfermline *v.* Glasgow Parkgrove), which should have taken place on New-Year's Day was unfortunately put off. The Secretary for the Dunfermline Club received a late telegram from the Parkgrove, saying that owing to the weather, some of their men did not turn out. We trust that nothing will prevent the match advertised in our columns from coming off to-day at Lady's Mill park, as a good game is expected. We give the teams that are to contend :–

Dunfermline Saturday Press – *Saturday, 3 January 1880*

Perhaps the poor weather, the fixture cancellations and subsequent loss of revenue created problems of a financial nature. Historian Sean Damer has researched the Broomloan estate, where Trinidad Park was situated, and he may have identified a possible contributory factor.[113] Parkgrove paid rent on Trinidad Park to the property developer called Thomas Lucas Paterson, who owned Broomloan. If the club were unable to pay, Paterson, a highly mercenary individual, would have unhesitatingly evicted them. Later, when notices appeared in the Glasgow papers offering Trinidad Park to let, it became evident the facility remained available to anyone able to raise the money to hire it. The financial issues may have exacerbated other problems within the Parkgrove club.

Ground to Let.

TO Football Clubs.—Field to Let on Broomloan Estate; lately rented by Parkgrove Football Club. Use of Club house on ground.—A. K. Paterson, 517 Govan Road, Govan.

Glasgow Evening Citizen – *Friday, 16 April 1880*

113 Damer (1989).

The Scottish Association Annual does not shed any light on the club's collapse, listing Parkgrove as a member from 1875 to 1879. Having lost the Trinidad Park ground, they did not appear in the 1879/80 annual. Even though there are newspaper reports of games played by a team called 'Parkgrove' after April 1880, this would not be Watson's club.

After the collapse, many of the players, including Watson, formed a new team called the 'Glasgow Pilgrims', taking the name of their English counterparts, for whom Watson would play in years to come. The formation of the club is recorded as April 1880, indicating that Parkgrove may have folded after their last game on 6 March 1880 against Kilmarnock Portland. Losing 3-1, this would be the last time Watson captained his club.

Queen's Park Football Club

> 'The Story of the Queen's Park is so interwoven with the history of Scottish football that the two cannot be disassociated. In writing the story of the club, the more the subject is studied, the more the impression must prevail, that were it not for the fostering care given to Association football in Scotland by this club, the game would never have taken the place it has in the world of sport, nor would Scotland stand where it does, as the nursery and home of football as at present played in all parts of the world. Foresight and enthusiasm enabled the great amateur combination known as the Queen's Park Football Club, to spring into being with a fixed object in view.'[114]

114 Robinson (1920).

It is no overstatement to say that Queen's Park were the forebears of the modern game. They were the first association football club in Scotland, founded in 1867, played as the first Scottish national team and were the principal force behind the creation of the Scottish FA. They were ambassadors of football, making 'missionary' trips to Scottish lowlands to demonstrate and promote the game. They invented 'combination' football, 'scientific' football, which the English would quickly realise was the future of the game.

The Queen's Park style of football included field positions, positional strategy, passing and tactical formations. In the 1870s, the English set out their players in a 1-1-8 formation, a shape that favoured the individual, the forwards, dribbling, and the kick and rush game that was characteristic of the public school system. Queen's Park lined up 2-2-6, and later 2-3-5, a formation favoured for decades after.

The club's motto, *Ludere causa Ludendi*,[115] identified the club as strictly amateur and, therefore, allied them to the gentlemen of southern England. Sandwiched between was the industrial north of England, where the desire for the business of football would successfully seduce a stream of Scottish players south. This exodus would prevent the Scots from fielding a national team representative of the quality of the players they were producing. However, they were still strong enough to regularly beat the English. But the steady stream of 'Scottish Professors' to the northern clubs would eventually influence the professional game and shape the sport now played the world over.

There is a suspicion that Watson might have been surplus to requirements at Queen's Park as they were already in

115 'To Play for the Sake of Playing'.

possession of several excellent full-backs. R.W. Neill, J.W. Holm and W.S. Somers were all experienced, and Somers and Neill were already internationals. Watson's Parkgrove friend and team-mate, J.J. Gow, would play at full-back alongside him and also become an international. As the favoured formation at the time only allowed for a pair of full-backs, Queen's Park would only be able to utilise two at a time.

For a game against the Edinburgh Association on the first Saturday after Easter, Watson played half-back, suggesting that they may have accommodated him into the team. Even though experiments with formations were taking place at that time, it would be unusual to have played both Watson and Gow out of position at half-back. In fact, in the next game, in the Glasgow Charity Cup, Gow was kept out of the team, and Watson once again played in midfield.

Watson's move may not have been as clean-cut as Richard Robinson states in his history of Queen's Park.[116] He said Watson became a Queen's Park player on 6 April 1880; however, Watson had already played for Queen's Park against the Edinburgh Association on 3 April, winning 16-0, and may have also made up the numbers for a game on Easter Monday against the Manchester Wanderers at Hampden. Curiously, two months earlier, in a match report for the Scottish Canadian victory over Nottingham Forest on 10 February, Watson had been labelled as a Queen's Park player. This could simply be an error or could suggest he had already been talking to Queen's Park, two months before joining them.

Later, in another game for the Scottish Canadian team on 17 April, Watson is listed as a Parkgrove player, and four days later he played for Pilgrims in a 5-2 triumph over

---

116 Robinson (1920).

Edinburgh Hibernians. There are references to a 'Watsonian-era' at Pilgrims, therefore his move to Queen's Park appears to be rather indistinct, especially considering they already had a wealth of defenders at their disposal.[117] However, the addition of Watson and Gow would appear to be justified, as, within a year, W.S. Somers would retire and R.W. Neill would suffer a knee injury in a charity match and disappear from the game.[118]

Perhaps Robinson's calendar of events was not as accurate as he believed, as he also stated that J.J. Gow joined Queen's Park from Pilgrims in 1879, but Gow was still a Parkgrove player in February 1880 when trials for the Scottish national team were held at Trinidad Park. Nine Parkgrove players were invited to attend, underlining the quality of the squad at the time of its collapse. Also, Pilgrims was not formed until April 1880, so Gow appears to have joined Queen's Park after Watson.

Nevertheless, on Saturday, 10 April 1880, Watson entered the Dunfermline FC athletic sports day, where his allegiances were confirmed. The suffix next to his name in the newspaper reports stated 'QPFC'. On the day, he won his trademark event, the standing high jump, with a relatively weak leap of five feet, considering his other triumphs.

The miserable winter had resulted in many games being postponed, forcing the fixture schedule to drag on into April and May, much later than usual. Watson played again on 24 April 1880, meeting the formidable Vale of Leven in the semi-final of the Glasgow Merchants Charity Cup. The game ended as a draw, but in the replay Queen's Park ended the game as resounding 4-0 winners.

---

117 *Athletic News*, Wednesday, 28 September 1881.

118 R.W. Neill reappeared in 1887, as goalkeeper for London Caledonians.

In February, before Watson joined, Queen's Park had beaten Thornliebank 3-0 to win the Scottish Cup. They were now looking to win the 'double' but would have to face a strong Rangers team looking for revenge for being dumped out of the Scottish Cup in the first round by Queen's Park.

The Saturday before the final, on 1 May, Watson competed at the Alexandra Athletic Club annual sports day. He entered the 100 yards race and won the high jump with a leap of 5ft 6in and may have also played for Queen's Park in the football competition. Perhaps he found activity the best way to manage nerves.

Saturday, 8 May 1880 was a big day for Watson, as not only was it the first time he had played in a major cup final, but he was asked to play as a third half-back, a new formation criticised for 'not being conducive to good play'![119] Until now, Watson had played as the second half-back and, obviously, to get him involved in the games, a new formation had to be considered. Adding a centre-half and losing a forward was a gamble, especially as this was the Glasgow Merchants Charity Cup Final.

A crowd of over 5,000 spectators turned out to witness a game predicted to be 'one of the best, if not the best, of the season', and it lived up to all expectations.[120] The best players in Scotland were on show, and all but four were playing or would play internationally. However, an exciting, evenly matched game ended as a 1-1 draw, so went to a replay.

Four days later, several thousand spectators squeezed into Kinning Park, some standing on wagons, others on rooftops, to get the best vantage point. Queen's Park not only fell behind by one goal in the first half but lost Neill to injury.

---

119 Potentially, the first introduction of a centre-half in a major cup final.

120 *Glasgow Evening Citizen*, Friday, 7 May 1880.

This meant completing the game with only ten players. However, after the break, Queen's Park came out and began pressurising the Rangers goal. When Geordie Ker got 'sorely lamed', it looked as if it was not going to be Queen's Park's day. But he carried on and, just before full time, as Rangers were beginning to believe they had won the cup, Queen's Park scored two goals in quick succession, the second the subject of protests by the Rangers players. Queen's Park had beaten Rangers 2-1 to win the cup. Unacknowledged at the time, Andrew Watson had become the first man of colour to win major silverware.

Along with Neill and Ker, Rangers' Archie Steel also sustained injuries. The match had been very physical and was criticised for the roughness of the play and for a disputed winning goal. However, the season was still not at an end.

Football Notices, &c.

GRAND FOOTBALL MATCH,
IN AID OF THE DICK MEMORIAL FUND.
CLAPHAM ROVERS
(Holders of the English Association Challenge Cup)
VERSUS
QUEEN'S PARK
(Holders of the Scottish Association Challenge Cup).
HAMPDEN PARK, SATURDAY, 15TH MAY, 1880.
Kick-off, 3.30 P.M.
Admission—To Ground, 1s.; to Stand, 1s.
Tickets for Ground and Stand to be had from Messrs. H. & P. M'Neil, 23 Renfield Street. Places Reserved on Stand for Ticketholders till 3.15 P.M.

Glasgow Evening Citizen – *Thursday, 13 May 1880*

A week later, Queen's Park played host to Clapham Rovers, the English cup winners, in a friendly fixture in Glasgow. The game between the Scottish and English cup winners was to raise money for the widow of William Dick, the late secretary of the Scottish FA, and was arguably more significant than the Charity Cup Final. For this game, Watson reverted to full-back. Although several of the Queen's Park players were still lame from the encounter with Rangers the previous week, the Scots beat the English cup holders 3-2. Watson was now a member of the best team in the world.

But there was one more match to be played before the season could conclude. This was played in Rothesay on the Isle of Bute. The fixture was another arranged to raise funds for a Scottish football tour of Canada. Even though it was only an exhibition game, the teams were divided into the 'Internationals' and the 'Non-Internationals'. Mostly from Rangers and Queen's Park, the Non-Internationals included J.J. Gow and Tom Vallance's brother, Alexander. Tom Vallance and Andrew played for the 'Internationals', who eventually lost 5-1.

Although this was only an exhibition match and perhaps a fun day out for the players, the inclusion of Watson in a team of 'Internationals' indicates the growing admiration for the young player, who was yet to achieve international honours. Five years after arriving in Glasgow, he had joined the elite of Scottish football and, by implication, world football. Watson was now one of the best players in the world.

Throughout the summer of 1880, Watson competed for Queen's Park in numerous athletic events. At the Kilmarnock Athletic Club, where, surprisingly, he came second in the high jump, the report explained:

> 'I have little doubt the Queen's Park man, who has been known to do 5ft 9in., would have won had he not had the misfortune to tear his shoe.'[121]

121 *Athletic News*, Wednesday, 26 May 1880.

Watson entered the Mauchline FC[122] athletic sports day, the Crescent Football Club athletic sports day, the Ardrossan and Saltcoats Club annual athletic sports day and won the high jump in each. In the Queen's Park Football Club athletic sports day, he again won the high jump with a leap of 5ft 5in and was probably included in the Queen's Park team that entered the four-a-side football competition.

In early September 1880, Queen's Park began their season with a cup tie win of 7-0 over John Elder. Watson was now playing full-back alongside his old Parkgrove team-mate, J.J. Gow, and by November he was listed as captain.

Watson captained most of the teams he regularly played for, and it is surprising how often this responsibility would be awarded to him. In many cases, he accepted the role after only a few games and, in the case of his first game for Scotland, on his debut. Watson was a leader and was comfortable with responsibility. As C.W. Alcock wrote about the captain's role:

> 'The qualities required for the proper fulfilment of a post requiring peculiar skill are not inherent; they are, in fact a gift. The power and ability to command are not given to everyone.'[123]

In the picture of the Scottish national team from 1881, Watson's body language and seating position perhaps confirm this. Not only does he look relaxed and comfortable, but he is also in the centre of the picture, the focal point, arms and legs casually crossed, and almost reclining. Obviously at

122 Founded by Watson's friend Dr John Smith.

123 Alcock (1906).

ease, this may reflect his relationship with his team-mates and their willingness to support and trust him.

The win over John Elder in September 1880 heralded a period of two seasons where Queen's Park played over 60 games, losing only once. Richard Robinson, author of a history of Queen's Park Football Club, wrote:

> 'At this period the team that represented the Queen's Park was one of the best, if not the best, that had appeared on a football field.'[124]

In the 1880/81 season, Queen's Park won the Glasgow Charity and Scottish cups and held on to both in the following season. In the autumn of 1880, Watson was regularly singled out for praise by the media:

> 'Of the Queen's Park backs none shone so well as Andrew Watson, who has made tremendous strides since beginning the season.'[125]

> 'Watson, the old Parkgrove man, has improved very much as a back since I saw him perform last year, and I should not be at all surprised to find him in the International team this season.'[126]

The second quote was prophetic, as in March 1881, after attending the trials again, Watson was selected to play for Scotland. He had trialled in February 1879, and he did so again in February 1880, but missed the next trials in March, due to the birth of his daughter, Agnes Maude. Being absent excluded him from selection, even though it was highly likely

124 Robinson (1920).

125 *Athletic News,* Wednesday, 3 November 1880.

126 *Athletic News,* Wednesday, 27 October 1880.

he would have been picked. But the arrival of a daughter would have been ample compensation.

The 1881 England versus Scotland game would be the tenth official meeting between the old enemies, Scotland having won six, England two, with two drawn games. The last two meetings had produced identical scorelines of 5-4, England winning in 1879, and Scotland in 1880. Even though the Scots had won the last match, these fixtures had been close affairs. There was a distinct uneasiness in the Scottish camp as, for the first time, the English had held trials, emulating the Scottish selection process. This did little to calm the Scottish nerves.

Even though this would be his international debut, Watson was selected as captain, the highest honour in Scottish football. Arguably, at that moment in time, Andrew Watson was the foremost association footballer in the world. The occasion would put Watson's name in the history books as the first man of colour to lead a British national team, to play for and captain Scotland, and the first man of colour to play international football.

At 10am on Friday, 11 March, Watson and the Scottish delegation left Central Station in Glasgow for London. Of the travelling party, only three were players, with seven more taking the night train, perhaps due to their day jobs, and three more were already waiting in London.

> 'A large crowd were on the platform and gave them three hearty cheers, indicative of their desire that a success should be won for Scotland.'[127]

On a foggy day at The Oval, the home of English football at that time, between 3,000 and 5,000 spectators turned

127 *Glasgow Evening Citizen*, Friday, 11 March 1881.

out to witness the game. The Scottish colours[128] were '... primrose (yellow) and rose (pink), blue knickerbockers and red stockings'. In contrast, England wore the familiar white jerseys, navy shorts and socks. Having won the toss, England took up their place under the gasometer and the Scots at the Crown Baths end. The game kicked off at 3.15pm.

From the very beginning, the Scots looked more potent than the English. At half-time, the score was a respectable 2-0 to the Scots, the goals scored by Dr John Smith and Queen's Park's Geordie Ker. After half-time, the passing game of the Scots began dominating the dribbling, kick and rush game of the English. After another Scottish goal, scored by David Hill of Rangers, E.C. Bambridge managed to pull one back for the English, to rapturous cheers and applause from the crowd. But by the time the final whistle blew, the Scots had 'lowered the English flag' three more times. Two goals each from Smith and Ker, one by Hill, plus an own goal by Edgar Field of Clapham Rovers, produced an emphatic, if somewhat unexpected, 6-1 rout.

In the evening, the Scots were entertained to dinner at the Freemasons' Tavern but left later to catch the train to Wrexham, where they were to face the Welsh on the following Monday.

English newspaper reports tried to soften the blow and pick out positives: '... anything but depressed by their ill-fortune, now played up brilliantly ...'; '... pluck and dash displayed by the English team ...'; '... with hereditary courage, they battled on ...'[129]

Some were cool, saying:

---

128 Archibald Philip Primrose (1847-1929), was the 5th Earl of Rosebery, 1st Earl of Midlothian, Old Etonian and Oxonian, Honorary President of the Scottish FA. He would later become the Prime Minister.

129 *The Referee,* Sunday, 13 March 1881.

> '… a much easier success, it must be admitted, than was ever expected in England.'[130]

Others were less gracious:

> 'On behalf of the home team, only one club was represented by more than a single player, while no less a number than five of the celebrated Queen's-Park (Glasgow) club assisted in upholding the honour of Scotland. This, as may readily be imagined, gave the Northerners a distinct advantage.'[131]

Others relegated the story to a single line below long reports of the games between Nottingham Wanderers and Aston Villa 2nd XI, or Nottingham Forest and Blackburn Rovers. But nothing could hide the superiority of the Scottish play.

The Scottish newspapers highlighted three disallowed, so-called 'offside' goals that had been dismissed by the English referee, Major Marindin, plus a goalbound shot that was deliberately handled on the line by Wilson, preventing a far greater humiliation. Having breached the English defence ten times was undoubtedly something for the Scottish to crow about.

It became one of the most meaningful results in the history of the fixture. Symbolic of the total superiority of Scottish football, it remains a defining landmark in the history of the modern game. The result also sent shockwaves through the English football community. Acknowledging the superiority of the Scottish game, it ushered in a change of mindset and a deep-seated desire by the English to develop their own game.

---

130 *Leeds Mercury,* Monday, 14 March 1881.

131 *Morning Post,* Monday, 14 March 1881.

For Watson, this would have been a truly memorable occasion and a highlight of his football career to date. He would have been unaware of his achievements as a man of colour, but might have recalled as a schoolboy at King's College, visiting The Oval to watch football or cricket, never once imagining he would play there himself one day, or that he would be the first man of colour to play at The Oval.

N.C. Bailey and E.C. Bambridge played for England that day, and Bambridge's brother, E.H. Bambridge, had been an umpire.[132] All were members of the English FA and were doubtless impressed by the new Scottish captain. Even though they may have believed they were prepared for a battle, few could believe that an England team could be beaten so emphatically.

Two days after the annihilation of England in London, the Scottish team defeated Wales in Wrexham 5-1. In some reports, Watson captained the Scots again, although Tom Vallance is officially recorded in the role in the history books.

On returning to Scotland, Watson finished the season with Queen's Park, winning both the Scottish Cup and the Glasgow Charity Cup again. Over the following summer, he continued to enter athletic competitions, continued to win the high jump and, over the year, he continued to attract plaudits from the press. He had convincingly proven himself as one of Scotland's best players.

In November 1881, Watson was 'persuaded' to take on the role of secretary at Queen's Park, confirming his ability to manage official positions and, apparently, underlining his commitment to the club.

---

132 There were two umpires: Bambridge and Donald Hamilton (former president of the defunct Parkgrove club), vice-president for the Scottish FA.

On 11 March 1882, Watson made his third appearance for Scotland, against England in Glasgow. The game was played at Hampden Park before a crowd estimated at between 12,000 and 20,000, significantly more than in London at the previous meeting. The *Glasgow Herald* described the scenes around the ground:

> 'Cabs, cars, omnibuses and every other conceivable sort of conveyance were utilised to carry the immense throng of people from the city ... the largest portion of the crowd elected to walk, and the result was that the roads converging on Hampden Park for a long time seemed but continuous streams of humanity.'[133]

There had been concerns that the game would not go ahead as the ground had frozen in the week, but the weather turned and became 'summerlike'. There were also serious concerns in the Scottish camp due to '... the vast strides made by the Englishmen of late in the dribbling and passing game...'[134] As London had beaten the Glasgow Representative team in Sheffield and the Scotch Counties team in Birmingham, the fear was that their recent performances heralded a new era of domination.

Even though the Scots were handicapped by having to play under the English rules, where throw-ins and offsides were different, they performed better in all other areas. The game ended with another win for the Scots, 5-1, the seventh time they had beaten the English. The score would have been six but for a rule, long since removed, that denied

133 *Glasgow Herald*, Monday, 13 March 1882.

134 *Manchester Courier and Lancashire General Advertiser*, Monday, 13 March 1882.

Football Matches.

GREAT INTERNATIONAL

FOOTBALL MATCH.

ENGLAND

VERSUS

SCOTLAND,

SATURDAY, 11TH MARCH.

HAMPDEN PARK.

Kick-Off 3.30 P.M.

Admission, 1s. — Grand Stand, 1s.6d. Extra.

QUEEN'S PARK GRAND STANCE will be Reserved till 3 P.M. Tickets to be had from H. & P. M'Neill, 21 and 23 Renfield Street.

Glasgow Evening Citizen – *Friday, 10 March 1882*

McIntyre's goal from a free-kick, as it was scored directly without touching any other player!

Two goals each for John Campbell McLeod McPherson of Arthurlie and Geordie Ker, plus one from William Harrower of Queen's Park, separated the teams. There were seven Queen's Park players in the squad and, once again, the result underlined Scottish prominence.

Perhaps unusually, Watson's part in the proceedings was limited to a few mentions, most references describing the strength and capability of the Scottish defence:

> 'Watson … was, as is usual with him, very steady and his speed aided Scotland a great deal.'[135]

---

135 *Athletic News*, Wednesday, 15 March 1882.

Another report said:

> 'I have seen A. Watson do very much better, but then we who are in the secret know how he did not shine with his accustomed brilliancy. For a week or so he has been ailing with a sore side, one of his rib bones having lately got a nasty smash, that in some measure accounts for his not doing, what we all know he can do.'[136]

Watson's injury had not prevented his selection, and Scotland had won convincingly. But a brief report in the *Athletic News* three days before the game, hints at the real cause of Watson's injury.

NEVER has it been my luck to meet a gentleman possessed of such abnormal vivacity "from morn till noon, from noon till dewy eve," and a' the nicht "Coupeau" kept at it. The powers of the cachinatory muscles of his auditors were taxed to the utmost. In fact it is believed Andy Watson has ruptured a legament in his side, the laugh which caused the accident being the loudest on record, not to mention the bell like intonation of same.

Athletic News – *Wednesday, 8 March 1882*

This defeat was the final straw for the English FA, who resolved that something should be done to reverse English fortunes.

The losses undoubtedly influenced the FA's decision to form a new 'Wednesday Club' who could regularly play together and form the nucleus of the English national squad. This team would later become known as the Corinthian Football Club.

---

136 *Athletic News*, Wednesday, 15 March 1882.

Watson was not selected for the game against Wales on 25 March 1882. However, that game clashed with the Scottish Cup Final between Queen's Park and Dumbarton. With the first game drawn, and facing a replay, Watson may have sacrificed a cap for loyalty to the club. Queen's Park won the replay 4-1, retaining the trophy for another year.

Watson had secured his place in Scottish hearts with defeats of the English and Welsh. He was also a successful member of the undefeated Queen's Park and Glasgow teams. But barely two months after Scotland's latest humiliation of the English, *Athletic News* printed a short paragraph:

> 'Glasgow is about to loose [sic] one of its most conspicuous football figures. Andrew Watson, who has played so well for Queen's Park, and also for Scotland, goes to London for good tomorrow (Thursday), having received an appointment in one of the Government offices. Their [sic] never was a kinder-hearted gentleman than Mr. Watson, and I am sure when he goes, many will miss him.
>
> A. Watson, I believe, is an Old Eton lad, and if the Etonians are in want of a reliable back, they should secure his services.'[137]

London

At the end of May 1882, Watson stepped down as secretary for Queen's Park, and moved his family to Tottenham in London, apparently for good. The suddenness and the

137 *Athletic News*, Wednesday, 31 May 1882.

complete lack of suggestion that Watson was planning to leave Scotland came as a shock to many.

While some were still reeling from the news, a month later Watson surprisingly reappeared in Scotland and competed at the South Western Football Club annual sports day, coming second in the 'Place kick at Football' competition with a kick of 196ft 2in. He also may have played for the Queen's Park team in the four-a-side football tournament. Unusually, there is no mention of a high jump competition.

This unexpected appearance in Scotland, so soon after moving to London, heralded a pattern of behaviour exhibited throughout his time in the south. Often, he would be in Glasgow when he had been selected to play for an English team. During his time in the south, there is a sense that the lure of Scotland was too irresistible.

Three months after arriving in London, Watson's wife Jessie became ill. Aside from the distress this would have caused both Andrew and the children, it would also disrupt his new standing as a civil servant. To a lesser degree, it would also interfere with any footballing commitments that he had arranged.

Perhaps unaware of the seriousness of her illness, on 21 October 1882, Watson took part in his first proper game in England, for an E.C. Bambridge scratch XI against Clapham Rovers. Rovers had won the FA Cup in 1880 and were still one of the best teams in the south at that time. In a report of his first game in England, Watson earned an acknowledgement:

> 'The game was played in a more or less incessant downpour of rain, but nevertheless some good form was exhibited on both sides, the back play of E.C. Bambridge and A. Weston, [sic] the

> Scotch International player, being very strong …'[138]

The match finished in a creditable one-all draw. It is noticeable that Bambridge, a famous striker, chose to play alongside Watson at the back, obviously intent on studying Watson in action and learning from the Scotsman. Also, captain of Clapham was Cecil Henry Holden-White, the English international, who would become the first captain of the Corinthian Football Club. He too would have been more than curious about Watson and what the new club could expect to see in their ranks.

The following week, Watson appeared in a game for Swifts against Bradfield College, Swifts winning convincingly, 4-0. A match report stated that 'the Bradfield forwards were unable to pass A. Watson …'[139]

In the days between the Rovers and Bradfield games, A.J Secretan's Corinthians played their first game, and had Jessie not been ill, it is highly likely Watson would have been invited to play his first game for the club.[140]

However, on 31 October, Jessie died, leaving Andrew without a wife, and Rupert and Agnes without a mother. Jessie's funeral was on 3 November and, shortly afterwards, Watson sent his children back to Glasgow to the care of his in-laws.

It is possible that Jessie and Andrew had come to London together to set up a home, leaving the children in the care of their grandparents, intending to send for them when the time was right. However, if they had done this, there would have

---

138 *Field*, Saturday, 28 October 1882.

139 *Field*, Saturday, 4 November 1882.

140 At this point, A.J. Secretan managed the team, but would later leave and pass the responsibility to N.L. Jackson.

been more sightings of Watson in the Glasgow media that summer, and he probably would have appeared in more sports days than the single appearance at South Western. If the children had remained in Glasgow, Watson would have had to endure the death of his wife without any family support.

Less than two weeks after Jessie's funeral, Watson returned to football and played five games in two weeks for both Swifts and Pilgrims. One of these was for Swifts against Upton Park in the second round of the FA Cup on 30 November 1884. Playing alongside E.C. and A.L. Bambridge, Swifts went two goals up in the first half, only for Upton Park to level the game after the break. Towards the end, Swifts player and England international, Clement Mitchell, broke free and shot at goal, the ball hitting the 'tape'.[141] The umpires and referee disagreed about whether the ball had gone over, and what would have been the winning goal for Swifts was not awarded. Upton Park suggested extra time, but Swifts refused, forcing a replay the next day. The general opinion was that if the game had gone to extra time, Upton Park would have won, but E.C. Bambridge, perhaps cunningly, refused to accept the offer.

Watson, still in mourning, received a few mentions in the press, saying he was 'most useful' and defended 'manfully'.[142],[143] A hundred years later the significance of his performance would be recognised, identifying him as the first black footballer to play in the FA Cup. Swifts won the replay 3-2 and progressed to the next round.

In December, Watson received his first call-up for Corinthian. His name was on the team sheet to play against Charterhouse School, but by making one of his unannounced

141 Crossbars were yet to be compulsory in the rules of the game.

142 *Sporting Life*, Saturday, 2 December 1882.

143 *Field*, Saturday, 9 December 1882.

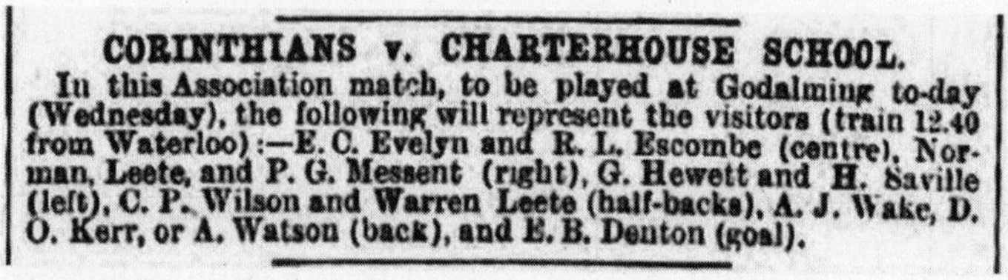

CORINTHIANS v. CHARTERHOUSE SCHOOL.

In this Association match, to be played at Godalming to-day (Wednesday), the following will represent the visitors (train 12.40 from Waterloo):—E. C. Evelyn and R. L. Escombe (centre), Norman, Leete, and P. G. Messent (right), G. Hewett and H. Saville (left), C. P. Wilson and Warren Leete (half-backs), A. J. Wake, D. O. Kerr, or A. Watson (back), and E. B. Denton (goal).

Sporting Life – *Wednesday, 13 December 1882*

trips back to Scotland, he missed the game. He also missed a game for Pilgrims arranged for three days earlier.

Possibly the most significant difference in terms of a football schedule for Watson was getting used to playing his football during the week. In Scotland with Parkgrove and Queen's Park, fixtures were mostly played on Saturday afternoons, with exceptions for cup replays or friendlies. In the south, most games were scheduled to take place during the week, with the weekends reserved for cup games. Throughout his first autumn in London, Watson only played five times on a Saturday, in cup matches, and all the other games were played on weekdays. No doubt Bambridge would have informed him that this would be the case and, if so, Watson's commitment to his new civil servant position would be only partial. His employers were either very laissez-faire or Watson would be stretching the bounds of acceptability. This brings into question the nature of his employment and whether Bambridge had made 'arrangements' before he arrived in London, or whether his career in London was shorter than originally planned.

Later in the month, Watson played at Charterhouse, but not with Corinthian. On 16 December 1882, he turned out for Pilgrims and his performance that day made a distinct impression. The press said:

> 'Andy Watson played magnificently at full-back, the boys noting him the finest back they have seen.'[144]

144 *Field*, Saturday, 23 December 1882.

> '... the boys voting him the best back player ever seen on their ground'.[145]

One reference to the occasion stated that Watson was carried in triumph from the field on the shoulders of the young Carthusians. Such adulation would have been a high point in any player's career, but for an institution so representative of the establishment to treat a black footballer with such high regard would have been unheard of at that time. Charterhouse was not only the home of many famous Corinthian and England footballers but was a bastion of 'Britishness'. The school represented an upper-middle-class elite, expected to 'go up' to university and accept prominent positions in government, business, the clergy or the military. This unique moment in football history was where, perhaps for the first time, a black athlete's ability eclipsed their colour or heritage.

Watson's movements around this time continued to be unpredictable, but it was becoming increasingly apparent that he was on course to become as popular in England as he had been in Scotland.

At Christmas 1882, having played for Swifts against Brentwood, Watson returned to Glasgow, this time taking the Swifts football team with him. Reports in the press said he had been instrumental in arranging a fixture with Queen's Park at Hampden and that he would play for the Englishmen against his old comrades, including his friend J.J. Gow.

On New Year's Day 1883, when Watson ran on to the field of play, the Queen's Park supporters warmly cheered him. The respect shown towards a man who could have been attacked for his colour, heritage and lack of allegiance

---

145 *Athletic News*, Wednesday, 20 December 1882.

to either Queen's Park or Scotland, conveys the esteem in which the Glaswegians held him. It is a remarkable testament to a person of colour to be received so warmly in a potentially hostile environment. The reaction of the Queen's Park supporters probably affected Watson, who had been struggling with his obligations on both sides of the border. He may have seriously considered abandoning his life in London and returning to Glasgow, to a city that counted him as one of its own.

The newspaper reports of the game were kind also, praising his clean kicking and splendid tackling. However, the game did not go to plan for the invincible Scottish side, and Swifts won 2-1, the first time an English team had ever beaten them on their own ground.

The reaction to the loss was felt deeply in Scotland. Almost a year later, a commentator wrote:

> 'The year 1883 opened very inauspiciously for the Queen's Park. On the first day they sustained the defeat at the hands of an English club, being the first time the foreigner had ever succeeded in desecrating the sacred ground of Hampden Park ... The club had only recently lost Andrew Watson, its best back ... Watson, on his removal to London, joined the Swifts, and was mainly instrumental in bringing them to Glasgow. The team that represented the Swifts was drawn from many clubs, it being the fashion in London apparently for one man to belong to several clubs. The Swifts came, saw, and conquered, and the Queen's Park was left crestfallen and defeated.'[146]

146 *Glasgow Evening Post*, Friday, 21 December 1883.

A week after the Swifts game, the following report appeared in the press concerning the Glasgow Association trials:

> 'As usual, a number of those players did not turn up. Mr McDowell had a very great difficulty in making up two teams, and he asked Andrew Watson, who is now on a visit to Glasgow, and who was one of the spectators, to play as forward, but, being without his football uniform, he could not oblige the Secretary of the Association.'[147]

Watson was clearly still taking an interest in Glasgow's football, and in the full knowledge he was ineligible to play in his homeland, had attended the trials anyway. There is a sense that he felt more at home in Glasgow than in London and that, even though he was not included in its footballing activities, he was still interested and cared for the city.

Returning to London, Watson continued to represent Pilgrims, Swifts and made his debut for Corinthian, against a formidable Upton Park side, losing 7-0. Six days later, Watson and Swifts lost 2-0 to Old Etonians in the fourth round of the FA Cup. The game is of interest because it was the first time Watson played against the famous bearded Hon. Arthur Fitzgerald Kinnaird, 11th Lord Kinnaird. He was a principal member of the FA and later became president, a position he held for over 30 years. He played in nine FA Cup finals, winning three, and, due to his father's parentage, like Watson, had played for Scotland.[148]

The following day, Watson appeared as an umpire for a match in the fourth round of the FA Cup between Old

---

147 *Athletic News,* Wednesday, 10 January 1883.

148 Mitchell, A., *Arthur Kinnaird: First Lord of Football* (2011).

Carthusians and Royal Engineers. So important was this game that the president of the FA, Major Marindin, was asked to referee and Watson and Morton Peto Betts were chosen as umpires. Betts, a close friend of Kinnaird, had scored the winning goal in the first FA Cup Final. Carthusians thumped Engineers 6-2, but by umpiring in this game, Andrew Watson became the first man of colour to officiate in an FA Cup game and any major cup competition. It was yet another 'first' for Watson to add to his list of achievements.

After officiating in the match, and apparently unannounced, Watson headed back to Glasgow for what the press called 'the most important football match in Scotland this season'.[149] The Scottish Cup quarter-final game pitched holders Queen's Park against Dumbarton at their Boghead Ground. The press mentioned that Watson had been 'specially brought from London' for the game and Dumbarton lodged an official protest at Watson's presence.[150] They need not have worried, as a combination of a muddy surface, underhand tactics from one or two Dumbarton players, and a partisan crowd, saw Queen's Park lose to the eventual cup winners, 3-1.

The significance of this game and Watson's importation is that he had been selected to play for West Surrey, Corinthian and Pilgrims, and turned his back on all three in preference to Queen's Park. Admittedly, it was a cup quarter-final, and even though the West Surrey fixture against South Essex was called off due to poor weather, Corinthian lost to Norfolk 3-1, and Pilgrims, with only ten men, faced Blackburn Rovers and were thumped 14-0. However, turning his back on these clubs does not appear to have had any consequences

149 *Dundee Courier*, Monday, 5 February 1883.

150 *Glasgow Herald*, Monday, 5 February 1883.

for Watson, as he was back with Pilgrims in March and with Corinthian for their first-ever Easter tour.

Watson's unpredictable behaviour continued, and the increasing frequency of his absences due to visits to Glasgow, if he were still employed, probably stretched his employer's patience. Indeed, there is little evidence that his career as a civil servant had any longevity. The demands of Bambridge's Swifts, Pilgrims, A.J Secretan's Corinthian, and Dr John Smith's Edinburgh University team would have required many midweek absences, perhaps only possible if Watson was leading an untethered existence. Even though he was drawn to Glasgow to be with his children, whenever he was there he would inevitably play for Queen's Park.

In March 1883, Watson was invited to tour the north of England with A.J Secretan's Corinthian team, playing Accrington, Bootle (who he would later join), Church and Stoke. Corinthian won two games and lost two, and perhaps due to the intense schedule, several other arranged fixtures were not played. Sadly, the tour did not capture the imagination of the public, nor did it presage the successes of future Corinthian tours.

Perhaps due to his kind nature, Watson appears to have had difficulty in refusing invitations from other clubs. At the end of the 1882/83 season, while still a member of Swifts, Pilgrims and Corinthian, he was elected as a member of Brentwood Football Club. The connection with Brentwood may have been his old Parkgrove team-mate, T.J. Britten, now a member of the Essex club. Later, Britten made an appearance for Bootle in 1887, probably under Watson's influence.

Watson presumably spent the whole of the autumn of 1883 in the south, as there are no records of him playing any games in Scotland. Of note, in one game on 22 December,

Pilgrims met the newly formed Casuals Football Club at Walthamstow and played out an exciting 4-4 draw, reported as 'the finest match seen on that ground this season'.[151] Pilgrims started the game with only nine players and were two goals down by the time they had a full complement. They also fielded four Queen's Park players, including Watson, Dr John Smith, J.W. Holm and W. Dunlop. Smith scored two of the Pilgrims' goals. *The Sportsman* reported that Watson 'fielded brilliantly'.[152] Appearing in the Casuals team were the club's founding fathers, Fred Bickley, who played close to 300 times for the club, and Tom Blenkiron.

A week later, Blenkiron played alongside Watson in a 5-2 win for Corinthian against the Sheffield Club. Watson appeared as captain of the club for the first time, and in doing so became the first black player to accept the captaincy of Corinthian.

Christmas 1883 followed the same pattern as the previous year, and Watson again played for Swifts on New Year's Day, but this time the result was reversed, Swifts losing 5-1 to Queen's Park. Later, the Scottish team entertained their English opponents to dinner at the Royal Hotel as a symbol of the respect they had for the London team. A few days later, Watson was asked to play for a weakened Queen's Park team that shockingly lost to Pollokshields Athletic, the result causing much commentary in the Scottish press.

Returning to London, Watson is recorded as playing several games for Swifts but, in February, the following advertisement appeared in the newspapers:

WANTED.—Mr. Andrew Watson to inform Mr. E. C. Bambridge of his whereabouts immediately by wire.

Nottingham Evening Post – *7 February 1884*

---

151 *Athletic News*, Wednesday, 26 December 1883.

152 *The Sportsman*, Friday, 21 December 1883.

Not only is this a little alarming, as Watson had played for Swifts in the previous month, but it also confirms that Andrew was no longer living in Tottenham and no longer a civil servant. Nevertheless, Bambridge obviously managed to contact him as Watson played for Swifts a week after the advert appeared. In October, Bambridge would use the same technique to contact Watson in connection with the forthcoming Corinthian tour.

Surrey County

On 9 February 1884, Watson was double-booked. He had been chosen to play for Surrey County against a combined Berkshire and Buckinghamshire team, but with Bambridge's advertisement successful, he joined Swifts in their FA Cup quarter-final against Notts County, drawing 1-1, but lost the replay four days later. This was not the first time he had been asked to play for Surrey County, as in the previous January he had been selected for a game that was eventually postponed. He had been listed in Surrey team sheets several other times but had failed to show. But making amends, on Monday, 3 March 1884 Watson played for Surrey County against the Nottinghamshire Association, winning 6-2. This was the first time a man of colour had played for a senior county team, and Watson would turn out again three days later in the 3-0 defeat of Essex County.

The rapid growth of the game had increased pressure on the FA to organise and administrate the game regionally, consolidating their power through local associations. In the 1880s, over 30 county associations were created, all under the governance of the English FA. Associations were given the power to organise competitive cup competitions, elect officers and administer the clubs in their county, reporting back to the governing body. Representative teams played inter-county fixtures and drew on the best players in the county.

One of the first of the kind was the Surrey County (Association) Club, founded in 1879, after a meeting at The Oval. The club included, among others, E.H. Bambridge, N.C. Bailey and C.W. Alcock, but this failed to become established. In March 1882, another attempt was made, and the Surrey County Football Association was founded, affiliating to N.L. Jackson's London FA. The added kudos of appointing Queen Victoria's favourite son, His Royal Highness the Duke of Connaught and Strathearn as the royal patron of the association, firmly established Surrey as one of the leading associations in the country.

Ranald Robert Hamilton Lockhart-Ross, a Scotsman like Watson, and a member of the East Sheen Club, was the first general secretary and captained the early games for the county. Including more clubs than any other association, they could draw upon hundreds of players, so fixtures were arranged under subsidiaries such as East Surrey and West Surrey, as well as Surrey County. They were allowed to draw upon players with family or business connections to the county.

Team lists in the newspapers included the Surrey-based club or the town the players were associated with. This was necessary due to complaints appearing in the press about so-called county teams populated by players with little or no relationship with the county they were representing. In response to this was an equal number of complaints about the difficulty of selecting players when county cup fixtures clashed with games for their chosen club.

Nevertheless, it appears that the vice-presidents of the Surrey County Association, N.C. Bailey and C.W. Alcock (previously secretary of the FA), were willing to accept Watson based on his father's residence in the county. On the various Surrey team sheets where Watson's name appears, the suffix refers to not just one, but several towns in Surrey. Confusingly,

SURREY COUNTY v. OXFORD UNIVERSITY.
For this match, to be played at Oxford to-day (Monday), the teams will be as follow:
Surrey: W. Underwood (Reigate Priory) (goal), A. Watson (Dorking and Swifts) or W. B. Hobbs (Reigate Priory) and C. W. Pearson (Surbiton Wanderers) (backs), F. Eldridge (Weybridge), C. H. Russell (East Sheen), and E. J. Diver (Reigate Priory) (half-backs), R. S. Ibbs Barnes) (centre), D. Patrick (Casuals) and W. J. Anderson (Farnham) (right wing), H. W. Bainbridge (Weybridge) (captain), and Capt. Barker (East Sheen), or J. G. Ferns (Barnes) (left wing) (forwards).
Oxford University: A. W. Osborne (Hertford) (goal), P. M. Walters (Oriel) and L. T. Thring (New) (backs), R. S. King (Hertford) (captain) and W. H. Edgar (Balliol) (half-backs), A. H. J. Cochrane (Hertford) and O. Scoones (Christ Church) (right wing), T. Pellatt (Trinity) and Hugh Guy (Hertford) (centres), F. W. Bain (Christ Church) and another (left wing) (forwards).
Train 1 p.m. from Paddington to Oxford.

The Sportsman – *Monday, 2 February 1885*

Swifts also appears as a suffix for Watson, even though the club was based in Berkshire. Dorking, Godalming and Worplesdon were cited as towns with which Watson was associated, all within proximity of each other. Watson's father, Peter Miller Watson, lived in Worplesdon for ten years before his death, and this suggests Watson cited his father's last address for his eligibility to play for the county. There are no records of Watson playing for Dorking, Worplesdon or Godalming, and it is unclear why he chose to name more than one town.

Watson played five times for Surrey, although he was selected eight times for the county and four times for West Surrey. He played alongside N.C. Bailey, E.C. and A.L Bambridge, and A.M Walters, brother to P.M. Walters. The Walters brothers would make the full-back positions at Corinthian their own in the following years and became the full-back stalwarts for the England team. Fred Bickley and Tom Blenkiron, the founders of the Casuals Football Club, both played alongside Watson in the county teams, along with other Corinthians, such as R.H. Mills-Roberts, C.A. Lloyd-Jones, and Norman Leete. In several team sheets,

Watson is listed as captain and would continue his history of administrative responsibilities in accepting a role on a player selection sub-committee.

Of note, on 14 March 1884, in a Surrey Association Challenge Cup game between Barnes and Reigate Priory, Watson made his second appearance as a match official. Alongside H. Nichols, he took on the role of 'umpire', with E.C. Bambridge as the referee. March 1884, was a busy month for Watson. He played once for Corinthian, beating Charterhouse 2-1, four times for Surrey County, winning two, losing and drawing one, and a friendly for an obscure team called Friar Park at Henley. He played twice for West Surrey as captain, once beating Oxfordshire 7-0, and although selected he failed to appear for another fixture against West Sussex. Missing two more Surrey County fixtures, he probably watched Queen's Park lose to Blackburn Rovers in the FA Cup Final before returning to Glasgow for a series of cup games. After Easter 1884, he remained in Glasgow until the autumn, confirming he was no longer a civil servant or a resident of the London metropolis.

The 1884 Corinthian Tour

During the autumn of 1883, A.J. Secretan, the first honorary secretary of the Corinthian Club, was 'called abroad' and had to relinquish his responsibilities.[153] Although Nicholas Lane 'Pa' Jackson had previously been offered but excused himself from the role, he now relented and agreed to take on the management of Corinthian.[154] He was well aware

---

153 Archer Jeston Secretan (1857–1910). In June 1883, he was in Manitoba, Canada and had filed for a Homestead Grant.

154 The nickname 'Pa' was given him on one of the early Corinthian tours when, during a night journey, he asked a player to stop singing and disturbing the other players. He received the reply, 'Oh Pa, don't be cross.' The name stuck.

the club had not lived up to anyone's expectations and had struggled to attract players. In one game against Brighton College, they were compelled to include 33-year-old Pa Jackson himself. F.N.S. Creek would repeat a quote from a member when asked about how the team had performed in recent matches:

> 'Not badly, considering that our team generally consists of three men, seven telegrams, and an apologetic letter which arrives the next morning.'[155]

It was apparent the club needed better management, and Jackson was the obvious choice. He had proven his abilities at the Finchley Club, at the FA, the London FA and with a scratch team bearing Jackson's own name.

Jackson discovered that poor administration had caused issues with the organisation of the team and had even breached the club's rule book. It was too late in the year to arrange a proper fixture schedule, so Corinthian only played three games in their second season. Watson played in two of those games.

Having already toured with Secretan's Corinthians in the spring of 1883, Watson was selected to play against Cambridge in November, but he not only failed to show for the game but had also gone missing for fixtures with Brentwood, Swifts, Pilgrims and a London representative team.

Selected again in December 1883 when Corinthian met the Sheffield Club at Upton Park, Watson was honoured with the captaincy, leading them to a 5-2 victory.[156]

---

155 Creek (1933).

156 Watson was the first black player, as well as the first Scot, to play for and to captain the team.

His next game for the club was three months later, on 5 March 1884 against Charterhouse, and perhaps only notable as a young Charles Wreford Brown was in the Charterhouse team that day. It would be Wreford Brown who, 15 years later, would publish his opinion of Watson's footballing abilities:

> '... he never kept himself in proper condition, and was therefore unable to utilise to the full, the abilities he possessed'.[157]

Charterhouse lost 2-1.

No longer a civil servant, Watson spent the next seven months in Glasgow, winning the Glasgow Charity Cup again and continuing to play for Queen's Park. His absence from the London circle meant that at the beginning of October 1884, E.C. Bambridge found it once again necessary to insert adverts in the newspapers requesting that Watson contact him:

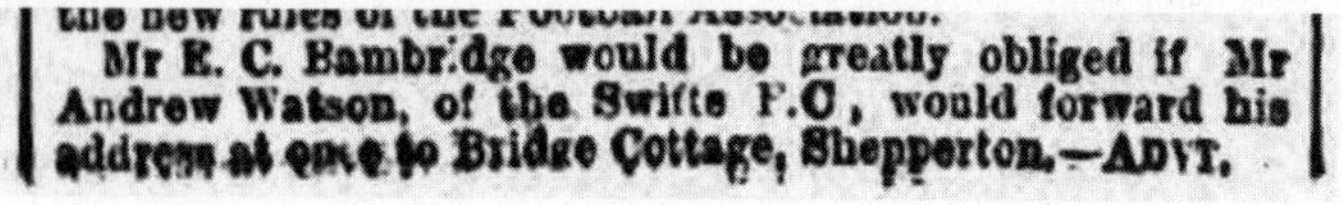

Mr E. C. Bambridge would be greatly obliged if Mr Andrew Watson, of the Swifts F.C, would forward his address at once to Bridge Cottage, Shepperton.—ADVT.

The Sportsman – *Thursday, 23 October 1884*

It may be significant that Bambridge and not Jackson placed the advertisements, as Bambridge was not at that time a regular for Corinthian, having announced his retirement from football before they played their first game in October 1882. However, in a little over a year, Bambridge would become a regular Corinthian player.

The first two games of the Jackson era appear to have been commitments made before he took over. Of the players

157 *Dundee Evening Telegraph*, Friday, 16 December 1898.

used in these two games, only two would be invited on the forthcoming tour. Watson, although selected, failed to show for either game, and Corinthian lost both games emphatically, the first 7-1 to Notts County and, a week later, 5-0 to Cambridge University.

On the day before the Notts County game, Watson, although on the team sheet for Corinthian, had chosen to play for Queen's Park against Aston Villa in Birmingham. After losing 2-1, he returned to Glasgow for two more Queen's Park games. It seemed that Watson was now a Glasgow resident again and his footballing career would be played out north of the border. But, surprisingly, he arrived in London in time to play one game for Swifts on 10 December and would be ready and available to begin his second tour with Corinthian on 15 December.

Jackson's plan was to arrange fixtures between amateurs and professionals, obviously intended to prove that players who played for free and the love of the game could not only match but beat teams where players were paid for their services. His first tour would be his only tour before professionalism was legitimised the following year.

Corinthian fixtures proved to be immensely popular due to the connotations they represented. In retrospect, these fixtures may have also paved the way for the foundation of the Football League, which looked to replace the amateur-friendly games with more exciting regular spectacles, where teams competed for more than just pride.

The '1884 Northern Tour' was Jackson's first, subsequent tours would follow a similar format. He would arrange matches against professional teams of the highest quality, organising fixtures on each day, occasionally leaving one day free for travel, if necessary. The 1884 tour lasted eight days, with seven fixtures. It was a heavy schedule that would be reflected in the results as the days passed. However, this was probably one of the most impressive tours the Corinthians made, setting the amateurs against several of the loudest supporters of professionalism.

As Corinthian had been created by the English FA, these games may also have been a veiled attempt to undermine professionalism. For many, these games represented more than just amateurs versus professionals. They were viewed as a series of battles between the south and the north, 'gentlemen' versus 'players', upper class versus working class, rich versus poor and, for some, good versus bad. On a lesser scale, it perhaps cemented N.L. Jackson's reputation as the champion of amateurism, and even though he was not a member of the ruling elite he aspired to, based on the Corinthian successes, he would be accepted into their ranks.

But, perhaps unexpectedly, the fixtures were also instrumental in smoothing the division between the amateurs and the professionals. Most of the games were played in friendly competition, bringing the two sides of the debate together. Corinthian won some games and perhaps lost more, but their gentlemanly code was welcomed wherever they played. Under their influence, peace was maintained, avenues of communication kept open and discussion centred on the quality of the football. If there had been a rugby version of Corinthian, perhaps the two sides in the rugby code may have remained whole.

Of the Corinthian team that played the opening game of the tour, nine were or would become internationals. The two eldest were both Scottish, Andrew Watson and Dr John Smith. The youngest was Tinsley Lindley, only 19 and still at Cambridge University. The son of a lace dresser in Nottingham, Lindley would have a sparkling career, playing for England 13 times, scoring 14 goals. He would play for Casuals, Swifts and Cambridge University, but also played as an amateur for professional clubs such as Aston Villa, Preston North End and Nottingham Forest. On his debut for Forest at the age of 16, he scored a hat-trick. He never wore football boots but preferred to wear his brogues, claiming boots prevented him from sprinting!

In the team for the opening game was the only survivor of the first Corinthian game, and first captain, Cecil Henry Holden-White, a wine merchant from London, and an England international. There was also Andrew Amos from London and Francis William Pawson from Sheffield, both bound for the clergy, William Nevill Cobbold, a schoolteacher from Suffolk, Benjamin Ward Spilsbury from Derbyshire, who would become a farmer in Canada, and Montague John Rendall from Oxfordshire, who would become a schoolmaster at Winchester. William Frederick Beardshaw was a general manager of a steel manufacturing company and was not a public schoolboy or university graduate, but a member of the Sheffield Club and a representative for Sheffield at FA meetings. Later, he would put his name to the documents that would establish a new football club called Sheffield United.

Of the eleven who played that first game, five were from the south, two from the north, two from the Midlands and two from Scotland. This was a reasonably balanced team considering the regional divisions that had plagued the game for years. Seven of the party were Cambridge University men, four 'blues', who had played five days earlier for the university against Aston Villa, losing 3-0.

Other players in the travelling party included John Wilson Holm, the Queen's Park full-back, who had played at Parkgrove with Watson and J.J. Gow. Holm's brothers,

Andrew Hair and William Alexander would also play for Corinthian, and Andrew Hair Holm, like Watson, had also captained the Scottish national team. Beardshaw, Watson and Holm were the only survivors from Corinthian's first Northern Tour over the Easter period in 1883.

Others in the touring party were John Leaver Nickisson, the Essex cricketer who would go on to play 13 times for Corinthian, and Thomas Pellatt, an Oxford graduate who would become headmaster at Durnford School.[158]

Jackson named his tour party of 16 players in the weeks before the team set off, but of those originally named, only four would appear on tour. As obligations changed, injuries occurred and players dropped out, Jackson was able to find competent and capable players to carry the Corinthian flag.

Jackson also supplemented players on tour, and for the Sheffield Club game, probably due to the exhaustion of his team, he drafted in three players: Charles William Richard Tepper, an old Westminster and Brentwood team-mate of J.L. Nickisson, John Auger Dixon, the Notts County player, and Arthur William Ward, who would only play for Corinthian twice but would be a lifetime member, and also a founding member of the Nottingham Forest Football Club.

Jackson also brought in players for the Preston North End game, drafting in Edgerton Stewart-Brown from the Liverpool Ramblers and Stuart Macrae, a Scot who played for England, settled in Nottingham and became a Notts County player. He may also have been the first Scot to play for England.

158 Ian Fleming of James Bond fame was a pupil at Durnford School in Pellat's time and described it as a 'traditionally brutal prep school' – *Daily Echo*, 9 September 2008.

The tour struggled with goalkeepers, with Dr John Smith taking on the role in the Sheffield game and Jackson drafted in Liverpool Rambler, James Heald, for the Bolton Wanderers game.

With so much to manage, it is remarkable that Jackson was able to organise all the details of the tour, from travel to accommodation, to player availability. But when they arrived in Blackburn, probably on the morning of the game, they would be ready to face their first opponents.

Blackburn Rovers had beaten Queen's Park in the FA Cup Final and would do so again in the next. Having beaten Queen's Park, Rovers were *ipso facto* the best team in the world. With home advantage and support, the champions prepared to meet the rambling amateur gentlemen. Almost overlooked by the press, who had focused on the previous week's Rovers versus Blackburn Olympic Cup game, and with a sense of a David and Goliath mismatch, most assumed Rovers would sweep aside the unknown posh southern outfit without too much effort.

The day was cold with a strong wind, and snow in the air. Having won the toss, Corinthian kicked off with the wind at their backs. Within 17 minutes, they had scored four goals and were outclassing Rovers in every area of the pitch. Rovers managed to get one goal back before half-time but were unable to use the wind in their favour in the second half and failed to score any further goals. Corinthian, on the other hand, with the wind in their faces, continued to dominate and scored four more in the second half.

The emphatic 8-1 victory beggared belief, but it had announced the arrival of the Corinthian Club. Even though Fergus Suter and Hugh McIntyre, two of the first Scottish Professors, were in the Blackburn team, some newspapers in the north suggested that Rovers were weakened by the absence of players. In truth, although two regular players were missing, they had been replaced by players of an equally high standard. One press report said:

> '... nobody would have believed for a moment that the best team in the world could have thrashed the Blackburnians so severely. It is difficult, nay impossible, to account for it ...'[159]

On the day, Dr John Smith, using his famous *nom de guerre*, 'J.S. Miller', Tinsley Lindley and Francis Pawson scored two apiece, Cobbold one, and an own goal had completed the rout.

Of note, Rovers' only previous defeat of similar standing was on a visit by Tom Vallance's Scottish Canadians in 1880, when Blackburn suffered an 8-1 loss to a team containing Dr John Smith and Rangers' Moses McNeil. A regular member of the Scottish Canadians, Watson would have played that day had he not remained behind to trial for the Glasgow team to face Sheffield.

After the Rovers game, Watson was singled out for praise for his 'great service' to the team. The defeat of Blackburn would have been one of his proudest football achievements, along with captaining Scotland and winning silverware with Queen's Park. Whatever Bambridge had said to him to convince him to uproot his family, renounce the national team and move to London may have been ratified by this success.

On the following day, making two changes to the team, Corinthian met Darwen and lost 2-1. The last-minute

---

159 *Wigan Observer and District Advertiser*, Friday, 19 December 1884.

Darwen goal was reported as 'fortuitous' in the southern press. On the next day, Corinthian made three changes and drew 4-4 with Blackburn Olympic, another previous FA Cup holder and the first northern team to win the trophy. The following day, with Watson and five others rested, Corinthian beat Sheffield 2-1. By now the gruelling schedule was beginning to take its toll on the players and exhaustion began influencing the results. They lost either 6-0 or 7-0 to Bolton Wanderers, where a newspaper commented that Watson, Amos and Beardshaw 'seemed quite worn out'.[160]

After losing 3-1 to Preston North End, then 3-2 to Notts County at Trent Bridge, the tour ended. Corinthian had originally arranged to play Queen's Park in Glasgow on the last day, but it was said they could not 'come to terms', and they played Notts instead. However, after six days of games and then third-class train travel to Glasgow, the exhaustion would have made them easy pickings for the Glaswegians.[161] Nevertheless, on account of the Blackburn Rovers rout, the tour was considered a resounding success.

Had the fixture schedule allowed for rest and recuperation days, then it is conceivable that Corinthian would have achieved better results. However, punishing schedules would become a characteristic of all future Corinthian tours, as Jackson would attempt to play as many games as possible in a short period.

As 1885 began, Watson remained in the south and joined up with Swifts again. He was in demand and his name appeared on team sheets for Upton Park, Surrey County

160 *Manchester Courier and Lancashire General Advertiser*, Saturday, 20 December 1884.

161 Player expenses allowed for third-class travel only. However, many players would have paid for their own first-class tickets.

and a London Representative team. A month after their last meeting, Corinthian avenged their defeat by Preston North End on the Northern Tour, securing a famous 3-2 win at The Oval.

Jackson would arrange over a dozen fixtures with North End over the next few years, each game eagerly anticipated and attended by many tens of thousands of spectators. Having been expelled from the 1884 FA Cup for professionalism, Jackson appears to have favoured fixtures against North End, perhaps seeing them as the embodiment of professionalism.

Watson had played for Corinthian in their first game against the 'invincible' Preston North End, and his second appearance would prove to be his last game for them. He had played for Corinthian 14 times and will forever be associated with the club. His record is moderate – seven wins, six losses and one draw – but he could have added more appearances, failing to materialise for four or five other games, and but for the loss of Jessie, he may well have played in Corinthian's first-ever game.

The Corinthian influence on football in general cannot be understated. Popularising the game around the world and influencing the formation of teams and football associations in numerous countries, they functioned as ambassadors for the sport and their code of sportsmanship and fair play still echoes throughout the world wherever a British athlete competes.

The Corinthian ethos became the code that all players, amateur or professional, would uphold, and the philosophy would disseminate to schools and universities, in friendly or competitive games. Generations of pupils and students that followed would adhere to the code, that for them would identify the hero from the villain, the gentleman from the cad, the sport from the cheat. To this day, the word 'Corinthian' continues to embody all that is good and honest in all sport. This would have been Andrew Watson's code too.

Return to Glasgow

Beginning in the summer of 1884, rumours had began to appear in the press, suggesting Watson's southern sojourn was coming to an end:

> 'There is some word of Andrew Watson coming back to Glasgow again, and if that be true, we will no doubt find him in his old position. Watson is not yet "wound up". With a little practice, he would be as brilliant as he was in his most palmy days.'[162]

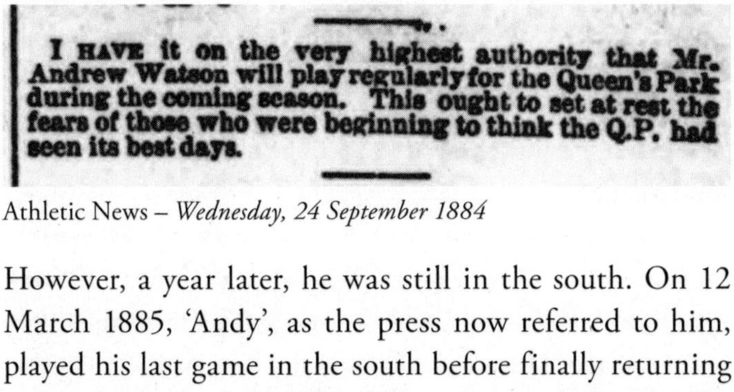

I HAVE it on the very highest authority that Mr. Andrew Watson will play regularly for the Queen's Park during the coming season. This ought to set at rest the fears of those who were beginning to think the Q.P. had seen its best days.

Athletic News – *Wednesday, 24 September 1884*

However, a year later, he was still in the south. On 12 March 1885, 'Andy', as the press now referred to him, played his last game in the south before finally returning north. In another outing for a Surrey County representative team, against Cambridge University, he faced a team containing several good friends – Rendall, Amos, Spilsbury and Tinsley Lindley from the 1884 Corinthian tour, and A.M. Walters and Tom Blenkiron in the Surrey team – and even though this probably made it an enjoyable game, Surrey lost 2-1.

162 *Athletic News*, Wednesday, 30 July 1884.

After Easter, having assisted in the 5-0 thrashing of Northern FC, Watson went straight into the Queen's Park team to face Scottish Cup holders, Renton, in the semi-final of the Glasgow Charity Cup. The papers said Watson had been 'brought down' from London for the game as several Queen's Park players were cup-tied but, in the end, Queen's Park came from behind to win 3-2. Two weeks later he helped Queen's Park beat Dumbarton 1-0 in the Glasgow Charity Cup Final.

On 11 May 1885, he took part in a friendly game for the 'Queen's Park Smokers' versus 'Non-Smokers'. No reason was given for the fixture, but it was probably an end-of-season celebration involving all the club's players, even though there were still competitive games to be played. Perhaps unsurprisingly, the non-smokers won 3-0 but, revealingly, Watson played for the smokers!

By the time Watson began the new season, professionalism in England had been legitimised. Scotland would have to wait another eight years before recognising the pro footballer.

The first game of the 1885/86 season was against Strathmore in Dundee, and Watson was now a talisman for Queen's Park – whenever he was on the team sheet, the belief was that Queen's Park could not lose. As if confirming this, for the rest of the autumn, Queen's Park won all but three of their 18 games, once recording a 16-0 win against St Peter's.

Watson continued to receive accolades in the press:

> '... Watson at the back deserves special mention ...'[163]

---

163 *Dundee Evening Telegraph*, Monday, 26 October 1885.

The Glasgow team that beat Sheffield 1-0 at Sheaf Grounds, Sheffield, St Valentine's Day, 1880 . Back Row (l-r): George Gillespie (gk) (Rangers), (poss.) John Campbell (South Western), Alex Kennedy (Third Lanark), Donald Hamilton (President: Parkgrove FC), Andrew Watson (Parkgrove), (poss.), John Phillips, (South Western), James A.K. Watson (Rangers). Middle Row: Charles Campbell (Queen's Park), Moses McNeil (Rangers)
Front Row: (poss.) Robert Alexander, (Mauchline), reserve, M.J. Eadie Fraser (Queen's Park), (poss.) James McAdam (3rd Lanark), William 'Daddy' Dunlop (Rangers), Peter McNeil (SFA treasurer, secretary and founding father of Rangers FC) © Scottish Football Museum

The Scottish team that beat England 6-1 on 12 March 1881 at The Oval. Back Row (l-r): William McGuire (Beith), George Ker (Queen's Park), Donald Hamilton (SFA – Scottish umpire), Tom Vallance (Rangers), John Smith (Queen's Park), Joseph Lindsay (Dumbarton), William McKinnon – Reserve (Dumbarton)
Front Row: David Hill (Rangers), Charles Campbell (Queen's Park), David Davidson (Queen's Park), Andrew Watson –Capt. (Queen's Park), George Gillespie (Rangers), Harry McNeil (Rangers) © Scottish Football Museum

The Scottish team that beat Wales 5-1 on 14 March 1881 at Wrexham. Back Row (l-r): David Hill (Rangers), Andrew Watson (Queen's Park), Tom Vallance – Capt. (Rangers), Donald Hamilton (SFA – Scottish umpire), John Smith (Queen's Park), Geordie Ker (Queen's Park), George Gillespie (Rangers). Front Row: William McGuire (Beith), William McKinnon (Dumbarton), Harry McNeil (Queen's Park), David Davidson (Queen's Park), Joseph Lindsay (Dumbarton), Robert McPherson (Vale of Leven). © Scottish Football Museum

The Scottish team that beat England 5-1 on 11 March 1882 at Hampden
Back row: (unknown), John Leck Kay (Queen's Park), Andrew Watson (Queen's Park), Eadie Fraser (Queen's Park), Andrew McIntyre (Vale of Leven), John Campbell McLeod McPherson (Arthurlie). Middle Row: William Harrower (Queen's Park), (unknown), Charles Campbell – Capt. (Queen's Park), William Anderson (Queen's Park), Peter Miller (Dumbarton). Sitting on floor: George Gillespie (Rangers), George Ker (Queen's Park). © Scottish Football Museum

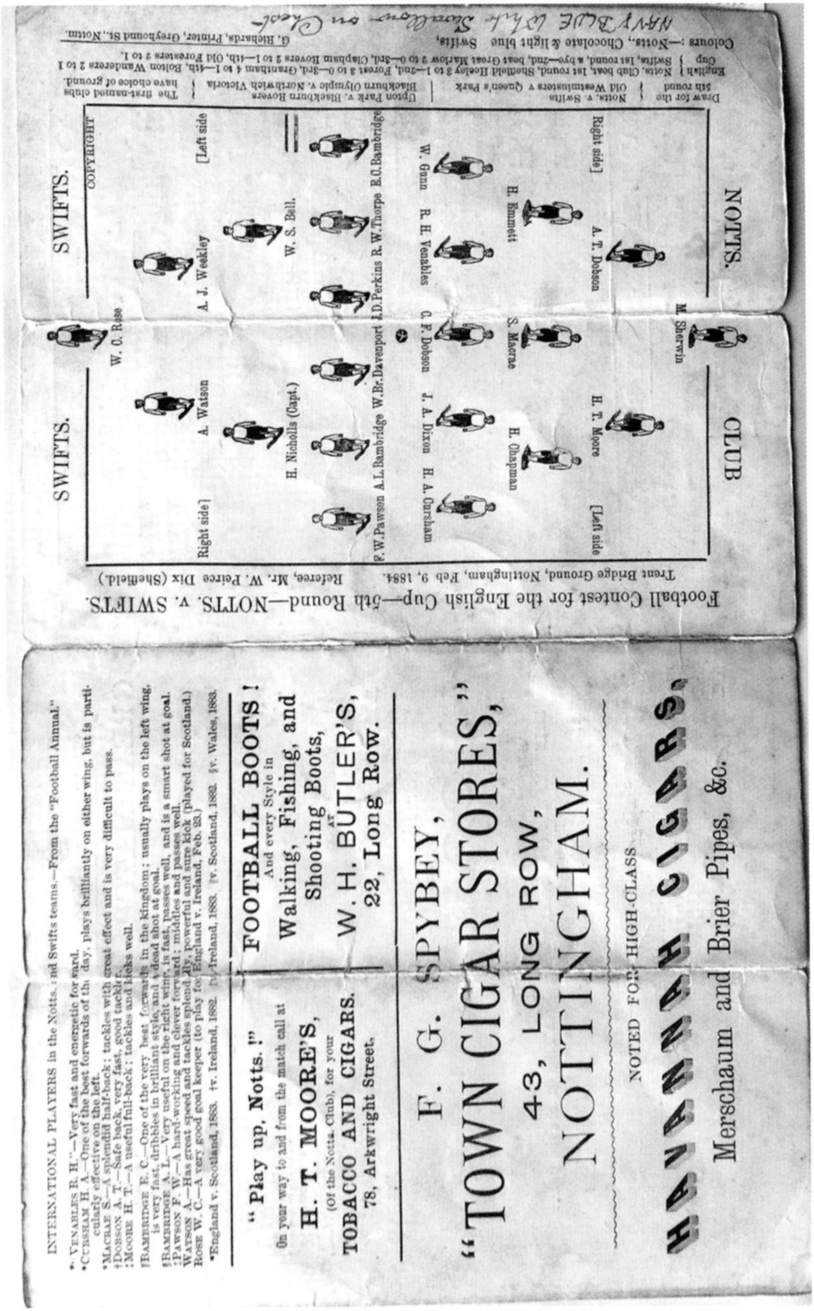

Programme for the FA Cup fifth round tie between Notts Club and Swifts – 9 February 1884. This game resulted in a draw, with Notts winning the replay. Permission: Andy Mitchell

Jessie's grave in Abney Park, Stoke Newington, London. Inscription says, 'Her sun went down while it was yet day'.

Dumbarton v Queen's Park – 3 February 1883. Over 10,000 spectators attended the game. The first time Queen's Park had visited Dumbarton and, specifically for this match, an elevated platform was erected along one side of the pitch

Nicholas Lane 'Pa' Jackson Junior (1849–1937)

Tinsley Lindley (1865–1940)

Cecil Henry Holden-White (1860–1934)

Watson top left, and Tom Veitch rear centre

The 'Scottish Crusaders', an unofficial Queen's Park team that beat Aston Villa 2-1 on 24 April 1886, at Perry Barr, Birmingham. Back Row (l-r): Andrew Watson (Queen's Park), William McGregor, (President Aston Villa, founder of the Football League), Victor Jones, (Director, Aston Villa), Jack Hughes, (co-founder Aston Villa), (unknown), William McLeod (Queen's Park,) George Ramsey, (Manager, Aston Villa). Middle Row: Robert Fraser (Queen's Park), John Alexander Lambie (Queen's Park), Archibald Rowan (Queen's Park), (unknown), David Hill (Rangers), (unknown). Front Row: (poss.) W. Hastings (Airdrieonians) John Kevan McDowell, (SFA), (poss.) J. Sneddon (Airdrieonians). © Scottish Football Museum

This detail from the Scottish Crusaders picture shows two of the most important figures in the early days of football standing side-by-side. William McGregor, the founder of the Football League, a competition that changed the game forever. Watson, an amateur, next to the man who paved the way for professional football. Perhaps the arrangement of players and officials in this picture was not accidental?

Forest Road, Kew, Surrey

Charles Campbell (1854–1927)

The Louisianan. *http://www.titanicinquiry.org/ships/louisianian.php*

SS West Indian

An unusual picture, missing not only Andrew Watson, but goalkeeper George Gillespie, and Walter Arnott, both international players.

Benjamin Francis 'Fred' Bickley (1861–1927)

Thomas Walter Blenkiron (1864–1934)
© Charterhouse School

'... Watson being conspicuous at the back.'[164]

'... Arnott and Watson appeared to take matters very coolly, but it was at once apparent that there was no mediocrity of football talent about them.'[165]

'... Watson at the back kicked with capital judgement and unerring accuracy.'[166]

In December 1885, an article appeared in the *Scottish Athletic Journal* under the heading 'Modern Athletic Celebrities – Mr Andrew Watson – Queen's Park Football Club'.[167] It was for this article that the only known engraving of Watson was produced by an unknown artist. It is a flattering piece that praises Watson's footballing and athletic prowess but is somewhat spoilt by the author's licence with the facts.

It begins by stating that Watson had been on Hamilton Crescent practising his high jumping at the age of 17 in 1873. It also says he was educated at Glasgow College and goes on to say he joined Parkgrove in 1874 and captained the side for six years, won over 40 prizes for the high jump, clearing 5ft 10in at the Queen's Park athletic meeting in 1879, and that he competed in boat races on the Thames.

'His aquatic enthusiasm as well as his physique, however, being considerably reduced by an unfortunate upset in the above-mentioned river, resulting

164 *Glasgow Herald*, Monday, 16 November 1885.

165 *The Courier and Argus*, Tuesday, 1 December 1885.

166 *Glasgow Herald*, Monday, 7 December 1885.

167 *Scottish Athletic Journal*, Tuesday, 15 December 1885.

> in a very dangerous attack of rheumatic fever, which he has only recently thoroughly recovered from.'

No records of Watson participating in rowing, sculling or boating have come to light, and if he did contract rheumatic fever in December 1885, he made a remarkable recovery, playing in all 18 games for Queen's Park during that period, without missing a single weekend. He had also not been in London since the previous April.

What is notable about this article, is that, even then, facts about Watson's life were in short supply. In 1873 he was at King's College School in London, and unlikely to have been practising on Hamilton Crescent, home of the West of Scotland Cricket Club. He was not captain of Parkgrove in 1874, and even if he was in Glasgow in that year, he would have been with Maxwell. His winning jump at the Queen's Park athletic meeting on 6 September 1879 was 5ft 4in. However, the piece ends:

> '... he is the embodiment of rare geniality and kind-heartedness, affording a "feast of reason and flow of soul" to which the dull eyes of superficial critics are blind.
>
> Farewell, dear friend, may guid luck hit you
> And 'mang her favourites admit you.
> If e'er Detraction shore to smit you,
> May nane believe him;
> And ony de'il that thinks to get you,
> Good Lord deceive him!'

What is perhaps remarkable about this piece is that, although it is a personal biographical remembrance, and full of errors, nowhere does it mention his colour or the land of his birth. Several articles express admiration for Watson's kind-heartedness and geniality, and even though other players were complimented regularly in the press, none received the warmth and affection preserved for Watson.

As if not to be outdone by Corinthian, Queen's Park visited the home of Blackburn Rovers on Boxing Day 1885 and beat the English Cup holders 3-0. A few days later, on New Year's Day, Corinthian replaced Swifts as visitors to Hampden in the first of an annual fixture that would in the years to come become much anticipated, well attended and, for many, a better representation of England versus Scotland than the national teams' battles. On this occasion, the teams drew 2-2, and Andrew played for Queen's Park against E.C. Bambridge, Tinsley Lindley and William Nevill 'Nuts' Cobbold, his Corinthian team-mates from the side that beat Blackburn Rovers the previous year.

Immigration

Watson was now 29 years old and, although he was a regular for Queen's Park, in January 1886 more rumours began appearing in various newspapers that he was planning to emigrate to America. This also failed to materialise, and his name continued to appear on the Queen's Park team sheets. At the beginning of February, Queen's Park won the Scottish Cup again, beating Renton 3-1 in the final. This was the fourth time Watson had collected a Scottish Cup winners' medal.

A week later, Queen's Park entertained Notts County in Glasgow losing both games 1-0, but the report mentioned that Watson was not on form and had picked up an injury.

On 6 March 1886, *The Sportsman* published a single line stating that Watson had resigned from Queen's Park. The lack of interest in the story of Watson's retirement is striking. A few years earlier, he had been the darling of Scottish football, but now the end of his footballing career was worthy of only a single line.

On the same day as this news appeared, Queen's Park were due to play Corinthian at The Oval in London. Oddly, Watson's name was on the team sheet for Queen's Park but they withdrew from the fixture at the last minute, citing the lack of available players. Notts County stepped in as a replacement and on a freezing day, with the ground covered in snow, County lost 7-0. Obviously, Queen's Park made the correct decision.

Watson's retirement may have been a contributory factor in Queen's Park scratching the game, but it was probably also damage limitation, as for a club proud of its history, a humiliating defeat would have put a severe dent in their reputation.

Of note, on 20 March 1886, a fixture was arranged between the Glasgow Pilgrims and a team of 'Ancients', made up of old Parkgrove players. Although Watson was mentioned, he did not play, having stepped out of retirement again for Queen's Park in their 6-0 dismantling of Third Lanark. The article said:

> 'The Parkgrove was in its day a really first-class club and had in it many players who afterwards obtained international distinction. The most notable of these are A. Watson and J.J. Gow, both now members of the Queen's Park eleven.'[168]

---

168 *Glasgow Evening Post,* Friday, 19 March 1886.

As if to underline the statement, Old Parkgrove won 3-0.

Two weeks later, and for the first time in three years, Watson played again for Edinburgh University in a charity game to raise money for the Edinburgh Association.

> 'Watson played a finished game and put in a lot of sound work.'[169]

Soon after, news broke that Dr John Smith and Watson had signed up to join a tour by a new London Scottish team called the Caledonian Football Club, an organisation of Scotsmen living in the London metropolis. They did not appear in any of the games. The 1923 history of the London Caledonians makes no mention of this team, identifying an 1889 tour as the first time the 'Caleys' travelled, even though the history includes many of the same players that toured in 1885.[170]

Watson's absence from the Caledonian games was related to a match Queen's Park had arranged against Aston Villa in Birmingham. Queen's Park had wanted to withdraw from this game also but, inexplicably, some of the Queen's Park players were determined to fulfil the fixture. As this was not an official Queen's Park team, the players chose to call themselves the 'Scotch Crusaders', although the press reported the game as a legitimate Queen's Park fixture. Even though the side was not strong, it managed to win 3-0, with the retired Watson being singled out for praise:

> '... Watson, as usual, played a superb defensive game … whenever Allen came down the wing, Watson

169 *Edinburgh Evening News*, Monday, 5 April 1886.

170 Old Member (1924).

> was always ready to dispossess him, and he invariably succeeded.'[171]

A few days later, and perhaps related to the Scotch Crusaders game, a report appeared in *Athletic News* that suggested Watson, along with a player from Cowlairs (McLeod[172]), was moving to Birmingham to accept 'a situation'.

> 'These men will probably be found in the ranks of the Aston Villa, as it is from one of the greatest supporters of that club that they have got business appointments.'[173]

Like the previous rumours, these proved to be erroneous, and even though the suggestion that Watson was moving to Birmingham to accept an 'appointment' was false, there was an echo of Watson's previous move to London with Bambridge. The echo would ring true again in the months that followed.

Watson was due to make one final appearance that season, in an exhibition game on 19 June 1886 in Dundee for a team called 'I Zingari' ('The Gypsies'). Watson had been listed as the goalkeeper, suggesting he was injured or unfit. However, in the match reports the following day, his name did not appear, so he had either pulled out or failed to show.

Reports in the press during June 1886 stated that Watson was in training to enter the National Championships at the Powderhall Grounds in Edinburgh as a high jumper. This

---

171 *Athletic News*, Tuesday, 27 April 1886.

172 William 'Wiggy' McLeod (1860–1943) signed for Aston Villa, with Tom Robertson (1864–1924). Both would be investigated as professionals. George Kynoch MP, president of Villa, found them work in a local ammunitions factory. An international, McLeod played for Notts Forest, Glasgow, Blackburn Olympic and Queen's Park.

173 *Athletic News*, Tuesday, 4 May 1886.

would be his final athletics competition. He implied that he was hoping to match 5ft 8in, and perhaps even the 5ft 10in he had managed years earlier. The report revealed that there would be four entries in the high jump and that the battle would be between Watson and J.N. MacLeod of Glasgow University, as J.W. Parsons, the world record holder, would be absent.

On the day, Parsons showed up and thrilled the crowd with a winning jump of 5ft 11in. He attempted but failed three times to jump 6ft. MacLeod came second with a jump of 5ft 7in and A.G.G Asher third with 5ft $6^{1}/_{4}$in. Watson failed to record a jump. Parsons also won the 'broad jump' with a leap of 21ft 8in, a foot better than his closest rival. It was an end to an athletic career that had lasted for ten years, and Watson would be remembered in Glasgow as much for athletics as he was for football.

A year later, a sportswriter reminisced:

> '... A. Watson and Dr Smith, who also could sprint a bit, and many men whose names do not occur to us at the moment. These were individuals who stood forth as giants amidst other competitors and whose sideboards are loaded with trophies obtained in the athletic arena.'[174]

In September, at the beginning of the 1886/87 season, Watson returned to Queen's Park and played two games, against Vale of Leven and Preston North End. The report on the Preston match stated that Watson had been pulled out of retirement, along with two other players, and would play out of position, as one of three half-backs.

---

174 *Glasgow Evening Post*, Saturday, 23 April 1887.

Five thousand spectators watched Queen's Park put on a 'miserable display', losing 6-1.[175] This was the last game Andrew Watson played for Queen's Park and, as with his final appearance for Corinthian, the opponent was Preston North End.

GRAND FOOTBALL MATCH.
QUEEN'S PARK
Versus
PRESTON NORTH END,
AT HAMPDEN PARK,
ON SATURDAY FIRST.
Kick-off at 3.30 P.M.
Admission 6d. Ladies Free.
Grand Stand, 6d Extra Each Person.

North British Daily Mail – *Monday, 20 September 1886. Watson's last game for Queen's Park. 5,000 spectators watched them lose 6-1.*

Even though Watson spent the rest of the season in retirement, in January 1887 his name appeared on the team sheet for a New Year's Day game for a team called Battlefield. Although a heavy frost prevented the game from going ahead, this may have indicated that Watson was considering returning to the game.

In February, Watson married his second wife, Eliza Kate Tyler, an English shop girl, who was living and working in Glasgow. Now 30 years old, Watson's new circumstances may have put any thoughts of football on hold, for a while at least.

Three months later, his name appeared again on a Battlefield team sheet to play against Cliftonville in Belfast. This appearance was probably at the request of Watson's friend, Dr John Smith, who acted as the goalkeeper on the day. Battlefield was an offshoot of Queen's Park, but there

175 *The Sportsman*, Tuesday, 28 September 1886.

had been tension between the two clubs since Battlefield had unexpectedly defeated Queen's Park in the third round of the Scottish FA Cup in 1884. Watson had played for Queen's Park that day, but as each team comprised Queen's Park members, both teams wore Queen's Park shirts, probably causing great confusion and contributing to the shock of the scoreline.

Bootle Football Club

In May 1887, and after more than a year with no competitive football, a newspaper report in Liverpool mentioned that Watson had appeared in a scratch game for a team called Garston against Bootle FC. Organised by Evertonian founder Thomas Evans, a keen footballer, referee and enthusiastic athlete, the game was arranged to launch the new Garston Cricket, Tennis and Football Club. As the Garston team contained several well-known Everton players, the event attracted over 1,000 spectators.

Watson was on the losing side as Bootle won 1-0, but it would be to Bootle that Watson would next turn. At the end of the summer, the news leaked that Watson had signed for Bootle. He packed up with his new wife and left Glasgow for a second time, this time for Liverpool.

Bootle's new signing played his first game on 23 August 1887, at Bootle's new ground. It was a charity match to raise money for W. Spence, a Bootle cricketer. The game finished 1-1, with Watson playing alongside ex-Dumbarton player, Tom Veitch, Bootle's captain. In the previous season Tom and his brother William had made up the back line, but William had 'gone to sea as an engineer' and it would be Watson's job to replace him.[176] Later, Watson would also go

176 *Athletic News*, Tuesday, 23 August 1887.

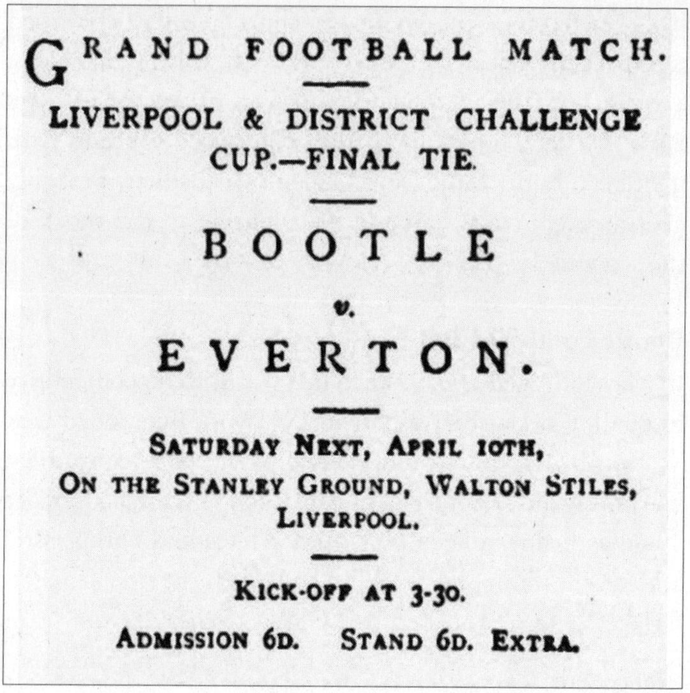

GRAND FOOTBALL MATCH.

LIVERPOOL & DISTRICT CHALLENGE CUP.—FINAL TIE.

BOOTLE

v.

EVERTON.

SATURDAY NEXT, APRIL 10TH,
ON THE STANLEY GROUND, WALTON STILES,
LIVERPOOL.

KICK-OFF AT 3-30.

ADMISSION 6D. STAND 6D. EXTRA.

Having lost 1-0 in 1886, this would be the cup Watson would help Bootle win in 1887. Cricket and Football Field – *Saturday, 3 April 1886*

to sea as an engineer, suggesting it may have been the same employer that had arranged Watson's career move.

Even though Veitch had played several times for Dumbarton against Queen's Park, he had never faced Watson in any of the dramatic cup games between the two sides, but he would have known of Watson's pedigree. Veitch was a devout man and would later in life become a lay preacher. With Watson's religious upbringing, they perhaps found a common bond, as they would go on to form a formidable pairing at the back for Bootle.

Another new face in the Bootle team was Robert Calderwood from Renfrewshire, a Scottish international with three caps, who had played for Cartvale and Cowlairs. Having responded to an advertisement, Calderwood had arrived in Bootle and been given a job as a labourer at the docks, loading grain ships at 26 shillings a week. Borrowing five pounds, Calderwood left the city three days later, promising to repay the loan on his return. He never came back. Sending a telegram to Cowlairs Football Club, he had asked for them to send him the cost of the fare back to Scotland, after which he would become a Cowlairs player. For this, Calderwood was found guilty of professionalism and suspended from Scottish football for two years. Arriving around the same time, and also from Scotland, Watson was not investigated.

TO FOOTBALL PLAYERS.—WANTED, a First-class CENTRE FORWARD and CENTRE HALF-BACK to join a Club in a Town in the Midlands. Work will be found, but for good players only.—Apply, with full particulars and reference, K.O., *Athletic News* Office, Manchester.

Athletic News – *Tuesday, 13 December 1887*

Bootle was a well-funded club, and even though they claimed to be strictly amateur and would fiercely deny paying players, there were the usual tell-tale signs of Scottish or non-local players in the ranks of both Bootle and Everton. Although a form of professionalism had been legalised, the FA endorsed strict policies.

Bootle had been in existence for under ten years and were fierce rivals of the other new club on Merseyside, Everton. At the outset, both Bootle and Everton were amateur sides, and 'borrowing' star players to guest in big fixtures had been traditionally acceptable. However, the commercial pressure of football had begun to change these arrangements, and 'importation' of players took on a more discreet and permanent flavour, especially after the 'legitimisation' of professionalism in 1885.

What followed in the years after professionals were accepted into the ranks of the FA were tales like Calderwood's on the previous page, many of which would resemble witch hunts. At one point, Everton were thrown out of the FA Cup, and their ground closed for one month for paying seven players but declaring three to be amateurs. Their accusers also said that Bootle had offered these players situations (jobs) as an inducement to join.

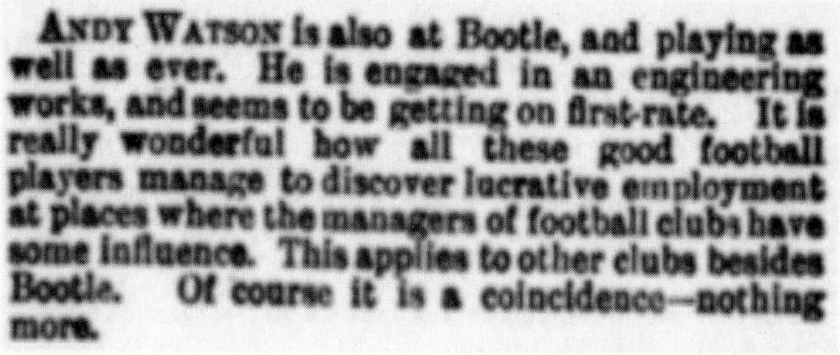

Andy Watson is also at Bootle, and playing as well as ever. He is engaged in an engineering works, and seems to be getting on first-rate. It is really wonderful how all these good football players manage to discover lucrative employment at places where the managers of football clubs have some influence. This applies to other clubs besides Bootle. Of course it is a coincidence—nothing more.

Athletic News – *Tuesday, 6 September 1887*

A report appeared in the press in September 1887, implying what many people believed was happening, and by explicitly naming Watson in the investigation. Nevertheless, Watson's move to London in the summer of 1882 was of a similar nature, and although it was far less noticeable, it was undoubtedly a career opportunity coupled with footballing opportunities. However, at that time, professionalism in the south was not under the same scrutiny, and as Bambridge, a senior member of the FA, had assisted in the arrangement, Watson obviously believed it was not professionalism. Any suggestion of this would have been profoundly insulting and strenuously denied.

Having retired from football a year earlier, Watson's future was unsure. Like the move to London, the Bootle opportunity may have been too attractive to ignore. So, for the second time,

Watson uprooted his family and headed south to Liverpool, where he would stay for over a quarter of a century.

In December, Bootle were due to play Great Lever Unity in the FA Cup, but even before the game had kicked off, Great Lever protested the presence of Watson as that of a professional. According to Tony Onslow, in the days before the fixture, Great Lever received a telegram from an anonymous source, calling themselves 'Smith of Oakfield', stating that Bootle were intent on playing two players, Watson and Hastings, who were ineligible to play, both being professionals.[177]

Later, the FA appointed a commission to investigate the accusation. The protest against Watson and Hastings was dismissed, but they set up a second commission to examine the charge of professionalism. The FA Commission interviewed Watson's bona fide team-mates, Veitch, Holt, Armstrong and Lewis, along with two other players, Izatt and Weir.[178],[179] The second commission dismissed the allegations of professionalism, but not before Nicholas Lane 'Pa' Jackson of Corinthian had written to the Athletic News:

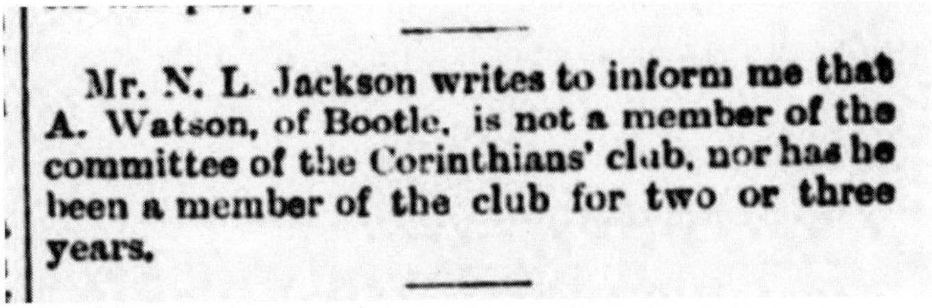

Mr. N. L. Jackson writes to inform me that A. Watson, of Bootle, is not a member of the committee of the Corinthians' club, nor has he been a member of the club for two or three years.

Athletic News – *Tuesday, 10 January 1888*

---

177 Onslow (2005).

178 Izzat would later join Bootle.

179 Izatt and Weir had agreed to 'sign' for Bootle, but on the day of their arrival in Liverpool, they had chosen to go to Everton instead.

How Watson was affected by this is unknown, but as an honourable gentleman, the accusation of professionalism would have wounded him. To have Jackson publicly disassociate the Corinthian Club from Watson implied the charges were truthful, increasing the humiliation. Watson may have dwelt upon this and felt the need to react, but there is no record of any response from him. Even though his honour had been tarnished and reputation damaged, it appears, like a true gentleman, he preferred to remain silent.

Having played over 100 times for Queen's Park over several years, Watson would play close to half that number again for Bootle in one season. The stress of playing so many games in such a short period would expose his 31-year-old body to an enormous strain.[180] Predictably, towards the end of the season, injuries prevented him from seeing the season out. However, he only missed two games in the autumn, due to having his nose broken in an accidental coming together with his team-mate, John Holt. He nevertheless continued to receive plaudits in the press:

> '... it is quite refreshing to see the Scotch International (Andy Watson) as good as ever.'[181]

> 'Andy Watson's back play was the predominant feature of the game.'[182]

> 'The Bootle defence was excellent; Watson in big form and it was rather surprising to observe

180 Research has identified 42 games in which Watson took part between August 1887 and April 1888.

181 *Athletic News*, Tuesday, 10 January 1888.

182 *Athletic News*, Tuesday, 13 September 1887.

> several Burnley forwards palpably "funking"[183] the imperturbable Andrew, who was extremely active for a veteran.'[184]

> '... at full-back, the play of Andy Watson was worth going miles to witness.'[185]

However, Watson's failing fitness also began to appear:

> 'Immediately on restarting, Andy Watson falls to pieces, and gathering himself together retires to the pavilion for repairs, nor could he be induced to lose his hold of the fragments even when the Church forwards ran past him with the ball.'[186]

> 'Andy Watson ... has grown big and fat, but he is no means so sure as when he wore the uniform of the Swifts ...'[187]

The first notification to appear in the press concerning Watson's second retirement from the game appeared in July 1888. It was once again a single line that said:

> 'Andy Watson is retiring from football.'[188]

Watson had not played since picking up an injury in April, during the defeat of the 1886 Lancashire Cup winners,

---

183 Failing.

184 *Cricket and Football Field*, Saturday, 17 December 1887.

185 *Cricket and Football Field*, Saturday, 25 February 1888.

186 *Cricket and Football Field*, Saturday, 18 February 1888.

187 *Athletic News*, Tuesday, 10 January 1888.

188 *Cricket and Football Field*, Saturday, 7 July 1888.

Bolton Wanderers. This would prove to be Watson's last competitive game. A month before his retirement, and eight years since his previous child was born, Watson became a father again, to Henry Tyler.[189] His second daughter, Phyllis Kate would be born in 1892, four years after he hung up his boots.[190]

Seven days after Bootle's triumph, on 17 April 1888, William McGregor, the chair of Aston Villa, officially established the Football League, changing the course of football in England, and laying the foundations for the game we know today.

Five days after this announcement, Bootle defeated Stanley in the Liverpool Cup, and although Watson was injured and did not play, as team captain, he is pictured with the winning team (see page xii of plate section).

FA Cup

For all his achievements, Watson had little or no FA Cup success. Having appeared in the cup for Swifts and Queen's Park, his record is weak. Examining his FA Cup pedigree, a pattern emerges. The year after leaving a club, the club he departed would go on to have an unbeaten cup run.

Of the teams he played for, Queen's Park had the most impressive FA Cup history. A founder member, they had reached the semi-finals, meeting Wanderers at The Oval in London. The game ended in a draw but, being unable to afford another trip from Scotland, they were forced to scratch the replay.

This provided Wanderers with a bye to the final, where they beat Royal Engineers. Many believe Queen's Park

---

189 Henry Tyler Watson (1888–1975).

190 Phyllis Kate Watson (1891–1957).

would have beaten Wanderers in the replay and gone on to beat Royal Engineers in the final, becoming the very first FA Cup winners, but it was not to be.

Over the following years, Queen's Park were often forced to scratch to teams in the south, as the cost of travel was beyond their resources. However, in March 1884, they met Blackburn Rovers in the FA Cup Final. Although Watson was ineligible to play, having appeared for Swifts earlier in the competition, it is highly likely that he was at The Oval to witness the game.

However, they lost 2-1 to Blackburn Rovers in a similarly disappointing manner to that of 1872. The contest was heavily criticised for the poor refereeing and decision-making of the FA president, Major Sir Francis Marindin, who disallowed several Queen's Park goals. Later, Marindin informed the team that if they made louder appeals, he would have allowed two goals to stand and the game would have been theirs.

It is worth considering that if Watson had not moved to London but had remained in Glasgow with Queen's Park, he could have become the first black man to win an FA Cup medal. His presence may even have been enough for a Queen's Park success.

When Watson played for Swifts in the FA Cup the following season, he again made himself ineligible for Queen's Park. The year after the 'Marindin final', Queen's Park went on another cup run, reaching the final but losing to Blackburn Rovers again, this time 2-0.

When Watson returned to Scotland apparently for good at the end of his southern sojourn and re-joined Queen's Park, their FA Cup ended in the first round, withdrawing because they could not afford to send a team south. Conversely, Swifts had a good cup run, reaching the semi-finals but losing to the eventual champions, Blackburn Rovers. Similarly, the year after Watson left Bootle, they enjoyed the best cup run in their history. That year they reached the quarter-finals, only to be beaten by the eventual winners, again Blackburn Rovers.

When, in 1887, the Scottish FA amended their rules and forbade any Scottish clubs from holding membership of any other football association, Queen's Park were unable to enter the competition, denying Watson a final shot at an elusive FA Cup medal.

A Player

In 1882, Watson's name appeared in the minutes of a Scottish FA meeting. Walter Arnott, who later become Watson's team-mate, had overheard disparaging remarks made by the then vice-chair, John Wallace, referring to Watson's unavailability for the upcoming Glasgow game against Sheffield. Wallace had joked that if Watson had been available, he would have drugged Arnott, incapacitating him, substituting Watson into the team. Even though this was idle talk overheard in a public smoking room of a hotel, Arnott took offence and reported Wallace to the Scottish FA, who reprimanded Wallace. However, the comment reveals Watson's standing and how highly he was regarded in Glasgow football circles.

Watson's footballing ability, or the type of player he was, are hard to discern. He had a good physique and was an effective tackler, but was also a good header of the ball, and hard to beat for speed. His kicking ability was already apparent from his time at King's College School, and frequently mentioned in press reports, like this one from a match where Watson appeared for Brentwood against Notts County:

> 'Time after time, Watson was too much … and though the ball weighed 3 cwt[191] – more or less – it was nearly always returned half the length of the field.'

D.D. Bone wrote:

> 'Mr Watson was a rare "header-out", and was famed for his fine tackling and neat kicking. He had one fault, however, and this consisted in kicking over his own lines occasionally when hard pressed by a dashing forward.'[192]

Today, avoiding danger by kicking the ball into touch would be considered safe defending, allowing the defenders and midfield to regroup. For this, Watson could be regarded as ahead of his time or an early tactician. At that time, the style of football favoured by the English consisted of being able to 'dribble' or 'kick and rush', like the kicking game in rugby. Therefore, the ability to kick a ball a long way, and accurately, would be considered not only a skill but an asset to any defence.

Arguably, the dribbling and rushing game in Scottish football had never existed, having used a passing game from the early days. But, in England, the defender's job was to clear the ball from danger and get it to the forwards, where the dribbling and rushing could commence. Therefore, if the ball ended up in the opponent's half, then all the better. But a good kick was also an effective method of distributing the

---

191 Weight measurement equal to over 300lb (136kg). This humorous remark refers to the leather balls used at the time that would soak up water, increasing the ball's weight on a wet surface or rainy day.

192 Bone (1890).

ball and would have been essential in the passing game that the Scottish players preferred.

There are several mentions of Watson taking free kicks, and one of him scoring. By the rules of the time, the goal would not have counted as it would today, as the ball had to touch another player to be allowed. Perhaps luckily, the ball bounced off a couple of defenders before crossing the line. But a goal by a defender was a rare thing, and most of the full-backs at the time would rarely cross the halfway line. Watson would also attempt shots from a distance, occasionally scoring, requiring not only a powerful kick and proper technique but accuracy too.

Heading the ball was a reasonably new technique, and when it was first utilised in the mid-1870s, it brought chuckles of laughter from the spectators. Bearing in mind the balls produced during that period were not waterproof and would gradually become heavier, sometimes doubling or tripling in weight on rainy days, the practice could be painful and potentially dangerous, as medical research would later discover.

Watson's ability to use this tactic would have been considered a useful defensive device, and along with his ability to kick the ball some distance, he would have been an asset to any team. Having a physically powerful stature would allow him to use his weight and charge players, with or without the ball, something he would have learned in his rugby days. Gradually, the rugby influence on the game would wane, and this kind of physicality would be outlawed.

Many comments made about Watson's game describe him as mature and self-assured. The following paragraph was printed in the lead-up to the England versus Scotland game at The Oval, Watson's first appearance for Scotland:

> 'Watson, even in the early days of his captaincy of the young Parkgrove, showed that he had not mistaken his place in the field at back, and latterly in the Queen's Park has proved one of the best men in that crack team. For coolness and judgement, we go the length of saying he will not be surpassed today by any of the 21 players.'[193]

An article from 1925 in the *Slough, Eton & Windsor Observer* by 'An Old Stager', remembered Swifts from their heyday and said:

> 'The best of their backs was "Andy" Watson, a coloured player who ridiculed the use of pads and as a consequence I have seen his shins streaming with blood ...'

To be named as the best back in one of the best teams in England corresponds with many other comments made about Watson. The reference to the injuries he sustained refers again to the physicality that lingered in the association game, and serious injuries occurred. In 1890, the younger brother of A.M. and P.M. Walters, Hugh Melmoth Walters, died from a kick in the stomach received during a game for Casuals against St Bartholomew's Hospital. The elder two Walters brothers retired because of their loss.

Coda

Even though Andrew Watson's top-flight career lasted only 13 seasons, during that time, he played over 300 games for

193 *Bell's Life in London and Sporting Chronicle*, Saturday, 12 March 1881.

close to 20 different clubs and teams.[194] But it would be the legitimisation of the professional game and the introduction of the Football League that would usher in a new era.

Watson would be too old to play league football, but his career had witnessed many significant changes. He had been a Scottish Professor and brought his knowledge south to the gentlemen amateurs. Many would learn by playing alongside him and would practice the passing game, beginning to understand formations and tactics.

Under his captaincy, he would direct the team on the field of play. Many would go on to play for the English national team and others would become the administrators of the game, governing the sport and leading it into the new century. Not only was Watson a gentleman and an amateur, but he was also a leader, a pioneer, and an innovator.

But the tartan army in the north vastly outnumbered the handful of Scots, like Dr John Smith and Watson, who journeyed south to play amateur football. They were perhaps too late to effect an immediate change in the southern amateurs when, after ten years of southern dominance, Blackburn Olympic won the FA Cup and took it north for the duration. It would remain there for 18 years before returning south with Spurs in 1901. By that time, the style of football invented by Queen's Park over 30 years earlier had spread far and wide and had evolved into the much-changed game.

Watson was associated with two major clubs of the age, on either side of the border. He was considered the best full-back in Scotland, and one of the best full-backs of that era. His footballing career bridged the chasm between a gentleman's pastime and a national obsession.

---

194 From August 1875 to April 1888.

It is sad to acknowledge that the last year of his playing career was marred by allegation of professionalism, but there can be no doubt that all who knew him would never believe he would have accepted money to play the game he loved. Equally, the accusations would have wounded him deeply, and he would have to carry the humiliation with him.

Perhaps going to sea was a method of dealing with this. He would now embark on a career in the maritime, leaving Liverpool for most of the year, requiring him to accept a confined and monastic existence on transatlantic ships, a life more of a recluse than a famous, educated gentleman footballer.

In 1893, a year after he became qualified as a First-Class Engineer, Bootle Football Club folded due to financial difficulties. A year earlier, a dispute between the Everton directors led to the foundation of Liverpool Football Club. They would replace Bootle as the primary opponent to Everton on Merseyside.

Mariner

It is not entirely clear what career opportunity Watson had accepted at Bootle, but he was not the only player to follow the path from football into marine engineering. His new team-mate Tom Veitch's brother, Dumbarton's Bob Jamieson, W. Hastings and 'Watty' Campbell, among others, were all Scotsmen who came to Bootle to play football and ended up as marine engineers or serving on ships. Even after Watson had hung up his boots, there were occasional mentions of his whereabouts in some newspapers:

> * * *
>
> **Friends of Mr. Andrew Watson, late of the Queen's Park, will be pleased to hear that he is doing well as an engineer on board one of the Liverpool and South American liners.**
>
> * * *

Glasgow Evening Post – *Friday, 11 January 1889*

As it turned out, Watson had chosen a career path culminating in the position of Chief Engineer for the West Indian and Pacific Steamship Company. This would require him to spend three or four years as an apprentice, firstly sitting his Second Engineer, then his First Engineer qualification. He would need to spend several years at sea, gaining the necessary experience on several ships, including time spent on a steamship called *William Cliff*, which sailed out of Liverpool to the West Indies and South America.

The ship was named after a Liverpudlian merchant from Liverpool, William Cliff, the son of Adam Cliff, a shipping merchant. William's father filed claims for over 1,000 slaves when the Slavery Compensation Act was introduced in 1837. He collected over £20,000 in payments, equivalent to £23m in 2018. William used his enormous inherited wealth for 'munificent acts of beneficence in Liverpool and the neighbourhood'.

After his death, William was praised for 'giving away' over £100,000. His 'open-hearted generosity' founded and endowed the Home for Ancient Mariners, the Gordon Boys' Home on Stanley Road, and he was on the board of the India and Pacific Steamship Company Limited, the company that owned the ships that employed Watson.

When *William Cliff* had docked in Liverpool on 1 April 1889, Watson would have received the news that his sister Annetta had died the previous day. He would have around two weeks to settle her affairs before *William Cliff* returned to the sea.

In February 1891, three years after retiring from football, Watson sat his Board of Trade Examinations and received his Second-Class Engineering certification. The fee to sit the examinations was £1, and a condition of eligibility to sit them, both verbal and written, was four years at sea, or three years with a year's service as an apprentice. It would appear that Watson's acceptance for the examinations may have been expedited, perhaps due to having enrolled in the University of Glasgow to study engineering in 1875.

Or his performance and work ethic was such that he impressed the Company and was accepted as a bright and promising candidate.

Watson's daughter, Phyllis Kate, had been born a few weeks before he sat the examinations and, in her early years, she would become accustomed to her father's absences, leaving the parenting to Eliza. He was fortunate that when Phyllis was born on 11 January 1891, *William Cliff* was in its home port at the time, leaving for Panama soon after.

Two years later, on Monday, 8 May 1893, the *Liverpool Echo* published a list of Masters, Mates and Engineers who had passed examinations in the previous week, and Andrew Watson appears in the list of successful candidates as a First-Class Engineer. This achievement was unusual, as three years' service was usually required between sitting the second- and first-class examinations.

Of note, a few days earlier, on 2 May 1893, the Scottish FA legitimised professionalism in Scottish football. The game in Scotland would never be the same again.

The work as an engineer may have suited Watson, who had previously proven his administrative and organisational abilities during his football career. The ship's engineers are critical on board any vessel and require competence, knowledge and people skills. The fact that Watson only held the position of Chief Engineer on two voyages could suggest that he preferred life as a Second Engineer. The chief's role was more administrative, whereas the Second Engineer was more hands-on. They would be responsible for a variety of tasks, including the overall management of the engine room, passenger and crew safety, repairs, maintenance of machinery, scheduled and unscheduled maintenance, staff management, duty rotas, and the supervision of the watch.

Obviously, the financial rewards were not as good as for a Chief Engineer. Watson earned £11 a month, rising to £15 for taking on the role of Chief Engineer, which in today's money would be around £17,000, rising to £23,000 per annum. Not a fortune by any standards, and the records indicate that, for all his voyages, Watson requested a month's salary in advance, which probably went to Eliza.

On 7 October 1883, *William Cliff* arrived in New Orleans on 7 October 1893, where another ship, the *Louisianian* was also in port. According to logs of the *Louisianian*, on 20 October 1893, the Second Engineer, William Cameron, became sick and was admitted to hospital in New Orleans. On the same day, Watson signed on as the Second Engineer. There seems to have been trouble on the ship, as eight members of the crew deserted in Barbados, and two had been 'left imprisoned due to wilful disobedience to lawful commands' in Panama.

Watson remained loyal to the West India and Pacific Steamship Company Limited, which owned *William Cliff*, the *Louisianian*, and a ship that Watson would later join, *West Indian*.

The *Louisianian* was almost new, a steel steamer built in 1891 in Glasgow, and would have had the most modern and sophisticated systems of any ship afloat. It would, therefore, need a highly skilled and trained crew. Watson remained as the Second Engineer on this ship from 1893 to 1895.

Meanwhile, the English national team had the upper hand over the Scots. Of the ten games played in the 1890s, England won six, Scotland two and two were drawn. In the days before Wembley became England's home stadium, their games were played at various locations, such as Blackburn, Crystal Palace and, in April 1895, Goodison Park, Liverpool. The Scots lost 3-0, but amongst the analysis of the failings of the Scottish team, the Glasgow press reported a sighting of Andrew Watson at the game:

> 'Andrew Watson, late of Queen's Park, and International back in 1881-82, was a notable figure

> in the Compton lobby. He is voyaging between the Mersey and India. He shook hands warmly with J.L. Kay [sic], and asked for all the old boys.'[195]

> 'Andrew Watson, the old International and Queen's Park player, witnessed the match. His old friends will be glad to hear that he is in splendid health and looking younger than ever.'[196]

Watson signed on with *West Indian*, a merchant steamer, in 1896. It would be five years after receiving his First Engineer's certificate before he assumed the position of Chief Engineer, and then only for one trip, resuming a Second Engineer's position at the end of the voyage. In 1898 he accepted the chief's role again, but no records appear for any further travels. It is not clear why Watson chose to remain a Second Engineer for so long, and why he decided to stay on the same ship and not attempt to find an appropriate position elsewhere. For him to achieve promotion, he may have been content to wait for the old chief to step down or move on.

Both the *Louisianian* and *West Indian* followed the same itinerary, calling at Belize, Tampico, Santa Marta and Trinidad, Colon, and Barbados, returning to Liverpool via Kingston (Jamaica), Port-au-Prince (Haiti) and New Orleans. The trips usually took around three months, and Watson made two or three journeys a year.

West Indian also called at Demerara, and considering Watson spent over ten years and made multiple voyages on this routes, and it is conceivable he visited his ancestral home. If so, he may have met relatives or people who knew

195 *Scottish Referee,* Friday, 12 April 1895.

196 *Scottish Referee,* Monday, 8 April 1895.

his family and may have discovered the fate of his mother, Hannah, or Anna Rose.

Watson's family would also have felt the effect of his absences due to his occupation. It meant that as the children grew older, he was missing their childhood and development, much as he had done with Rupert and Agnes.

Watson does not appear on the 1901 census, but in 1911, he was 54 years old and stated he was a 'retired sea-going chief engineer'. It is likely he had retired in 1905, at the age of 50, as this was the year the *West Indian* was sold to the Red Cross Line and renamed *Cearense*. Perhaps Watson felt this was the right time to retire instead of changing shipping line allegiances. In 1911, his family were living in a terraced house in Mossley Hill, Liverpool, situated about three miles from the Royal Albert Dock. The house still stands today.

However, before this, in 1901, the Watson family had left Liverpool on *Waesland* for America. Why they had decided to make the journey is unclear, but this is the only family-orientated event to be found in Watson's historical register. This may have simply been a family holiday, or perhaps Andrew had been presented with another opportunity, and he was travelling to explore possibilities.

All four members of the family travelled second class, heading for Philadelphia on their way to New Orleans. Andrew was 45 years old, Kate 35, Harry 11 and Phyllis 10. Strangely, and perhaps in error, Watson lists his place of birth as England. It also says that he had never been to America before, confirming that the rumours of his travelling to California in the spring of 1886 were false.

The Philadelphia Passenger List Index Cards, one for each member of the family, state that they intended to stay with J.D. Cannell on 1207 Peter Street in New

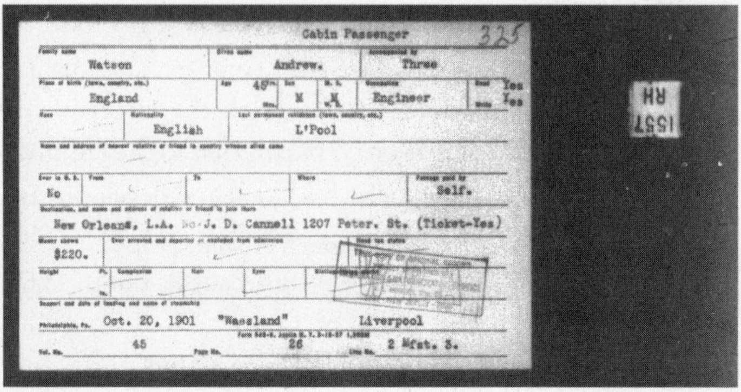
Cabin Passenger 325
Watson Andrew. Three
England 45 M M Engineer Yes Yes
English L'Pool
No Self.
New Orleans, L.A. to J. D. Cannell 1207 Peter. St. (Ticket-Yes)
$220.
Philadelphia, Pa. Oct. 20, 1901 "Waesland" Liverpool
45 26 2 Mfst. 3.

Philadelphia Passenger List Index Card

Orleans. However, oddly, research has failed to identify 'J.D. Cannell' or the house on Peter Street, but two doors down from their home on Cranborne Road in Liverpool lived a John Cannell, and this might be the same person. Their return trip is unregistered in the archives, but return they did, and a few years later they moved to Surrey from Liverpool.

All four Watson children would have experienced a similar childhood, where their father was absent for lengthy periods. Both sets of children were deprived of a paternal presence. The inaccurate reference to his father's occupation on Rupert's death certificate where it stated he was a civil servant could represent a disassociation and lack of contact between father and son, and it may be that only Phyllis enjoyed a meaningful relationship with her father.

Rupert and Agnes may have considered that they had been deserted, but the years Watson spent in London after Jessie's death also show a concerted effort to spend as much time as he could in Glasgow, even though many trips seem to have occurred when Queen's Park needed his services.

Numerous studies have indicated that fatherless children can suffer from difficulties such as self-loathing, depression, delinquency, and physical and mental health problems.[197] Perhaps this explains why Phyllis never left home, why Rupert died alone and in poverty, why Agnes all but completely disappeared, and why they all not only kept low profiles throughout their lives but why only Rupert got married to his step-cousin. None had any offspring. If these children suffered from the effects of an absent father, then coupling this to social attitudes towards their father's mixed heritage, the Watson children may have suffered from more complex issues.

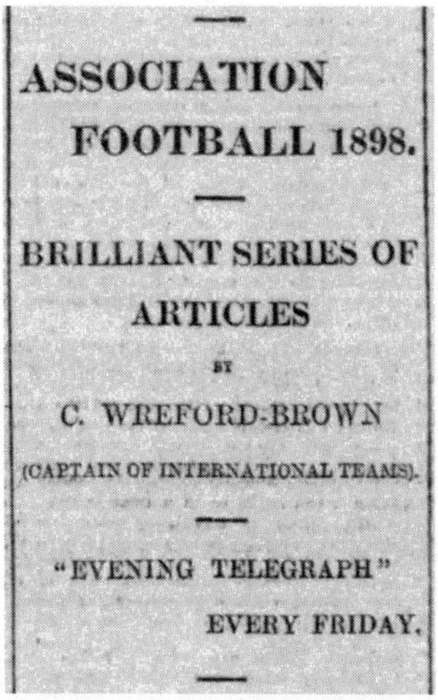
ASSOCIATION FOOTBALL 1898.

BRILLIANT SERIES OF ARTICLES

BY

C. WREFORD-BROWN

(CAPTAIN OF INTERNATIONAL TEAMS).

"EVENING TELEGRAPH"

EVERY FRIDAY.

Dundee Evening Telegraph – *Wednesday, 9 November 1898*

Watson's time at sea lasted longer than his football career and, after he retired from football, his name often appeared in the papers, referring to the Queen's Park, Swifts or Corinthian teams of the 1880s and Scotland's dominance over the English. Often, his remarkable talent and genial personality were also mentioned. But one of the very last times his name appears in the press was his obituary in the *Twickenham and Richmond Times* in 1921. After that, he is forgotten.

197 https://www.all4kids.org/2018/06/07/a-fathers-impact-on-child-development/https://www.psychologytoday.com/gb/blog/ co-parenting after-divorce/201205/father-absence-father-deficit-father-hunger

Gentleman

Even though photography in the 1880s was accessible to most people, only a few pictures of Andrew Watson have come to light. The grainy image of the Bootle team posing with the Liverpool Cup in 1888 (page xii) is the last, most recent image found. Watson was injured and unable to play in the final, but his inclusion in this photograph shows the respect afforded him by his team-mates.

After this picture was taken, Watson lived for another three decades, and even though he had a sparkling football career and was one of the greatest footballers of his age, he would almost disappear, leaving few traces. Having posed for this picture, he would begin a maritime career and spend the next dozen years living out of the public eye, criss-crossing the Atlantic, away for months at a time and separated from his family.

In modern times, he would have reappeared as a coach, pundit or manager and shared his knowledge and experience with new generations. However, choosing a monastic existence at sea suggests atonement or regret and having two families to support would obviously place a considerable financial burden on him. Even if he had investments, the income from seafaring would not go far.

Later still, he left Liverpool, where he had been living for over a quarter of a century and moved to Kew in Surrey, a town that he had no apparent connection with. Kew is some distance from Worplesdon, Surrey, where his father had lived and was buried, so there is no discernible reason for him to move to this part of Surrey. Perhaps it offered a fresh start for the family or was related to occupational or educational needs of Harry or Phyllis. Or maybe with his 60th birthday looming large, he simply felt the need for a new horizon. It may be a coincidence that his move south occurred around the beginning of the First World War, but being in his fifties, his use to the war effort in a naval capacity would have been minimal.[198]

There may never be an explanation for Watson's move to Kew, but there can be no doubt that by doing so he would be partly responsible for his own disappearance from the public record. Separating himself from the community he and his family had lived in for 27 years meant that he would eventually be lost to friends or colleagues. Until recently he was believed to have died in Australia or Mumbai. Equally, there are no indications that he tried to correct any information about himself or where he was living.

Andrew Watson died on 8 March 1921 at his family home in Forest Road, Kew. No post-mortem was necessary. Pneumonia and heart failure were noted as the cause of death, certified by the attending doctor, E.W. Lowry MCRS. The death certificate indicates Henry T. Watson as being present at the end, and presumably Phyllis and Eliza were there too.

Forest Road is a cul-de-sac, and the semi-detached, turn-of-the-century house is the last in the row. It is as picturesque and peaceful now as it must have been when the Watson family lived there. Beyond the end of the road is a tennis club that was in existence during Watson's time

198 Both of Watson's sons would serve; Rupert as a driver in the Australian 5th Field Artillery Brigade, and Henry saw action with the Argyll and Sutherland Highlanders and rose to the rank of corporal.

there. Two minutes away is the River Thames, which may have appealed to the mariner in Andrew, who is described on his death certificate as a Marine, not a Chief Engineer, as he had often stated previously.

Even though Watson's achievements are mostly centred in Scotland, in truth he only spent a short period of his life there and, although open to debate, he probably spoke with an English accent. His English background and public school education endowed him with a demeanour and confidence that endeared him to all who met him. This may account for the number of compliments he received in the press during his career.

In an article in *Athletic News* referring to Watson's decision to move to London in 1882, the author says:

> 'Their [sic] never was a kinder-hearted gentleman than Mr. Watson, and I am sure when he goes many will miss him.'[199]

Later that year in another report, this statement appeared:

> 'Never has it been my luck to meet a gentleman possessed of such abnormal vivacity "from morn till noon, from noon till dewy eve". And a' the nicht "Coupeau" kept at it. .'[200]

On 5 April 1884, this remarkable piece appeared:

> 'Andrew Watson ... And here I may pause to recall the pleasant reflection that we have seen a great

199 *Athletic News*, Wednesday, 15 March 1882.

200 *Athletic News,* Wednesday, 8 March 1882.

deal of this grand back in Nottingham during the season, and he has been associated with a variety of interests. He first came to us as a representative of the Brentwood (Essex) Club, afterwards, he visited us as a "Swift" playing in the cup tie with the Berkshire and Buckinghamshire team. Later on, he was with the heterogeneous lot that visited us to do services for Surrey, and finally he comes back with his early love the Queen's Park division. But in whatever character he comes, Andrew Watson is always welcome in Nottingham, where we love good football as dearly as we love all other good sports. Perhaps the most striking feature of play in Thursday's match was the fine defensive show made by Watson and W. Arnott and seeing them we probably saw the two very best backs in the United Kingdom associated.'[201]

At the end of his career, in 1888, this appeared:

> 'Andy Watson, the man of many clubs, who, though he has been lost to the sight of many of his southern friends, is still to their memory "Dear" ...'[202]

Few players accumulated as many public statements of fondness and admiration as Watson did throughout his career. The staggering quantity of accolades he received in newspaper reports records an athlete who impressed on the pitch as much as he was admired off it.

---

201 *Nottingham Journal,* Saturday, 5 April 1884.

202 *Athletic News,* Tuesday, 10 January 1888.

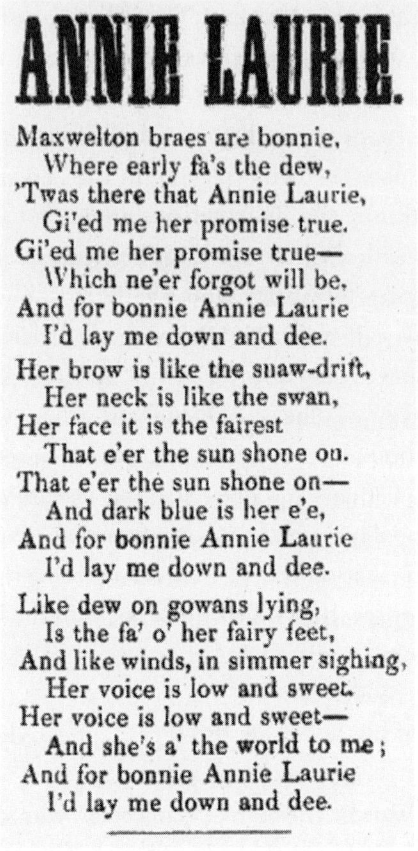

ANNIE LAURIE.

Maxwelton braes are bonnie,
Where early fa's the dew,
'Twas there that Annie Laurie,
Gi'ed me her promise true.
Gi'ed me her promise true—
Which ne'er forgot will be,
And for bonnie Annie Laurie
I'd lay me down and dee.

Her brow is like the snaw-drift,
Her neck is like the swan,
Her face it is the fairest
That e'er the sun shone on.
That e'er the sun shone on—
And dark blue is her e'e,
And for bonnie Annie Laurie
I'd lay me down and dee.

Like dew on gowans lying,
Is the fa' o' her fairy feet,
And like winds, in simmer sighing,
Her voice is low and sweet.
Her voice is low and sweet—
And she's a' the world to me;
And for bonnie Annie Laurie
I'd lay me down and dee.

Annie Laurie

In January 1888, Bootle held a 'Smoker',[203] and towards the end of the evening, fellow full-backs Tom Veitch and Watson stood up and sang the famous Scottish folk song, 'Annie Laurie'.

It is hard to imagine a ballad about unfulfilled love failing to remind Watson of his first wife, Jessie. Their marriage lasted only five years and perhaps the choice of this ballad is a testament to his perception of his own nationality. Conscious that his football career was coming to an end and, having set

203 A social gathering, usually formal, consisting of food and drink, speeches, and musical performances by members of the club.

up home in Liverpool with his English wife and children, it may not have occurred to him that he would live in England for the rest of his life. Perhaps he believed Scotland could still be an option for him.

Newspapers

Around the time that Watson's football career was beginning, Scottish newspapers offered little coverage of football. If a report appeared, it usually played second fiddle to curling or coursing, or under paragraphs on horse racing, draughts, fishing or quoiting. The coverage of football might run to only a single sentence or, if the game was an international or inter-city game, a whole paragraph. While Watson was a Parkgrove player, newspapers in Glasgow began to recognise the public interest and coverage gradually increased and improved.

Many journalists were unfamiliar with the sport and lacked even a basic knowledge, satisfying themselves with a description of what they saw from the side of the pitch. But

THE PILGRIMS v LEYTON.

These powerful London clubs opened their season last Saturday afternoon with a contest played on the grounds of the last named, which eventually resulted in favour of the visitors by two goals to nil. The Pilgrims were but weakly represented forward, though the splendid back play of Watson and Rogers and the goal keeping of Swepstone fully made up for any deficiency in this respect. During the latter part of the game the visitors were somewhat pressed. Barbour, a recent importation into the club ranks from Scotland, particularly distinguishing himself. No point, however, was scored, and at the call of time the state of the game was as above mentioned.

THE PILGRIMS.—H. A. Swepstone (captain) (goal), Andrew Watson and C. R. Rogers (backs), A. H. King and A. C. S. Stone (half backs), W. E. Fry, J. H. Bennett, C. H Owen, J. Armstrong, and J. H. Roberts.

LEYTON.—G. H. T. Lee (captain) (goal), G. Smith and J. Barbour (backs), E. Pracy and C. Sienesi (half backs), A. Henderson, C. Vasey, A. Anderson, F. Sayer, H. Piggott, and C. Westfield.

Bell's Life in London and Sporting Chronicle – *Saturday, 6 October 1883* while column inches increased, some players' names began to appear regularly in the press. Watson was often mentioned and, although we are accustomed to it today, at that time 'media exposure' of this type was foreign to football.

Players were usually referred to in match reports using their initials and surname, or only their surname. However, the press often referred to Watson using his full name, or the familiar 'Andy', and often including comments on his character and popularity. These reports are early signs of 'celebrity', making Andrew Watson one of the first, if not the first, football superstar.

Famous Players by 'Bauldie'

What follows is a reproduction of an article published in *Scottish Referee* on Friday, 27 June 1902 by 'Bauldie', the pen name of James Shaw Carmichael, considered one of the finest sports journalists at the end of the 19th and early 20th century. It is worthy of reproduction only because it captures the esteem and the respect Watson instilled, and even though there are some errors, it is an appropriate homage to Andrew Watson by someone who saw him play.

> Andrew Watson, of Queen's Park F.C.
> *"Ay, he was a king" – Shakespeare*

I have selected this once famous player in a week when the world's sovereigns have made this little sceptred isle, the silver gem of the sea, their home to do homage to King Edward and his Royal Consort.[204] I can think of no other player as

---

204 King Edward VII was crowned on 9 August 1902. Originally scheduled for 26 June of that year, the ceremony had been postponed at very short notice, because he had been taken ill with an abdominal abscess that required immediate surgery.

a back, save, it may be, Michael Paton, of Dumbarton, who bore himself with equal dignity, courtliness, and composure on the football field. I could cite you many instances in the career of Andrew Watson in proof of this estimate of his character, but I will let one suffice. It was in that memorable Scottish final in 1882, when the hardy 'Sons of the Rock' led by the late William McKinnon, bore down upon the Queen's defence as Rob Roy's raiders did on a Hielan' shieling. Like a wall, Andrew Watson stood up to the raiders and beat them back time and again. Irritated by his …

Cool, Cultured, Reposeful

… style, well do I remember McKinnon raising his hand to strike the noble back. With a calm smile that betokened complete control of temper, the Queen's back bore the insult offered to him and did nothing in return but smile, a fact that irritated his opponent all the more, and made them easier prey to his powers. Andrew Watson's bearing was that of a gentleman both on and off the field of play. If he charged an opponent, (and he sometimes did, you know), he did not, after the manner of some modern boorish backs, glory in the act, for he was ready with a kindly, 'Beg your pardon; are you hurt?' if his opponent seemed to be so. His sympathetic nature and polished style were the result partly of intuition and partly of a superior education and upbringing.

Educated at Halifax Grammar School, he migrated to Rugby School,[205] thence to King's College, London, and finally to Glasgow University, where the copestone was placed upon his mental training. No past Scottish Association player to my knowledge has had such a varied

205 There is no record of Andrew Watson in the Rugby School registers.

education, and I am not surprised that it had such a refining influence on his character. Association football one would have thought hardly suited to a gentlemanly nature such as his, and I question but for the influence of certain plebeian[206] acquaintances, he formed with members of …

Old Parkgrove FC

… if he would have deigned to play the game. These, however, overcame his modest scruples, and he was induced to join the ranks in which T.J. Britton, J. Docherty,[207] and others were shining lights. It was in the year 1874 that he threw in his lot with Parkgrove, and his kingly demeanour so won for him the admiration of his clubmates that for six years he captained them and led them on to victory. Gifted as he was, man and player, Parkgrove's narrow limits did not suit the growth of his undeniable powers, and nobody was surprised when he joined the Queen's Park and became the successor of the late Joseph Taylor as a right back. Inspired by the traditions of oldest Hampden, and fired by the idea of following in the steps of the man who made these, Andrew Watson's powers developed rapidly, and he was ere long regarded as Scotland's most judicious, most powerful, and most cultured back. The Scottish Association rightly interpreted the vox populi when in the year 1881 in the International v England, played at Kennington Oval, he was appointed captain of the Scottish eleven.

This distinguished honour was fully justified by the success of him and his men, for they routed the Saxons by no less than 6 goals to 1, and so put on the first record for this

---

206 Lower class

207 W.T. Docherty?

match, and one of the best results that have so far attended it for our country. I have already in other matches given you this renowned team, but there is no harm in giving you a good thing twice, and so I do so.

Goal – George Gillespie, Rangers
Backs – A. Watson and T. Vallance, Rangers
Half-backs – C. Campbell and D. Davidson, Queen's Park
Forwards – D. Hill, Rangers; W. McGuire, Beith; George Ker and John Smith, Queen's Park; J. Lindsay, Dumbarton; and H. McNeil, Queens Park.

I think you will remember me telling you that there were four centre forwards in this eleven, and that it was thus one of the most experimental ever crossed the Border. The quartette [sic] were: W. McGuire, G. Ker, John Smith, and Joseph Lindsey. I am trusting to memory, but I think it was in this great '81 year that our King, then Prince of Wales, patronised the match, in company with Lord Rosebery. Be that the case or not, this glorious Scottish victory was worthy of such exalted and Royal patronage. In this same year, Andrew Watson also played for Scotland v Wales, when the Thistles representatives also won handsomely, by 5 goals to 1.

He took part in the then Inter-City fixtures of London v Glasgow and Sheffield v Glasgow. In 1882 he again played on Hampden Park v England and curious to tell, a similar happy numerical result attended the Scottish arms – viz., 6 goals to 1.

These two victories are …

So Magnificently Beautiful

… that I give you the '82 eleven as well:

Goal – G. Gillespie, Rangers
Backs – A. Watson, Queen's Park, and A. McIntyre, Vale of Leven
Half-Backs – C. Campbell, Queen's Park and Peter Miller, Dumbarton
Forwards – Eddie Fraser and W. Anderson, W. Harrower and G. Ker (all of Queen's Park); R. McPherson, Arthurlie; and J.L. Kay, Queen's Park.

That was a grand team, too, my master, and I think, considering the unique performances of both that they should be placed side by side in the National Portrait Gallery of the Scottish FA.

For his club, Andrew Watson rendered yeoman service, notably in the hard battles v Dumbarton for the Scottish Cup. The last of these in which he figured was on fatal Boghead in 1883, when he came down to play centre-half for the Queen's, he is the first to fill that position for them. Unfortunately, the Queen's were beaten in that Scottish tie, 3-1, and so his last appearance for the premier club was associated with defeat.[208]

Apart from football Andrew Wilson [sic] was a grand athlete, and it may interest Messrs J.B. Milne and R.G. Murray to learn that as the Queen's Park Sports, he topped 5 feet 10 inches for the high jump.

The fortunes of business took him to London town, and so it came that Scottish football and athletics lost the adornment of one of the most gentlemanly sportsmen who has footed it on Scottish soil. He is now, I believe, located in Bombay, and I am sure it is the wish of all who knew him in the days of auld lang syne, or who appreciate the true

208 Watson's last appearance for Queen's Park was on Saturday, 25 September 1886.

manliness and beauty of character that he may be prosperous in the battle of life.

The Corinthian Football Club

Like many Scots, the pursuit of employment would require Andrew Watson to leave his homeland. Accepting a job in London with the civil service provided him with a career that, up until that point in his life, he had failed to establish. By the time he was 26 years old, he had been a student, a merchant, an apprentice engineer, and a warehouseman. His footballing reputation would precede him, and the southerners would be conscious of his involvement in the recent English humiliations, but as the first Scot to bring the art of Scottish football to the English amateurs, he would become one of, if not the first 'Scottish Professor' to introduce the Scottish innovations to the English amateurs.

In 1882, the game was rapidly evolving, and the English FA was being forced into a period of self-reflection. On the one hand, the two maulings by the Scottish had painfully exposed the inadequacies of the English game, and on the other, the influx of Scottish players and the practice of 'shamateurism' was not only flouting the laws on professionalism but improving the quality of the football played in the provinces. The increasing number of northern teams reaching the latter stages of the FA Cup was a testament to this. However, the FA feared a loss of governing power if they confronted these 'pro-amateurs', and there was already talk of a separate association for northern clubs if the southern FA did not recognise professionalism. Facing subjugation to the northern business ethic was one thing, but perhaps more disturbing for the amateurs would be the loss of footballing credibility.

After England's 5-1 defeat to Scotland in March 1882, the visitors were entertained to dinner at the Grand Hotel in Glasgow. When the speeches began, the chairman of the Scottish FA, Colonel Carrick Buchanan, casually voiced an opinion. He said:

> '… that the Englishman laboured under a great disadvantage of not knowing each other's play like the Scotsman, coming as they did from all parts, and everyone would admit that had something to do with their success, although they had played as well, if not better individually, than their Scottish brethren.'

N.C. Bailey, the English captain, responded:

> '… remarking that he had gone to Glasgow 3 or 4 times and have always got jolly well thrashed. They might play the game individually as well as their friends but could not look at them in combination and more particularly when they had so many members of Queen's Park in their eleven who had defeated England that day.'[209]

It was N.L. 'Pa' Jackson who later credited himself with identifying the problem and coming up with the solution was to create an English team in the Queen's Park mould. This would not only allow the English amateurs to develop a similar understanding and combination to the Scottish side but would also be able to feed these players to the national team.

At the time, this would be considered a radical and somewhat desperate solution to the FA's problems. For the

209 *North British Daily Mail,* Monday, 13 March 1882.

sport's governing body to create a football club with the primary aim of improving the quality of the English amateur game and resisting the Scots, was not only self-serving but undeniably preferential. For a governing body, claiming to represent the sport throughout the land, this plan would appear to only favour the southern amateurs.

Earlier in the year, Blackburn Rovers had reached the FA Cup Final, the first northern team to do so. Even though they had lost to Old Etonians, the only possible explanation for the presence in the Blackburn team of Fergus Suter, Hugh McIntyre, Thomas Strachan and Jimmy Douglas, all talented Scottish players, was that they were professionals and being rewarded for playing. But to confront their suspicions, the FA could potentially destroy everything they had worked so purposefully to achieve over the previous 20 years.

It had taken a lot of hard work, including the foundation of the FA Cup, to bring the ranks of association clubs under the controlling power of one governing body, and confronting the 'shamateurism' in these artisan teams could result in a regional split and the loss of governing monopoly. It would be better if they could find a solution that put the north in their place, preserving the FA Cup for the amateur clubs and 'old boys' teams of the south. Therefore, the creation of a 'super-team' of amateurs, linked to the best amateur teams in the country, might not only help to improve the quality of the amateur game, and the fortunes of the English national team, but it might also subdue the would-be professionals.

Over that summer, the idea was set aside while Jackson went about setting up the London Football Association. But on Monday, 13 September 1882, the FA called a meeting to make the draw for the first round of the FA Cup. At the meeting, a select group of members were invited to meet at A.J. Secretan's offices 'to consider the desirability of forming a new Wednesday Club'.[210] Jackson advertised the meeting in his *Football* magazine.

> NEW ASSOCIATION CLUB.—A club including in its ranks some International and many well-known players has just been started. It will play only the strongest matches, and its fixtures will be principally on Wednesdays. There is some probability that it will amalgamate with the old "Wanderers," and if so a club historical in football annals will be revived. A general meeting will shortly be held. A. J. Secretan, 2, Draper's-gardens, E.C., is the Hon. Sec. *pro tem.*, and N. L. Jackson, Hon. Sec. London Football Association, has undertaken to arrange matches, some of which will be with strong provincial clubs.

Football, *October 4, 1882*

The group met on 11 October 1882, at 28 Paternoster Row, London, not Secretan's office, and the new 'Wednesday Club' came into existence.[211] Present at the meeting with N.L. Jackson were England internationals N.C. Bailey, C.H. Holden-White, H.A. Swepstone, A.J. Secretan and W. Leete, brother of Norman. All but Jackson had played against Watson and all would become Corinthians.

The Wednesday Club would become known as the 'Corinthian Football Club' at the suggestion of H.A. Swepstone.[212] Jackson declined management of the team, claiming to be too busy, so the responsibility fell to A.J. Secretan. It would have the full support of the FA and all

210 *The Sportsman,* Wednesday, 11 October 1882.

211 Players were usually involved in club games on Saturdays, but could be free to play midweek.

212 Recent research has identified the source of the name as being a reference to Shakespeare's *Henry V, Part I.*

the southern amateur teams and be able to select the best players from the clubs and universities.

Corinthian would not only aim to develop players who could improve the quality of the English national team, but they also would uphold the southern gentleman's amateur ethos. It was a 'hail-Mary play', but it was believed to be worth the risk. The Corinthian players would also return to their clubs and share the new knowledge, feeding the grassroots and generally improving the quality of amateur football in the south.

As the Corinthian Football Club would be seen as the FA's own representatives, it would be necessary to deflect accusations of bias. The team would need to distance itself from the governing body, and introduced self-imposed restrictions, such as limiting the number of members and not charging a subscription or membership fee. The club would have to be self-financing, lease no home ground or possess any tangible assets, and as if to confirm its autonomy from the FA, the club would not compete in any cup competitions.

Unfortunately, the first season was poorly managed, and Corinthian failed not only to attract the best players but had little impact on the amateur game. History has reflected that if Corinthian had entered the FA Cup, with the players it had at its disposal, the cup might have remained in the south for years. But by the time the team came under the control of N.L. 'Pa' Jackson in late 1883, it was too late to save the FA Cup from going north, first to Blackburn Olympic, then to Blackburn Rovers, as they ushered in an era of northern supremacy.

However, the battles with the Scots became less one-sided, and although the English failed to assert the hoped-for dominance, and perhaps influenced by Jackson's presence on the selection committee, the English team swelled with the selection of Corinthian players. The results of the next few Scottish matches saw margins of loss reduced to a single goal or drawn matches. In two games against Wales, the whole English team would comprise Corinthian players, but as Wales were not considered high-class opposition, the experiment with squads full of Corinthians was not seen as a gamble. England won the first game in 1894, 5-1, but drew the other 1-1 in 1895 at The Oval.

The composition of the English teams to face Scotland reflected the arrival of the Corinthians, and in 1883 there were nine Corinthians in the English squad to face the Scots. There were six in 1884 and 1885, nine in 1886, seven in 1887 and five in 1888, when England won for the first time in nine years. This team was a mix of the best northern players and amateurs and produced a resounding 5-0 success on Scottish home soil, at Hampden Park. From then on, the Corinthian content in the England squad to face Scotland gradually reduced, as the legitimisation of professionalism and the foundation of league football began to assert a more significant influence on the national game.

Similarly, the presence of Queen's Park players in the Scottish team also decreased until, in 1902, a year after Spurs had returned the FA Cup to the south of England, a Scottish team faced England without any Queen's Park players.

The Corinthian Football Club continued to carry the flag for amateur football and played dozens of games against teams with a professional element, sometimes scoring historic successes over their professional cousins.

Playing for Scotland in the two thrashings of England in 1881 and 1882, Watson had unintentionally played a role in the creation of the Corinthian Club and the evolution of English football. As the first man of colour to play for the Scottish team, he would also become the first man of colour and first Scot to play for and captain Corinthian.

Watson was not the only Scottish Professor to come to the aid of the southern amateurs. Charles Campbell, the captain of Scotland and Queen's Park, also played in the 1881 and 1882 thrashings, and although he only played two games for Corinthian, he was accepted as a member of the club. Others who brought their knowledge to the English amateurs were Dr John Smith, Andrew Hair Holm and his brother John Wilson Holm, David Steel Allan, Alexander Hamilton and Walter Arnott, mostly internationals, and all Queen's Park players.

Watson's footballing influence on both sides of the border would mark him as a singularly unique person in the history of the early game. He helped bring the Scottish footballing innovations to the English and he played alongside the best English amateur players, many of whom went on to represent their country.

By the time Watson retired, the Scottish innovations had been fully absorbed, and the individual kick and rush dribbling style of the English was well on the way to extinction. The team game, positional play and short passing now became the dominant techniques used by most football teams. Sadly, this skill transference became so absorbed in the English game that they would later claim ownership, tipping their hats to the contribution made by the Scots, but taking credit for what they considered to be 'The English Game'.

Arguably, the FA's attempts at self-preservation and to stem the tsunami of professionalism had long-term effects for the fortunes of the teams in the south. Not until 20 years after the foundation of the Football League, in 1904/05, were Arsenal the first southern club accepted into the Football League. Up to that point, it only contained teams from the Midlands and the north of England. Arsenal were also the first southern club to win the league, in the 1930/31 season, over 40 years after its foundation.

Corinthian, however, would continue to keep the amateur flag flying and play an influential role in spreading the gospel of football around the world. Ironically, after a falling out with the FA, they were exiled from the association and were unable to play games against any teams affiliated with the FA. Their response was to look abroad and arrange tours through Europe and the other continents. They inspired the foundation of many national football associations, cup competitions and numerous football clubs around the world.[213]

Even after professionalism was firmly ensconced in the public appetite, Corinthian remained the shining light of amateur football. The team introduced one of the most significant elements in the world of sport: the 'Corinthian Spirit'. This code of conduct represents fair play, sportsmanship and honesty in the game, and this etiquette remains in the DNA of all British athletes.

Today, the club continues to play football in the lower echelons of the English Football League. Having merged with their fellow amateurs, Casuals Football Club, after the Second World War, the club became known as the Corinthian-Casuals Football Club, based in south London, in Tolworth, Surrey.

The Casuals FC has been mostly overlooked by football historians. Even though any link between the clubs was vociferously denied, recent research suggests an 'arrangement' may have existed. Founded in 1883, a year after the unsatisfactory first season, where Corinthian struggled to attract players, the Casuals acted as a feeder club, drawing

213 Corinthians Paulista in Brazil are perhaps the most significant legacy of the Corinthian Club tours in South America.

on the best university and club footballers. They would boast the largest membership of any amateur football club, and on numerous occasions would field three or more teams and more than once, they fielded five teams on a Saturday. From this vast pool of players, Corinthian would select the best for their fixtures and tours, guaranteeing a squad of talented, fit and committed players. Being chosen to play for Corinthian was an honour and considered a potential stepping-stone to the national team, so membership of the Casuals was the first step for any ambitious young player looking for football glory.

Coda

When Henry Tyler Watson died in 1975, the Watson family lineage appears to have ended. Watson's uncles did not register any offspring, and it is probable that if there were any, like Miller Watson, the father would have felt morally obligated to accept the responsibility for their care and schooling, and like Andrew and Annetta, they would have been sent back to Britain to be raised and educated. However, no records have been discovered of any other Watson children returning to these shores.

Of Andrew Watson's four children, we can be reasonably confident that three did not produce offspring, and if Henry married and had children, none have been found in research or have come forward to claim his name.

All of Watson's children left a low profile, with only a scattering of indications of their existence. This low profile and the absence of any grandchildren may have been one of many factors that contributed to Andrew Watson's disappearance from the historical record. Even though members of his extended family were immensely wealthy, none of their affluence appears to have filtered down to Watson's children, as none exhibited any signs of prosperity. In fact, for a family with such a distinguished heritage, the Watson family members all lived modest and unremarkable lives.

The decades following Watson saw the game change from a gentlemen's pastime to a global obsession, and as attendances, revenue and media focus grew, the sport would eventually evolve into the phenomenon it is today. This evolution would gradually conceal Watson's achievements, and those of his contemporaries, from the collective memory. As a result, it is perhaps understandable that there was an absence of any national obituary at the passing of Andrew Watson in 1921.

However, the work of Ged O'Brien, Tommy Malcolm and the Scottish Football Museum, Andy Mitchell and Tony Talburt, has restored Andrew Watson to his rightful place, not only in the history of the beautiful game but as a relevant and cultural icon.

We know very little about Watson's last years in Kew, but the hope is they were peaceful and untroubled. His life ended unaware that his brilliant and exceptional career in football was as ground-breaking and significant as is now appreciated. Had he not left Glasgow, how many more trophies would he have won at Queen's Park, how many more times would he have captained his country, and how much more of an imprint would he have left to assure his achievements would be recognised in the history of the game?

Similarly, if he had remained in London with Corinthian, would he have further enhanced his reputation and, as many Corinthians did, assume a role in the governance and development of the game. Even though he later returned to the city where his talent had matured, he did not stay long. Moving again, this time to Liverpool, a gateway to the maritime, where he would board ships, disappearing for months at a time, distancing himself from his own history.

He eventually returned to the county where his father had settled, severing any remaining links with a city where he last played football. Perhaps this final move helps to explain why the memory of the immensely talented and much-loved footballer became lost and why he was omitted from the books that presumed to tell the glorious history of the game. Perhaps his place in history would have been more secure, had he not led a straggling life.

Appendices

Andrew Watson's Playing Record

(Figures based on available information)

Battlefield	1	
Bootle	42	
Brentwood	1	
London Caledonians	0	Smith and Watson named on team sheets several times, but neither played
Corinthian	14	
Edinburgh University	3	
Glasgow	4	
Glasgow Pilgrims	1	
Friendlies	6	
I Zingari	0	Advertised but did not play
London Representative	0	Selected three times but did not play
Maxwell	2	Assumed
Parkgrove	95	
Pilgrims	12	
Queen's Park	110	
Scotland national team	3	
Scottish Caledonians	8	
Scottish Corinthians	0	Selected but played for Queen's Park
South of England	0	Selected but played for Pilgrims
Surrey County	5	

Swifts	28	
Upton Park	0	On team sheet but did not play
West Surrey	1	
Total Games	336	
Athletic meetings	38	
Played in England	109	32%
Played in Scotland	227	68%
	Results	
Result unknown	11	3%
D	58	17%
L	77	22%
W	190	58%
Total Games	336	

Watson Family Tree

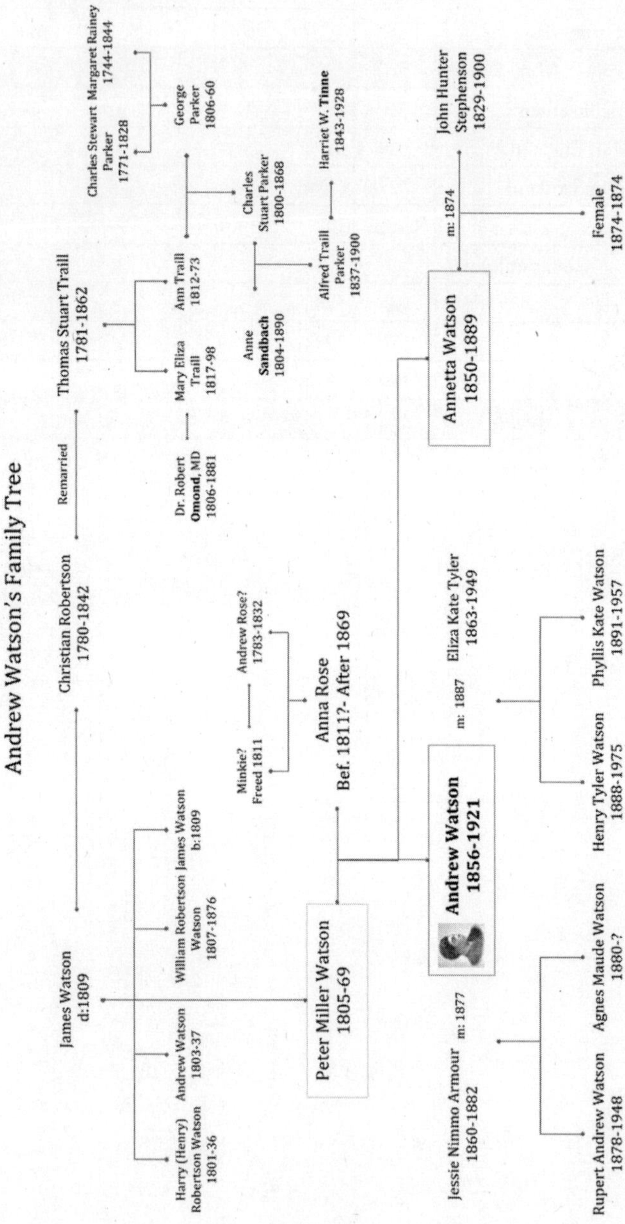

Watson Fixtures

The list of games below is incomplete, but contains all the games we can be sure of, or can be reasonably sure that Watson appeared in.

BF = Battlefield
BT = Bootle
BW = Brentwood
CFC = Corinthian
EU = Edinburgh University
GG = Glasgow Representative

GP = Glasgow Pilgrims
FRE = Friendly
MX = Maxwell
PG = Parkgrove
PLG = London Pilgrims
QP = Queen's Park

SN = Scotland national team
SC = Scottish Caledonians
SCY = Surrey County
SW = Swifts
WS = West Surrey

Date	Team	Notes	WLD
Sat, 3 Apr 1875	MX	Maxwell v Oxford Juniors played at Queen's Park. Lost 3-0. Maxwell would not leave the field in protest of the referee's decision to disallow a goal!	L
Sat, 1 May 1875	MX	Denniston v Maxwell at Queen's Park. Drawn 0-0.	D
Sat, 11 Sep 1875	PG	Oxford Juniors v Parkgrove at Queen's Park. Opening game of the season. A draw 0-0 but stopped in the second half after an injury to an Oxford player.	D
Sat, 25 Sep 1875	PG	Hamilton Academical v Parkgrove. Played in Hamilton. Lost 2-1.	L
Sat, 2 Oct 1875	PG	Parkgrove v Rosslyn. Played at Kinning Park. Drawn 0-0.	D
Sat, 23 Oct 1875	PG	Coatbridge v Parkgrove. Won 3-0. Watson listed.	W
Sat, 30 Oct 1875	PG	Abercorn v Parkgrove at Strathclyde Park. Result unknown.	unknown

Sat, 6 Nov 1875	PG	Ulva v Parkgrove. Won 3-0. Goals by Docherty, J. Miller, and G. Miller.	W
Sat, 13 Nov 1875	PG	Union v Parkgrove. Won 3-0. Goals by Penny, Millar and Docherty. Parkgrove keeper touched the ball once!	W
Sat, 8 Jan 1876	PG	Parkgrove v Ulva. Won 1-0. Goal scored by T.C. Urquhart.	W
Sat, 15 Jan 1876	PG	Parkgrove v Coatbridge. Played at Clifford Park. Result unknown.	unknown
Sat, 22 Jan 1876	PG	Parkgrove v Hamilton Academical. Played at Clifford Park. Drawn 0-0.	D
Sat, 29 Jan 1876	PG	Parkgrove v Abercorn at Kinning Park. 2-2 but mixed as Abercorn could not muster a team.	D
Sat, 5 Feb 1876	PG	Parkgrove v Union. Lost 1-0 at Kinning Park.	L
Sat, 12 Feb 1876	PG	Parkgrove v Bellahouston. Played at Summerton Park. Result unknown.	unknown
Sat, 19 Feb 1876	PG	Parkgrove v Carrington at Clifford Park. Won 1-0.	W
Sat, 4 Mar 1876	PG	Parkgrove v Union at Clifford Park. Result unknown.	unknown
Sat, 11 Mar 1876	PG	Parkgrove v Rosslyn at Clifford Park. Drawn 1-1. Parkgrove keeper never touched the ball!	D
Sat, 18 Mar 1876	PG	Parkgrove v Govan at Clifford Park. Won 2-1.	W
Sat, 25 Mar 1876	PG	Parkgrove v Gilbertfield at Clifford Park. Result unknown.	unknown
Sat, 8 Apr 1876	PG	Parkgrove v Queen's Park Juniors at Clifford Park. Won 1-0. Goal Docherty.	W
Sat, 22 Apr 1876	PG	Parkgrove v Bellahouston at Clifford Park. Won 4-0. Goals by John Millar, James Miller, Watson and Valentine. Goalkeeper did not touch the ball in the second half.	W
Sat, 16 Sep 1876	PG	Parkgrove v Helensburgh. Lost 3-1.	L
Sat, 23 Sep 1876	PG	Parkgrove v Roslin at Clifford Park. Won 3-0. Goals by James Millar, G. Miller and ?	W
Sat, 30 Sep 1876	PG	Parkgrove v Lancefield. Scottish Cup. Lost 2-1.	L

Sat, 7 Oct 1876	PG	Queen's Park Juniors v Parkgrove. Lost 1-0. Watson mentioned.	L
Sat, 14 Oct 1876	PG	Parkgrove v Hamilton Academical. Won 2-1. Watson listed.	W
Sat, 21 Oct 1876	PG	Parkgrove v Mount Vernon. Won 3-0. Played at Clifford Park.	W
Sat, 28 Oct 1876	PG	Parkgrove v 4th RRV (Pollokshaws) at Clifford Park. Won 2-0. 'A. Watson and R. Armstrong (backs) played in the usual brilliant and dashing style.'	W
Sat, 18 Nov 1876	PG	Parkgrove v Wanderers PG. Won 2-1 (or one goal and one disputed to none). Watson scored. '... being ably tackled by Armstrong, Watson secured the ball and by a splendid longshot he sent it under the Wanderers' tape, thus lowering their colours after twenty minutes play.'	W
Sat, 25 Nov 1876	PG	Union v Parkgrove at Queen's Park. Result unknown.	unknown
Sat, 9 Dec 1876	PG	Parkgrove v Abercorn at Clifford Park. Won 3-0. PG Junior played 2nd Benmore on Clifford Park, won 1-0.	W
Sat, 16 Dec 1876	PG	Craigpark v Parkgrove. Match drawn. No mention of Watson.	D
Sat, 30 Dec 1876	PG	Rosslyn v Parkgrove at Overnewtown Park. Result unknown.	unknown
Sat, 13 Jan 1877	PG	Parkgrove v Queen's Park Juniors. Won 2-0. Mentions solid back play.	W
Sat, 27 Jan 1877	PG	Parkgrove v Union at Clifford Park. Result unknown.	unknown
Sat, 3 Feb 1877	PG	Parkgrove v Shawfield at Clifford Park. Drawn 1-1.	D
Sat, 10 Feb 1877	PG	Helensburgh v Parkgrove at Helensburgh. Drawn 3-3.	D
Sat, 17 Feb 1877	PG	4th RRV v Parkgrove. Played at Pollokshaws. Won 1-0.	W
Sat, 3 Mar 1877	PG	Parkgrove v Shawfield at Clifford Park. Drawn 1-1.	D
Sat, 24 Mar 1877	PG	Parkgrove v Craigpark at Clifford Park. Result unknown.	unknown

Sat, 31 Mar 1877	PG	Parkgrove v 3rd LRV at Clifford Park. Lost 3-0. Watson listed. Raised £20 for Govan poor. '... Watson did many clever things as extreme back ...'	L
Sat, 15 Sep 1877	PG	Rangers v Parkgrove. Lost 5-0 or 7-0. 'Of the Parkgrove players, Watson (back) was undoubtedly the best man.' 'Parkgrove one of the coming young clubs.'	L
Sat, 22 Sep 1877	PG	Queen's Park v Parkgrove. Lost 1-0. Watson mentioned. Played at Trinidad Park, attendance 1,000.	L
Sat, 13 Oct 1877	PG	Partick v Parkgrove. Won 5-3. Partick played first half with ten men and were 3-0 up at half-time. They played the second half with nine men and leaked five goals.	W
Sat, 20 Oct 1877	PG	Parkgrove v Kelvinbank at Trinidad Park. Won or lost 2-1. Scottish Cup 2nd Round. Campbell and Walker mentioned.	W/L?
Sat, 27 Oct 1877	PG	Parkgrove v Arthurlie. Lost 1-0. Not listed in *Scottish Annual.*	L
Sat, 3 Nov 1877	PG	Parkgrove v Beith. Won 3-2. Also 2nd Parkgrove v 2nd Beith fixture. No mention of Watson.	W
Sat, 10 Nov 1877	PG	Parkgrove v Sandyford. Won 3-2. Scottish Cup 3rd Round.	W
Sat, 17 Nov 1877	PG	Parkgrove v Clydesdale. Lost 4-0.	L
Sat, 24 Nov 1877	PG	Govan v Parkgrove (in aid of the Blantyre Fund). Drew 4-4. Maxwell Juniors played this day also.	D
Sat, 1 Dec 1877	PG	Parkgrove v Drumpellier. Won 3-1. Played at Trinidad Park. Scottish Cup 4th Round.	W
Sat, 29 Dec 1877	PG	Parkgrove v Partick. Drawn 1-1. Scottish Cup 5th Round.	D
Sat, 5 Jan 1878	PG	Partick v Parkgrove. Won 2-1. Scottish Cup 5th Round.	W
Sat, 19 Jan 1878	PG	Vale of Leven v Parkgrove. Lost 5-0. Scottish Cup 6th Round (quarter-final).	L
Sat, 9 Feb 1878	PG	Alexandra Athletic v Parkgrove at Kennyhill Park. Lost 4-1.	L

Sat, 23 Feb 1878	PG	Parkgrove v Lennox. Won 5-0.	W
Sat, 9 Mar 1878	PG	Parkgrove v Lancefield. Won 6-?	W
Sat, 20 Apr 1878	PG	Parkgrove v Beith. Lost 6-0. Report said Watson's kicking was excellent.	L
Sat, 10 Aug 1878	PG	17th RRV v Parkgrove at Field Park. Lost 4-3. Watson mentioned.	L
Sat, 28 Sep 1878	PG	Parkgrove v 1st LRV. Cup tie.	D
Sat, 5 Oct 1878	PG	Parkgrove v 1st LRV. Cup tie replay. Won 6-2 (no mention of Watson).	W
Sat, 12 Oct 1878	PG	Parkgrove v Northern. Won 3-1 (no mention of Watson). '… back play was sufficiently effective…'	W
Sat, 19 Oct 1878	PG	Parkgrove v Union. Won 1-0.	W
Sat, 26 Oct 1878	PG	Parkgrove v Clydesdale. Won 3-0.	W
Thu, 31 Oct 1878	PG	Parkgrove v Shaftesbury. Won 4-0. First electric light game at Trinidad Park.	W
Sat, 2 Nov 1878	PG	Parkgrove v Rangers at Trinidad Park. Won 4-1. Watson captain.	W
Sat, 9 Nov 1878	PG	Parkgrove v Rangers. Lost 8-2. Scottish Cup. Watson played at back.	L
Sat, 16 Nov 1878	PG	Unreported game.	
Sat, 23 Nov 1878	PG	Parkgrove v Alexandra Athletic at Trinidad Park. Lost 3-2?	L
Sat, 30 Nov 1878	PG	Shaftesbury v Parkgrove at Ashton Park. Won 2-1. Watson mentioned. Absence of a referee!	W
Sat, 15 Feb 1879	PG	Unreported game.	
Sat, 22 Feb 1879	PG	Unreported game.	
Sat, 1 Mar 1879	PG	Unreported game – Partick?	

Sat, 8 Mar 1879	PG	Parkgrove v Northern. Game drawn 1-1.	D
Sat, 22 Mar 1879	PG	Kilbirnie v Parkgrove. Lost 1-0, playing a man short.	L
Sat, 29 Mar 1879	PG	Third Lanark v Parkgrove. Lost 3-0. Watson listed. Played at Cathkin Park.	L
Sat, 5 Apr 1879	PG	Dumbarton v Parkgrove. Played at Govan. Lost 2-0.	L
Sat, 19 Apr 1879	PG	Unreported game.	
Sat, 30 Aug 1879	PG	Preliminary 4-a-side football heats for Queen's Park Sports Day. Parkgrove lost to Govan 2-0.	L
Wed, 10 Sep 1879	PG	Queen's Park v Parkgrove. Charity game for Langside Dorcas Society. Result unknown.	unknown
Sat, 13 Sep 1879	PG	Parkgrove v Third Lanark at Trinidad Park. Lost 1-0.	L
Sat, 20 Sep 1879	PG	South Western v Parkgrove. Drawn 1-1.	D
Sat, 27 Sep 1879	PG	Parkgrove v Kilmarnock Portland at Trinidad Park. Won 7-3 with ten men for the most part.	W
Sat, 4 Oct 1879	PG	Govan v Parkgrove at Broomloan Park. Won 3-0. Goals by Campbell, McFayden and Galloway.	W
Sat, 11 Oct 1879	PG	Rangers v Parkgrove at Kinning Park. Drawn 1-1.	D
Thu, 23 Oct 1879	PG	Parkgrove v Dunoon Excelsior. Won 4-1.	W
Sat, 1 Nov 1879	PG	Parkgrove v Alexandra Athletic. Cup tie at Trinidad Park. Won 6-2. Goals by Barclay (2), Galloway (2), Kyle, Godwin.	W
Sat, 8 Nov 1879	PG	Dumbarton v Parkgrove at Dumbarton. Lost 4-2.	L
Sat, 15 Nov 1879	PG	Aston Villa v Parkgrove in Birmingham. Won 4-2.	W
Sat, 22 Nov 1879	PG	Hibernian v Parkgrove. Cup tie. Drawn 2-2. Played in Edinburgh.	D

Sat, 29 Nov 1879	PG	Parkgrove v Hibernian. Cup tie replay. Watson listed. Drawn 2-2 at Trinidad Park.	D
Sat, 20 Dec 1879	PG	South Western v Parkgrove at Trinidad Park. Lost 1-0. PG had a disputed goal disallowed. Led to replay.	L
Sat, 27 Dec 1879	PG	Parkgrove v South Western. Cup replay at Copeland Park. Watson scored, 'whose play throughout was very fine'. Lost 3-2.	L
Thu, 1 Jan 1880	SC	Scottish Canadians v Rangers. Watson listed as 'half-back', but also as 'back'. Won 3-2.	W
Sat, 10 Jan 1880	PG	Parkgrove v Kilmarnock Athletic. Lost 5-1.	L
Mon, 9 Feb 1880	SC	Scottish Canadians v Manchester Wanderers (Association) at Manchester Rugby Club. Won 8-1. Noted that the Scotch team was 'well-represented' by Watson. Brought in as replacement for Davidson.	W
Tue, 10 Feb 1880	SC	Scottish Canadians v Nottingham Forest. Won 2-1. Watson is listed as a Queen's Park player.	W
Sat, 14 Feb 1880	GG	Sheffield v Glasgow. Glasgow won 1-0. Watson listed. 'Watson got at the ball, and by pretty dribbling, carried it away...'	W
Sat, 21 Feb 1880	SC	Selected to play for the Scotch Canadians v the Ayrshire Association at Rugby Park. Won 3-1. Listed as a Parkgrove player. 'The English rule of throwing in was practised for the first time here.'	W
Sat, 6 Mar 1880	PG	Parkgrove v Kilmarnock Portland as captain. Lost 3-1.	L
Sat, 13 Mar 1880	SC	Played for Scottish Canadians v Hearts. Composed mainly of Rangers and Parkgrove players. Won 5-1.	W
Sat, 20 Mar 1880	SC	Scottish Canadians v Amalgamated Team from St Mirren and Abercorn at Thistle Park. Won 8-1.	W
Mon, 29 Mar 1880	QP	Queen's Park v Manchester Wanderers at Hampden. Won 2-0. Wanderers were several players short, so QP provided players. Watson not mentioned.	W

Sat, 3 Apr 1880	QP	Played as half-back for Queen's Park v Edinburgh Association. Won 16-0.	W
Tue, 13 Apr 1880	QP	Caledonian v Queen's Park. Lost 1-0. Watson listed.	L
Sat, 17 Apr 1880	SC	Scottish Canadians v Edinburgh Hibernians. Won 3-0. Watson listed as a Parkgrove player.	W
Thu, 22 Apr 1880	GP	Glasgow Pilgrims v Edinburgh Hibernian. Played at Easter Road. Won 5-2. 'Watson at back played "binding" game.'	W
Sat, 24 Apr 1880	QP	Queen's Park v Vale of Leven. Scottish Charity Cup. Won 4-0.	W
Sat, 8 May 1880	QP	Played in the Glasgow Merchants Charity Cup v Rangers. Drawn 1-1. Replayed on 12 May. Watson played as half-back.	D
Wed, 12 May 1880	QP	Queen's Park v Rangers. Glasgow Merchants Charity Cup replay. Won 2-1. Watson listed.	W
Sat, 15 May 1880	QP	Queen's Park v Clapham Rovers. English v Scottish Cup holders. Won 3-2. For the Dick Memorial Fund. First half Scottish rules, second half English rules. Watson played as forward but reverted to back in the second half and the game changed in favour of QP.	W
Tue, 18 May 1880	FRE	Kilmarnock Team v Internationals at Hamilton Park. Internationals won 1-0. Watson, Vallance brothers, McNeill brothers, McIntyre.	W
Thu, 20 May 1880	SC	Internationals v Non-Internationals. Played to raise funds for the international team going to Canada. Watson in Internationals team that lost 5-2.	L
Sat, 11 Sep 1880	QP	Queen's Park v John Elder at Hampden Park. Cup. Won 7-0. Watson played in a two-man half-back role.	W
Sat, 18 Sep 1880	QP	Hibernian v Queen's Park. Watson listed. Won 1-0.	W
Sat, 25 Sep 1880	QP	Queen's Park v Rangers, in front of 3,000 spectators. Won 5-0. 'Watson did great service.'	W
Sat, 2 Oct 1880	QP	Queen's Park v Possill Park in the Scottish Cup. Won 5-0.	W
Sat, 9 Oct 1880	QP	Queen's Park v Heart of Midlothian, in front of 3,000 spectators. Won 8-1. Watson listed. 74 games played in Glasgow this day!	W

Sat, 16 Oct 1880	QP	Queen's Park v Rangers. Drawn 2-2. Watson listed.	D
Thu, 21 Oct 1880	QP	Queen's Park in Sheffield v Sheffield Wednesday. Won 5-0. Watson listed. '... and got as far as Watson, who, in the coolest manner possible, relieved his side by a rare fine kick.'	W
Sat, 23 Oct 1880	QP	Queen's Park in the Scottish Challenge Cup v the Pilgrims. Won 8-1. Pilgrims players '... many of whom it may be stated, are old members of the late Parkgrove (Govan) Club'.	W
Mon, 25 Oct 1880	FRE	Played in the second 'Electric Light Match' for 'South' v 'North' even though it was predominantly Rangers and Queen's Park players. Drawn 1-1.	D
Sat, 30 Oct 1880	QP	Queen's Park v Vale of Leven. Won 2-1. Watson listed.	W
Sat, 6 Nov 1880	QP	Queen's Park v Nottingham Club. Watson captain. Won 4-3.	W
Sat, 13 Nov 1880	QP	Queen's Park in the Scottish Cup v Beith. Won 11-2. Watson as half-back.	W
Sat, 27 Nov 1880	QP	Queen's Park v Dumbarton. Won 3-1. Report stated that Watson was in rare form.	W
Sat, 4 Dec 1880	QP	Queen's Park v Alexandra Athletic. Won 4-0. Watson was described as playing particularly well.	W
Sat, 11 Dec 1880	QP	Queen's Park v Mauchline. Cup tie. Watson not mentioned. Won 2-0.	W
Sat, 25 Dec 1880	QP	Campsie Central v Queen's Park. Scottish Cup. Won 10-0.	W
Sat, 1 Jan 1881	QP	Played in a friendly game v Old Etonians at Hampden Park in front of 4,000 spectators. Won 4-0. No Kinnaird. Took their opponents for dinner afterwards at the Royal Hotel. 'The steady play of Watson and Holm at back ...'	W
Sat, 15 Jan 1881	GG	Lancashire v Glasgow. Won 8-1 on a pitch covered in four inches of snow!	W
Sat, 12 Feb 1881	GG	Glasgow v Sheffield in front of 4,000 spectators. Won 3-0. Watson listed.	W
Sat, 19 Feb 1881	QP	Queen's Park v Clapham Rovers at The Oval. Won 1-0. Watson listed.	W
Sat, 12 Mar 1881	SN	Scotland v England at The Oval. Watson's first cap. Won 6-1. Listed as captain.	W

Mon, 14 Mar 1881	SN	Scotland v Wales at Wrexham. Won 5-1. Watson listed as captain in some reports.	W
Sat, 19 Mar 1881	QP	Queen's Park v Barrhead Arthurlie at Hampden. Drawn 0-0.	D
Wed, 23 Mar 1881	QP	Queen's Park v Third Lanark. Practice match for the Dumbarton final.	W
Sat, 26 Mar 1881	QP	Queen's Park v Dumbarton in the Association Challenge Cup. Won 2-1. 'Watson kicked with unerring precision throughout and only once missed the ball.' Game disputed and replayed on 9 April.	W
Sat, 2 Apr 1881	QP	Vale of Leven v Queen's Park at Alexandria. Drawn 0-0. Watson listed.	D
Thu, 7 Apr 1881	QP	Edinburgh University v Queen's Park. Won 2-0. Watson listed.	W
Sat, 9 Apr 1881	QP	Queen's Park v Dumbarton. Replay for the Scottish championship at Kinning Park. Won 3-1 in front of a crowd estimated at 10,000.	W
Wed, 20 Apr 1881	QP	3rd LRV v Queen's Park at Cathkin Park. Lost 1-0, even though report says QP missed four of their 1st XI.	L
Sat, 23 Apr 1881	QP	Queen's Park v Vale of Leven. Glasgow Charity Cup semi-final. Won 3-1 or 3-0.	W
Sat, 30 Apr 1881	QP	Queen's Park v Rangers in the Glasgow Charity Cup at Kinning Park. Game drawn 1-1.	D
Sat, 7 May 1881	QP	Queen's Park v Rangers in the Glasgow Charity Cup replay at Kinning Park. Won 3-1.	W
Wed, 18 May 1881	GG	Glasgow v Kilmarnock Athletic played at Holm Quarry Ground. Watson listed. Won 3-1.	W
Tue, 23 Aug 1881	QP	Kilmarnock v Queen's Park at Rugby Ground, Kilmarnock. Won 5-1.	W
Sat, 17 Sep 1881	QP	Queen's Park v Caledonian. Scottish Cup. Won 14-0. 'Watson, who, with A Holm, played back, was quite in his old form, doing some really good work for this team.'	W
Sat, 24 Sep 1881	QP	Queen's Park v Darwen. Won 6-0.	W
Sat, 1 Oct 1881	QP	Queen's Park v Jamestown. Played at Hampden. Won 5-1.	W

Sat, 8 Oct 1881	QP	Queen's Park v Cowlairs. At Hampden in the Scottish Cup 2nd round. Drawn 2-2.	D
Sat, 15 Oct 1881	QP	Queen's Park v Cowlairs in the Scottish Cup replay. Won 9-0. Watson named.	W
Thu, 20 Oct 1881	QP	Aston Villa v Queen's Park. Watson captain and was 'brilliant'. Won 4-0.	W
Sat, 22 Oct 1881	QP	Renfrew v Queen's Park. Won 3-1.	W
Sat, 29 Oct 1881	QP	Vale of Leven v Queen's Park at Alexandra. Won 2-1 in front of 3,000 spectators.	W
Sat, 5 Nov 1881	QP	Rangers v Queen's Park at Kinning Park. 4,000 crowd. Won 2-1. 'Fine fly kicking of Watson.'	W
Sat, 19 Nov 1881	QP	Queen's Park v Johnstone. Scottish Cup. Won 3-1.	W
Thu, 24 Nov 1881	QP	Queen's Park v Dunfermline. Won 3-0.	W
Sat, 26 Nov 1881	QP	Queen's Park v Nottingham at Hampden. Won 10-1. 'A. Holm and the Queen's Park captain (A. Watson) never showed to greater advantage than in their defence of goal.'	W
Sat, 3 Dec 1881	QP	Queen's Park v Partick Thistle at Hampden. 5th Round SFA Challenge Cup. Won 10-0. Full team.	W
Sat, 17 Dec 1881	QP	Queen's Park v Third Lanark. Played at Hampden. Won 2-0. Bad weather kept spectators away.	W
Sat, 24 Dec 1881	QP	Darwen v Queen's Park. Won 2-0. '... and Watson being repeatedly applauded for their magnificence'.	W
Mon, 26 Dec 1881	QP	Queen's Park v Blackburn Rovers. Drawn 2-2. Watson lame in the second half. 12,000 crowd.	D
Sat, 31 Dec 1881	QP	Queen's Park (scratch team) v Hurlford. Won 3-1. Fixture listed as Cliftonville.	W

Sun, 1 Jan 1882	QP	Queen's Park v Old Carthusians (English cup holders) at Hampden in front of around 1,000 spectators. Won 8-0. Scored 12 but four deemed offside. 'The English Captain, in responding to the toast of the "Old Carthusians" remarked that he expressed the sentiments of his eleven men when he declared that they had never seen such players as they had met that day.' E.H. Parry	W
Mon, 2 Jan 1882	QP	Queen's Park v Helensburgh at Faslane Park, Gareloch. The team travelled by omnibus. Won 2-0.	W
Sat, 7 Jan 1882	QP	Queen's Park v Shotts at Hampden. Scottish Cup. Won 14-0.	W
Sat, 21 Jan 1882	QP	Bootle v Queen's Park. Won 2-0.	W
Sat, 28 Jan 1882	QP	Beith v Queen's Park. Won 11-2. Beith, '… the club having lost the services of some of its best players … having been induced to cross the Border'. Watson named.	W
Sat, 4 Feb 1882	QP	Queen's Park v Dumfries at Hampden. Won 15-1. Watson listed. A charity game for Dumfries Infirmary comprising of players from the three Dumfries clubs. 3,000 spectators.	W
Sat, 18 Feb 1882	QP	Queen's Park v Kilmarnock at Hampden. Won 3-2. Scottish Cup.	W
Sat, 25 Feb 1882	QP	Queen's Park v the Nottinghamshire Club in front of 3,000 spectators. Won 4-1.	W
Sat, 11 Mar 1882	SN	Scotland v England. Last cap came against England in Glasgow in front of 15,000 spectators and Scotland won 5-1. 'Watson, as is usual with him, very steady and his speed aided Scotland a great deal.'	W
Sat, 18 Mar 1882	QP	Queen's Park v Dumbarton in the Scottish Cup Final. The game was drawn 2-2. Scotland played Wales on the same day, but Watson chose to play for QP.	D
Sat, 1 Apr 1882	QP	Queen's Park v Dumbarton in the replay of the Scottish Cup Final. Won 4-1.	W
Sat, 8 Apr 1882	QP	Paisley Abercorn v Queen's Park at Blackstone Park. Charity match. Won 5-0.	W

Sat, 15 Apr 1882	QP	Queen's Park v Vale of Leven in the Scottish Charity Cup 2nd Round. Drawn 2-2. Watson listed.	D
Sat, 6 May 1882	QP	Queen's Park v Vale of Leven in Charity Cup 2nd Round replay. Lost 2-0. QP's first defeat in two years. Last defeat was against same team. Watson listed.	L
Sat, 21 Oct 1882	FRE	E.C. Bambridge's XI v Clapham Rovers on Swifts ground in Slough. Drawn 1-1. Watson listed. '… the back play of E.C. Bambridge and A. Watson, the Scotch International player, being very strong …'	D
Sat, 28 Oct 1882	SW	Swifts v Bradfield College. Watson listed. Won 4-0. 'The Bradfield forwards were unable to pass A. Watson.'	W
Wed, 15 Nov 1882	PLG	Pilgrims v United Hospitals at Walthamstow. Won 2-1. *The Sportsman* stated, 'On the side of the winners the back play of Watson (late of Queen's Park) was very safe.' T	W
Thu, 16 Nov 1882	SW	Oxford University v Swifts. Watson listed. Lost 8-1.	L
Tue, 21 Nov 1882	SW	Royal Military Academy v Swifts. Won 4-1. Watson listed as back.	W
Sat, 25 Nov 1882	PLG	Pilgrims v Old Foresters. Lost 3-0. *The Sportsman* stated that there were two A. Watsons playing, Arthur keeping goal the other playing full-back. '… the fine back play of A. Watson saved his side from further loss.'	L
Thu, 30 Nov 1882	SW	Swifts v Upton Park alongside the Bambridge brothers and became the first black player to play in the English Cup when he turned out for Swifts.	D
Sat, 2 Dec 1882	SW	Swifts v Upton Park in the cup replay at The Oval. Won 3-2. Watson listed.	W
Sat, 16 Dec 1882	PLG	Pilgrims v Charterhouse, including Blenkiron, A.M. Walters, G. Spring-Rice and the Vincent brothers. Won 2-0. '… best back player ever seen on their ground.' 'Andy Watson played magnificently at full back, the boys noting him the finest back they have seen.'	W
Sat, 23 Dec 1882	SW	Swifts v J.L. Nickisson's XI/Brentwood at Slough. Watson listed. Lost 1-0. Brentwood played a man short. Last minute replacement for the Old Foresters fixture.	L

Mon, 1 Jan 1883	SW	Swifts v Queen's Park at Hampden Park. Won 2-1 in front of 4,000-5,000 spectators. Watson 'warmly cheered' as he stepped on to the park. First time an English team had beaten QP at Hampden. Team left Sunday night at 8.50pm from Euston. S	W
Wed, 10 Jan 1883	PLG	Crystal Palace Rovers v Pilgrims. Won 4-1.	W
Thu, 11 Jan 1883	SW	Swifts v Old Carthusians. Watson Listed. Won 9-0.	W
Thu, 18 Jan 1883	CFC	Corinthian v Upton Park. Lost 7-0. Watson included.	L
Sat, 20 Jan 1883	PLG	Pilgrims v the Sheffield Club at Bramall Lane. Played alongside T.W. Blenkiron. Lost 4-2. 3,000 crowd. 'Andy Watson delighted the gallery with his perfect back play.'	L
Wed, 24 Jan 1883	SW	Swifts v Old Etonians. 4th Round FA Cup. The Oval. Lost 2-0. Watson listed in squad. Kinnaird listed.	L
Sat, 3 Feb 1883	QP	Queen's Park v Dumbarton. Report in *The Sportsman*: 'The third half-back was Andrew Watson, their old captain, who was specially brought from London for this game.' Lost 3-1. Dumbarton protested Watson's inclusion.	L
Sat, 17 Feb 1883	FRE	Listed as playing for Mr Let's Eleven against Bruce Castle. Won 4-0.	W
Sat, 3 Mar 1883	PLG	Pilgrims v Cambridge. Lost 2-1. 'The feature, however, was the defence of Watson.' 'Andy Watson played a brilliant saving game.'	L
Fri, 23 Mar 1883	CFC	Corinthian v Accrington. Lost 4-3. Played alongside J.W. Holm. 'Watson wasn't the Watson of old; he seemed quite stale and indifferent.'	L
Sat, 24 Mar 1883	CFC	Corinthian v Church. Won 2-0. Played alongside J.W. Holm.	W
Mon, 26 Mar 1883	CFC	Bootle v Corinthian. Won 2-0. 'Most assuredly we should have looked for a better result seeing that such noted players as Swepstone, Andrew Watson, JW Holm (Glasgow), Sorby and Beardshaw were included in the ranks of the rambling club.'	W
Tue, 27 Mar 1883	CFC	Corinthian v Stoke. Lost 5-3. Played with only ten men.	L

Thu, 5 Apr 1883	QP	Blackburn Rovers v Queen's Park in front of 2,000 spectators. Drawn 1-1.	D
Sat, 21 Apr 1883	EU	Edinburgh University v Darwin. Won 3-1. Played with J.W. Holm and Dr Smith. Holm and Watson played a 'rattling game'.	W
Mon, 23 Apr 1883	EU	Edinburgh University v Aston Villa in Birmingham at Perry Barr. Drawn 1-1 in a snowstorm!	D
Sat, 29 Sep 1883	PLG	Leyton v Pilgrims. Won 2-0. Watson listed.	W
Wed, 17 Oct 1883	FRE	Mr G. Stephenson's Team v Westminster School. Lost 3-2 with E.C. Bambridge.	L
Sat, 20 Oct 1883	PLG	Pilgrims v Ipswich Association. Watson listed. Lost 3-2. '… the splendid kicking of ex-Queen's Park player, Andrew Watson.'	L
Sat, 27 Oct 1883	PLG	St George's College v Pilgrims at North Park, Croydon. Won 2-0. 'Visitors were rather strong.'	W
Wed, 14 Nov 1883	SW	Swifts v Westminster school. Watson listed. Won 3-2.	W
Sat, 17 Nov 1883	BW	Brentwood v Notts Club. Watson 'brilliant' but lost 3-2. Pilgrims played this day too. T.J. Britten in the team also.	L
Sat, 8 Dec 1883	SW	Swifts v Great Marlow at Dolphin Ground. FA Cup 2nd Round. Won 2-0.	W
Tue, 18 Dec 1883	PLG	Pilgrims v Casuals at Walthamstow. Drawn 4-4.	D
Wed, 26 Dec 1883	PLG	Pilgrims v Ipswich Association. Benefit of East Sussex Hospital. Watson listed. Lost 3-1.	L
Fri, 28 Dec 1883	CFC	Corinthian v Sheffield Club. Won 5-2. Watson captain.	W
Sat, 29 Dec 1883	SW	Clapham Rovers v Swifts. 3rd Round FA Cup. Won 2-1.	W
Tue, 1 Jan 1884	SW	Swifts v Queen's Park. Lost 5-1.	L
Sat, 5 Jan 1884	QP	Queen's Park v Pollokshields Athletic. Lost 2-1. Watson listed. 'Watson was not in form and the right wing of Shields did what they liked on his side.'	L

Sat, 19 Jan 1884	SW	Swifts v Old Foresters at Slough. FA Cup 4th Round. Watson listed. Won 2-1. Watson scored with a direct free kick and it was disallowed.	W
Sat, 9 Feb 1884	SW	Swifts v Notts at Trent Bridge. Drawn 1-1. '… grand back play of Watson …'	D
Thu, 14 Feb 1884	SW	Swifts v Notts County. FA Cup quarter-final replay. Lost 1-0. '... but for Watson's magnificent back play, the result would have been far different.' 'Andy Watson was a tower of defence.'	L
Mon, 3 Mar 1884	SCY	Surrey County v Nottinghamshire Association. Lost 6-2. 'A.S. Watson (Swifts)' named. Also 'Andrew Watson' and 'A.E. Watson'.	L
Wed, 5 Mar 1884	CFC	Corinthian v Charterhouse. Won 2-1. Watson mentioned.	W
Thu, 6 Mar 1884	SCY	Surrey County v Essex. Won 3-0. *Surrey Mirror* lists 'A. Watson (Swifts)'.	W
Wed, 12 Mar 1884	FRE	Friar Park v W. Franklyn's XI. Played at Henley. Drawn 1-1. 'Friar Park who were assisted by A. Watson, a late International player.' Played as a back.	D
Sat, 22 Mar 1884	SCY	Notts v Surrey. Watson listed as a Swifts player. Lost 6-2.	L
Mon, 24 Mar 1884	SCY	Surrey County v Cambridge University in return match. 'A. Watson (Dorking)'. Game drawn 0-0. 'Watson was particularly smart.'	D
Thu, 3 Apr 1884	QP	Queen's Park v Notts County in a testimonial for A.W. Cursham. Won 3-0.	W
Sat, 12 Apr 1884	QP	Queen's Park v Rangers in a charity match at Cathkin Park. Won 2-1 in front of 10,000 spectators.	W
Sat, 26 Apr 1884	QP	Queen's Park v Third Lanark Volunteers at Cathkin Park in the Glasgow Charity Cup in front of 10,000. Drawn 1-1. Watson listed to cover for Holm. Smith could not play owing to the death of his brother. 'Watson came all the way from Paris to assist his old club ...'	D
Sat, 3 May 1884	QP	Queen's Park v Third Lanark Volunteers in the Glasgow Charity Cup. Won 8-0.	W
Sat, 11 Oct 1884	PLG	Pilgrims v Guy's Hospital at Walthamstow. Won 4-0. Watson's kicking noted.	W

Sat, 18 Oct 1884	QP	Queen's Park v Dumbarton in Glasgow. Watson named. Drawn 0-0.	D
Wed, 12 Nov 1884	QP	Queen's Park v Aston Villa in Birmingham. Lost 2-1. '... but Watson was the pick, his safe returns and cool tackling being one of the features of the match.'	L
Sat, 29 Nov 1884	QP	Queen's Park v Dumbarton. Drawn 1-1.	D
Sat, 6 Dec 1884	SW	South Reading v Swifts. FA Cup 2nd Round. Won 3-2. Watson listed.	W
Wed, 10 Dec 1884	SW	Swifts v Bradfield College. Lost 2-1. Watson named. 'But for some fine play by A. Watson, they would have scored freely.'	L
Mon, 15 Dec 1884	CFC	Corinthian v Blackburn Rovers. Won 8-1. Beat FA Cup holders.	W
Tue, 16 Dec 1884	CFC	Corinthian v Darwen. Lost 2-1.	L
Wed, 17 Dec 1884	CFC	Corinthian v Blackburn Olympic. Drawn 4-4.	D
Fri, 19 Dec 1884	CFC	Corinthian v Bolton Wanderers. Lost 7-0.	L
Sat, 20 Dec 1884	CFC	Preston North End v Corinthian. Lost 3-1.	L
Mon, 22 Dec 1884	CFC	Corinthian v Notts Club at Trent Bridge. Lost 3-2. The tour lasted a week and consisted of seven games. Corinthian won two, drew one and lost four.	L
Sat, 3 Jan 1885	SW	Swifts v Old Westminsters. Drawn 1-1. FA Cup 3rd Round. 'Andy Watson played magnificently.'	D
Sat, 10 Jan 1885	SW	Swifts v Clapham Rovers. Won 3-0. 'Watson was the pick of the winning backs.' 'Andy Watson kicked and stopped in his usual first-class style.'	W
Wed, 14 Jan 1885	SW	Swifts v Old Westminsters in the FA Cup replay at The Oval. Drawn 2-2. 'Andrew Watson played a magnificent game at the back …'	D
Sat, 17 Jan 1885	CFC	Corinthian v Preston North End at The Oval. Won 3-2. 'Watson did not show to his usual advantage.'	W

Wed, 21 Jan 1885	SW	Swifts v Old Westminster's in the second replay in the FA Cup 3rd Round. Won 2-1 and Watson scored from a free kick! 'Watson's back play was the next feature worthy of mention, indeed from start to finish he proved a "host in himself" behind.'	W
Sat, 24 Jan 1885	SW	Swifts v Notts Forest at Slough. FA Cup 4th Round. Lost 1-0. Watson played, although 'lame'.	L
Sat, 14 Feb 1885	SW	Swifts v Notts. Lost 3-1. Watson listed.	L
Wed, 25 Feb 1885	SW	Swifts v Oxford University. Watson listed. Drawn 1-1 (or 2-0?).	D/W?
Sat, 28 Feb 1885	SW	Swifts v St Barts at Slough. Played ten men. Won 4-2. Dr Smith played and scored.	W
Wed, 4 Mar 1885	SW	Swifts v Charterhouse. Won 4-1. Listed as 'Andy Watson'.	W
Wed, 11 Mar 1885	SCY	Cambridge v Surrey. Lost 2-1. Watson listed as Swifts. In Cambridge team: M.J. Rendall, A.M. Walters, A. Amos, F.E. Saunders, Blenkiron, Spilsbury, Lindley.	L
Sat, 18 Apr 1885	QP	Northern v Queen's Park at Hyde Park, Springburn. Won 5-0.	W
Sat, 25 Apr 1885	QP	Queen's Park v Renton. Glasgow Charity Cup semi-final. 'Andrew Watson was brought down from London to fill Arnott's place.' Arnott was ineligible. Won 3-2.	W
Sat, 9 May 1885	QP	Queen's Park v Dumbarton. Charity Cup Final. Won 1-0. Overall, £5,240 was raised for charity.	W
Mon, 11 May 1885	QP	Smokers v Non-smokers. Non-smokers won 3-0. Watson on the Smokers team!	L
Wed, 13 May, 1885	QP	QP v Rangers at Hampden. Lost 1-0. Watson good at the back.	L
Sat, 23 May 1885	QP	Queen of the South Wanderers v Queen's Park. Won 4-0.	W
Sat, 30 May 1885	QP	Queen's Park v Pollokshields Athletic. Won 3-0.	W
Sat, 30 May 1885	QP	Tournament at Hampden with QP, Rangers, Pollokshields and Third Lanark Rifle Volunteers. Final between Third Lanark and QP. Drawn 0-0. Proceeds went to new drill hall for 3rd LRV. 4,000 crowd.	D

Sat, 22 Aug 1885	QP	Queen's Park v Strathmore at Dundee. Watson reported as arriving back in Scotland on the Friday for the game. Won 3-1.	W
Sat, 29 Aug 1885	QP	Queen's Park v St Peter's. Won 16-0. Watson described as 'late of Swifts'. Scottish Cup.	W
Sat, 12 Sep 1885	QP	Queen's Park v Hibs. Watson listed. Lost 2-1.	L
Sat, 19 Sep 1885	QP	Queen's Park v Blackburn Rovers. Won 7-1.	W
Sat, 26 Sep 1885	QP	Queen's Park v Rangers. Won 3-2.	W
Sat, 3 Oct 1885	QP	Queen's Park v Pilgrims. 2nd Round Scottish Cup. Watson listed. Won 1-0.	W
Sat, 10 Oct 1885	QP	Queen's Park v Notts County. Won 5-1.	W
Sat, 17 Oct 1885	QP	Queen's Park v Dumbarton. Won 3-2. Watson listed.	W
Sat, 24 Oct 1885	QP	East Stirlingshire v Queen's Park. Scottish Cup. Won 3-0.	W
Sat, 31 Oct 1885	QP	Queen's Park v Partick Thistle. English FA Cup. Watson listed. Won 5-1.	W
Sat, 7 Nov 1885	QP	Queen's Park v Rangers. Watson listed. Lost 4-0.	L
Sat, 14 Nov 1885	QP	Queen's Park v Airdrieonians. Cup match. Won 1-0. Watson listed.	W
Sat, 21 Nov 1885	QP	Queen's Park v Pollokshields Athletic. Won 2-0. QP could not get a team to play Aston Villa at Birmingham on Saturday, so met Pollokshields at Hampden.	W
Sat, 28 Nov 1885	QP	Queen's Park v Dundee. Won 4-1. Watson played at half-back.	W
Sat, 5 Dec 1885	QP	Queen's Park v Arthurlie. Scottish Cup. Won 2-1. 'Watson at back kicked with capital judgement and unerring accuracy.'	W
Sat, 12 Dec 1885	QP	Queen's Park v Abercorn. Won 4-3. Watson listed.	W
Sat, 19 Dec 1885	QP	Queen's Park v Dumbarton. Watson listed. Drawn 2-2.	D

Sat, 26 Dec 1885	QP	Queen's Park v Blackburn Rovers. Won 3-0. Watson listed.	W
Fri, 1 Jan 1886	QP	Queen's Park v Corinthian at Hampden. Drawn 2-2.	D
Sat, 16 Jan 1886	QP	Queen's Park v Third Lanark. 6th round cup match. Won 3-0. Watson listed.	W
Sat, 30 Jan 1886	QP	Queen's Park v Cowlairs. Watson listed. Won 3-1. Watson playing half-back in a 2-2-6 formation.	W
Sat, 13 Feb 1886	QP	Queen's Park v Renton in the Scottish Cup Final. Won 3-1. Watson listed.	W
Sat, 20 Feb 1886	QP	Notts County v Queen's Park. Watson listed. Lost 1-0. At Trent Bridge.	L
Sat, 20 Mar 1886	QP	Queen's Park v Third Lanark. Won 6-0. Watson listed.	W
Sat, 3 Apr 1886	EU	Hibernians v Edinburgh University. Lost 3-1. 'Watson played a finished game and put in a lot of sound work.'	L
Sat, 24 Apr 1886	QP	Scotch Crusaders (took the place of QP) v Aston Villa. Won 2-1. Report says, '... Watson, as usual, played a superb defensive game … whenever Allen came down the wing, Watson was always ready to dispossess him, and he invariably succeeded.'	W
Sat, 18 Sep 1886	QP	Vale of Leven v Queen's Park at Alexandria. Watson listed. Lost 4-2.	L
Sat, 25 Sep 1886	QP	Queen's Park v Preston North End. Lost 6-1. *Cricket and Football Field* reported that Andy Watson played at half, an 'unusual position for him'. Watson's last match for QP. 'Watson in poor form ...'	L
Thu, 5 May, 1887	FRE	Bootle v Garston 1-0 Watson played for Garston. Report in the Liverpool Mercury stated that Watson was a last-minute inclusion...?	L
Sat, 9 Apr 1887	BF	Battlefield FC v Cliftonville FC in Belfast. Won 2-1.	W
Tue, 23 Aug 1887	BT	Bootle v Liverpool and District. Drawn 1-1. Watson's first game for BT. A charity game to raise money for W. Spence, the late professional cricketer.	D

Sat, 27 Aug 1887	BT	Bootle Wanderers v Bootle, at Marsh-lane. Won 2-0. Watson listed.	W
Tue, 30 Aug 1887	BT	Bootle v Preston North End. Lost 3-1. Watson listed.	L
Sat, 3 Sep 1887	BT	Stanley v Bootle. Won 1-0. Watson listed.	W
Tue, 6 Sep 1887	BT	Bootle v Halliwell. Lost 3-1. *Cricket and Field* reported that 'Andy Watson increased his circle of admirers by his cool and effective play'.	L
Sat, 10 Sep 1887	BT	Bootle v Crewe Alexandra. Won 2-1. Watson listed.	W
Tue, 13 Sep 1887	BT	Bootle v Bolton Wanderers. Won 3-2. Watson listed.	W
Sat, 17 Sep 1887	BT	Bootle v Blackburn Olympic. Lost 2-1. Watson listed. 4,000 crowd.	L
Tue, 20 Sep 1887	BT	Bootle v Blackburn Rovers. Watson had a broken nose and could not play in the second half. Lost 2-1. Holt's head smashed into Watson's face in a tackle with Townley.	L
Sat, 8 Oct 1887	BT	Bootle v Liverpool Blues. Liverpool and District Cup. Watson listed to play. Won 16-0.	W
Sat, 15 Oct 1887	BT	Bootle v Workington. Won 6-0. FA Cup. Watson listed.	W
Sat, 22 Oct 1887	BT	Bootle v Stanley. Won 4-1.	W
Sat, 29 Oct 1887	BT	Bootle v Witton. Drawn 2-2. Watson listed.	D
Sat, 5 Nov 1887	BT	Bootle v South Shore. Drawn 1-1. National Cup. Watson listed.	D
Sat, 12 Nov 1887	BT	Bootle v South Shore. Won 3-0. National Cup. Watson listed.	W
Sat, 19 Nov 1887	BT	Bootle v Halliwell. Lost 5-0. Watson listed.	L
Sat, 26 Nov 1887	BT	Bootle v Higher Walton. Won 6-1. Watson listed. 'Andy Watson was decidedly off-colour.'	W
Sat, 3 Dec 1887	BT	Bootle v Everton. Lost 2-0 in front of 12,000 spectators. Watson listed.	L
Sat, 10 Dec 1887	BT	Bootle v Burnley. Watson listed. Drawn 1-1.	D

Sat, 17 Dec 1887	BT	Bootle v Great Bridge Unity. Won 2-1. Watson listed.	W
Sat, 24 Dec 1887	BT	Bootle v Chirk. Drawn 1-1. Watson listed.	D
Mon, 26 Dec 1887	BT	Bootle v Bolton Wanderers at Hawthorne Road. Lost 2-1. Watson listed.	L
Sat, 31 Dec 1887	BT	Bootle v Thornliebank. Watson listed. Won 6-0.	W
Mon, 2 Jan 1888	BT	Bootle v Third Lanark. Watson listed. Lost 3-2. 'Watson got badly shaken at the beginning …'	L
Sat, 7 Jan 1888	BT	Bootle v Old Carthusians at The Oval. Lost 2-0. Watson listed. A.M. Walters dislocated his knee.	L
Sat, 21 Jan 1888	BT	Bootle v Southport High Park at Hawthorne Road. Won 9-0. 2,000 crowd. Watson listed. Liverpool Cup.	W
Sat, 28 Jan 1888	BT	Bootle v Bootle Wanderers. Liverpool Cup semi-final. Won 4-1. Watson listed.	W
Sat, 4 Feb 1888	BT	Bootle v Bolton Wanderers. Lost 2-1. Watson listed.	L
Sat, 11 Feb 1888	BT	Bootle v Church. Won 4-0. Watson listed. Reports state that Watson was absent temporarily, but nothing more. Another report said he fell to pieces at the beginning of the second half but came back on.	W
Sat, 18 Feb 1888	BT	Bootle v Witton. Drawn 2-2. Watson listed, and 'as good as ever'.	D
Sat, 25 Feb 1888	BT	Bootle v Newton Heath. Watson listed. Won 1-0.	W
Sat, 3 Mar 1888	BT	Bootle v Northwich Victoria. Won 7-0. Watson listed. *Football Field* said, 'Andy Watson improves with each game, his play on Saturday being a treat.'	W
Sat, 10 Mar 1888	BT	Bootle v Witton. Watson listed. Lost 5-0.	L
Sat, 17 Mar 1888	BT	Bootle v Burnley. Drawn 0-0. Watson played.	D

Tue, 20 Mar 1888	BT	Bootle v Accrington. Watson listed. Drawn 1-1.	D
Sat, 24 Mar 1888	BT	Bootle v West Manchester. Drawn 2-2. Watson listed.	D
Mon, 26 Mar 1888	BT	Bootle v Halliwell. Watson mentioned. Drawn 1-1.	D
Fri, 30 Mar 1888	BT	Bootle v Dumbarton Athletic at Hawthorne Road (Good Friday). Won 3-2. Watson listed.	W
Sat, 31 Mar 1888	BT	Bootle v London Caledonians. Won 3-2.	W
Mon, 2 Apr 1888	BT	Bootle v Notts Forest. Won 4-1. Watson listed.	W
Sat, 7 Apr 1888	BT	Bootle v Mitchell St George. Lost 4-3. Watson listed.	L
Tue, 10 Apr 1888	BT	Bootle v Bolton Wanderers. Won 2-1. Watson's last game? 31 years old.	W

Selected bibliography

Adams, T., 'The Unmarked Grave: What Really Happened to Andrew Watson, British Football's First Black Star', *The Blizzard*, 10 (2013).

Alcock, C.W., *The Book of Rules of the Game of Football.* (New York: Peck and Snyder, 1906).

Alcock, C.W., *Football: The Association Game* (Cambridge: George Bell, 1906).

Alston, D., 'A Forgotten Diaspora: The Children Of Enslaved And "Free Coloured" Women and Highland Scots in Guyana Before Emancipation', *Edinburgh University Press*, 6/1 (2015).

Belton, B., *The Black Hammers: The Voices of West Ham's Ebony Heroes* (Pennant Books, 2006).

Bilsborough, P., 'The Development of Sport in Glasgow 1850–1914', *University of Stirling*, (1983).

Birley, D., *Sport and the Making of Britain* (Manchester University Press, 1993).

Bone, D.D., *Scottish Football: Reminiscences and Sketches* (Glasgow: John Menzies 1890).

Brown, P., *The Victorian Football Miscellany* (Goal-Post, 2013).

Brumell, J., *British Guiana: Demerara After Fifteen Years of Freedom* (London: T. Bosworth,1853).

Cameron, J., *Association Football and How to Play It* (London: Health & Strength, 1908).

Carrington, B. and McDonald, I., *'Race', Sport and British* Society (London: Routledge, 2001).

Carter, F.W. and Capel-Kirby, W., *The Mighty Kick* (London: Jarrolds, 1933).

Catton, J.A.H. 'Tityrus', *The Story of Association Football* (1926).

Catton, J.A.H. 'Tityrus', *Wickets and Goals* (Chapman and Hall, 1926).

Cavallini, R., *A Casual Affair: The History of the Casuals Football Club* (Dog N Duck, 2009).

Cavallini, R., *Corinthian-Casuals – The First Seventy Years 1939–2009* (Dog N Duck, 2009).

Cavallini, R., *Play Up Corinth: A History of the Corinthian Football Club* (Stroud: Tempus Publishing, 2007).

Cox, T., *A Popular History of The Grammar School of Queen Elizabeth at Heath, Near Halifax* (Halifax: F. King, 1879).

Creek, F.N.S., *A History of the Corinthian Football Club* (London: Longmans, Green & Co., 1933).

Damer, S., *From Moorepark to 'Wine Alley': The Rise and Fall of a Glasgow Housing Scheme* (Edinburgh University Press, 1989).

Dick, W.M., *Rules of the Scottish Football Association* (Weatherston, 1875).

Dimeo, P. and Finn, G.P.T., 'Racism, National Identity and Scottish Football', in Carrington, B. and McDonald, I., (eds) *'Race', Sport and British* Society (London: Routledge, 2001).

English Football Association, *The Rules of Association Football* (1863).

Fabian, A.H. (ed.) and Green, G., *Association Football* (Caxton, 1960).

Giulianotti, R., *Football: A Sociology of the Global Game* (Cambridge: Polity, 1999).

Grayson, E., *Corinthians and Cricketers* (London: Naldrett Press, 1955).

Green, G., *The Official History of the FA Cup* (London: Naldrett Press, 1949).

Hern, B & Greave, D., *Football's Black Pioneers* (Conker, 2020).

Hinds, R., *Black Lions: A History of Black Players in English Football* (SportsBooks, 2006).

Hobsbawn, E, *The Age of Empire 1875–1914* (Abacus, 1987).

Holman, S.R., *God Knows There's Need: Christian Responses to Poverty* (Oxford University Press, 2009).

Jackson, N.L. 'Pa', *Sporting Days and Sporting Ways* (London: Hurst and Blackett, 1932).

Jackson, N.L., *Association Football* (London: Hurst 1899).

James, B., *Queen's Park Football Club* (Cheltenham: The History Press, 2007).

Lamming, D., *A Scottish Soccer Internationalists' Who's Who, 1872–1986* (Hutton Press, 1987).

Lamming, D., *An English Football Internationalists' Who's Who, 1872–1988* (Hutton Press, 1990).

Lorimer, D., 'Theoretical Racism in Late-Victorian Anthropology, 1870–1900', *Victorian Studies*, 31/3 (1988).

Malcolm, T., *Glasgow v Sheffield: A Tale of Two Footballing Cities 1874–1960* (2010).

Mitchell, A., *Arthur Kinnaird: First Lord of Football* (Andy Mitchell Media, 2011).

Mitchell, A., *First Elevens: The Birth of International Football* (Andy Mitchell Media, 2012).

Morris, T., *In a Class of Their Own: A History of English Amateur Football* (Shrewsbury: Chequered Flag, 2015).

Old Member, *The Story of the London Caledonians Football Club* (Procter, 1924).

Onslow, T., *The Forgotten Rivals: A History of Bootle Football Club* (Birkenhead: Countyvise, 2005).

Philip, G.E., *A Scots Boy's World Sixty Years Ago* (1922).

Rafferty, J., *One Hundred Years of Scottish Football.* (Pan Books, 1973).

Ralston, G., *The Gallant Pioneers: Rangers 1872* (Stirling: Ralston, 2007).

Renson, R., 'Fair Play: Its Origins and Meanings in Sport and Society', *Kinesiology*, 41/1 (2009).

Robinson, R., *History of the Queen's Park Football Club 1867–1917* (Glasgow: Hay Nisbet, 1920).

Ross, A.M., *The Genealogy of the Families of Douglas of Mulderg and Robertson of Kindeace with Their Descendants* (Dingwall: A.M. Ross & Company, 1895).

Ross, M., *50 Years of FA Cup Finals, 1883–1932* (Yore, 1932).

Russell, D., *Football and the English: A Social History of Association Football, 1863–1995* (Preston: Carnegie Publishing, 1997).

Sanders, R., *Beastly Fury: The Strange Birth of British Football* (Bantam, 2009).

Shearman, M., *Athletics and Football* (London: Longmans, Green & Co., 1887).

Shearman, M. and Vincent, J.E., *Foot-Ball: Its History for Five Centuries* (Leadenhall, 1923).

Smart, J.B., *The Founders of Soccer* (Blythe Smart Publications, 2008).

Steel, A. 'Old International', *25 Years of Football* (1896).

Sutherland, A. and Young, D., *Andrew Watson* (HarperCollins, 2013).

Talburt, T., *Andrew Watson: The World's First Black Football Superstar* (London: Hansib, 2017).

Taylor, D.J., *On the Corinthian Spirit: The Decline of Amateurism in Sport* (Yellow Jersey Press, 2006).

Taylor, R., Kafel, A. and Smith, R., *Crossley Heath School* (Stroud: The History Press, 2006).

Vanplew, W., *Pay Up and Play the Game* (Cambridge University Press, 1988).

White, O., 'The Football League and the Game it Made: A Study of the Development and Transformation of Association Football, 1888–1914', *Northumbria University* (2015).

Williams, G., *The Code War: English Football Under the Historical Spotlight* (Yore, 1994).

Young, G.M., *Victorian England: Portrait of and Age* (Oxford University Press, 1964).

Young, P.M., *Football on Merseyside* (Soccer Book Club, 1963).

Websites:
ancestry.co.uk
archive.org
archives.etoncollege.com
britishnewspaperarchive.co.uk
charterhouse.daisy.websds.net
crossleyheath.org.uk
efcheritagesociety.com
electricscotland.com
englandfootballonline.com
familyhistory.bdm.nsw.gov.au
familysearch.org
findmypast.com
freeBMD.org.uk
guyana.org
kingscollections.org
liverpoolmaritime.org
maps.nls.uk
newspapers.com
oocities.org/br1anmccoll
playupliverpool.com
scotlandspeople.gov.uk
scotsfootballworldwide.scot
scottish-football-historical-archive.co.nf
scottishsporthistory.com
spanglefish.com/slavesandhighlanders
theredcard.org
ucl.ac.uk/lbs/

Index